1925 Through World War II

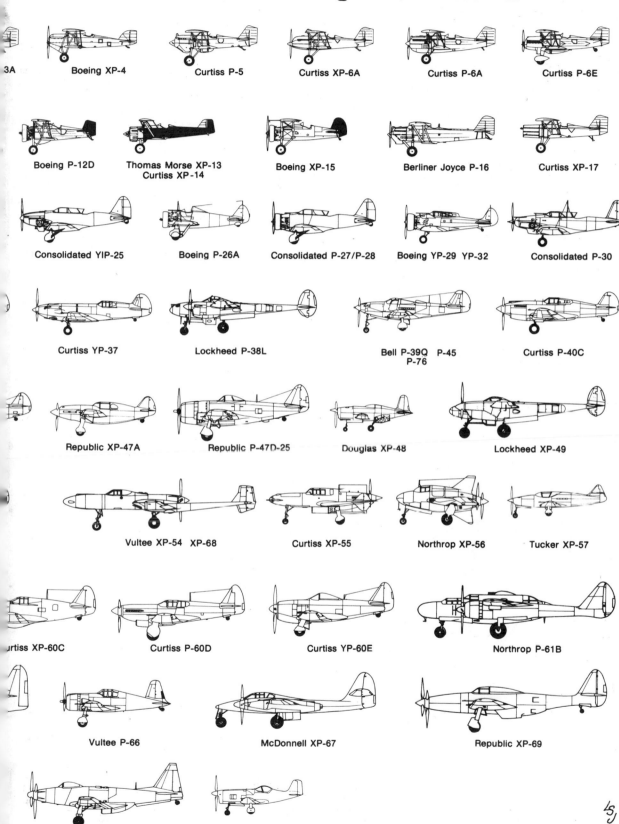

3A   Boeing XP-4   Curtiss P-5   Curtiss XP-6A   Curtiss P-6A   Curtiss P-6E

Boeing P-12D   Thomas Morse XP-13 Curtiss XP-14   Boeing XP-15   Berliner Joyce P-16   Curtiss XP-17

Consolidated YIP-25   Boeing P-26A   Consolidated P-27/P-28   Boeing YP-29 YP-32   Consolidated P-30

Curtiss YP-37   Lockheed P-38L   Bell P-39Q P-45 P-76   Curtiss P-40C

Republic XP-47A   Republic P-47D-25   Douglas XP-48   Lockheed XP-49

Vultee XP-54 XP-68   Curtiss XP-55   Northrop XP-56   Tucker XP-57

Curtiss XP-60C   Curtiss P-60D   Curtiss YP-60E   Northrop P-61B

Vultee P-66   McDonnell XP-67   Republic XP-69

Fisher P-75A   Bell XP-77

U.S. FIGHTERS

To my parents

U.S. FIGHTERS

By

LLOYD S. JONES

1975

AERO PUBLISHERS, INC.
329 West Aviation Road, Fallbrook, CA 92028

Library of Congress Cataloging in Publication Data

Jones, Lloyd S.
  U. S. fighters.

  1. Fighter planes—History. 2. Aeronautics,
Military—United States—History. I. Title.
UG1242.F5J66   358.4'18'3   75-25246
ISBN 0-8168-9200-8

Printed and Published in the United States by Aero Publishers, Inc.

TABLE OF CONTENTS

INTRODUCTION

The fighter airplane, as we know it today, had its beginnings in the First World War, but it was not initially an American development. In fact, no American-designed fighters were actually used in the war because they were years behind European technology. At the time America entered the war, the only suitable planes available were British and French machines, many already proven in combat. When the United States did start building fighters, they were license-built versions of European designs. The first American-developed fighters began to appear in 1918, but even these new planes drew heavily on established European patterns.

Gradually, American fighter development established a course of its own and distinctive new designs paralleled, if not led, world fighter technology. The first of these fighters carried rather complex designations denoting aircraft type, manufacturer, design sequence within the company, type of powerplant, etc. For example, the Packard-LePere LUSAC-11: the "L" represented its French designer, Capitain G. LePere; the "US" was for United States; "AC" for the Army Combat; and the number "11" indicated the eleventh design. This cumbersome method was replaced in September 1920, by one denoting aircraft type and the engine cooling system used on the airplane. In this case, the PW-9C was a *Pursuit*, *Water*-cooled, ninth PW type, third version (indicated by the "C").

In May 1924, the designating system was again simplified; the aircraft being identified by a single letter, followed by a number. Succeeding designs received the next number in the sequence. It is at this point that the series of fighters described in this volume had its beginning with the Curtiss P-1 Hawk. The "P" in this classification denoted pursuit. This arrangement for identifying fighters remained until 1948, when the pursuit classification gave way to

the more realistic "F" for fighter. This has caused some confusion among historians who use the "F-" designator for planes which became famous with their pursuit titles, the P-51 and P-47 for instance. Recently, these have been referred to as F-51's and F-47's. It is true that these fighters were still in service when the classification was changed, but in this accounting we have arbitrarily made the change with the Lockheed P/F-80 Shooting Star.

On September 18, 1962, the Defense Department took a step to eliminate conflicting designations by the Air Force and the Navy when referring to the same aircraft. The Air Force, upon acquiring the McDonnell Phantom II, identified it as the F-110A, while to the Navy it was the F4H-1. Under the 1962 system, the Phantom II became the F-4, a single letter after the "-4" denoting which version. The F4H-1 became the Navy's F-4B and the F-4C had been the F-110A. With this new classification, the entire military designation program began at "-1" again for every aircraft type. In the case of the fighters, the greatest effect was on existing Navy types—ten of which received new "F-" numbers. In order to maintain a continuity to the series, these Navy fighters are included in this history. All subsequent fighters now receive successive numbers regardless of the branch of service using them.

The progression of fighters is shown in this book in numerical sequence, not chronological order. This leads to a few planes appearing to be out of place or representing a technical step backward. If a new design, requiring extensive development, was ordered just before a revision to an existing airframe was requested, the revised plane with the later designation would probably be flying long before the new design with the lower number was completed. This is particularly true early in the series when revisions to the Curtiss P-1 were ordered at the same time as more advanced monoplanes were being designed.

Since 1928, the U. S. Army has assigned serial numbers to its aircraft by prefacing the number with the last two digits of the year in which the contract for the specific airplane was awarded. The serial number itself is the airplane's position in the entire quantity of planes ordered in the indicated year. For example, the serial number 48-129 applied to an F-86A identifies it as the 129th airplane ordered in 1948. The radio call number, carried on the tail, is 8129—the "4" being deleted because there would be no other plane with the same number for ten years. In this case, 58-129, a KC-135, would also carry the number 8129 ten years later. Since this could clearly lead to confusion if the F-86 was still in service, the older plane would then receive the tail number 0-8129, indicating it actually was built ten years earlier. If the plane remained in operation for a third decade, the number would become 00-8129. The entire serial number, 48-129, is located on the port nose near the cockpit in inch-high numbers for the life of the aircraft. During the American participation in the Vietnam War, only the last five digits of the radio call sign were painted on the fin of camouflaged fighters.

The specifications for the fighters described herein were obtained from official documents, either from military sources or company files, wherever possible. In a few instances, where the official figures were not available, they were taken from other sources accepted as factual in historical circles. In any case, the speeds and weights given are often average figures since few planes of a given type are likely to have the exact performance characteristics, even in the same production block.

Fighter armament seemed to lag behind the progress made in the airframe and powerplant. Through the twenties and thirties, the Army stubbornly adhered to the single .30 calibre and .50 calibre machine gun armament for each plane. It wasn't until the outbreak of the Second World War that American fighter weaponry became realistic and some fighters carried enough firepower to knock out 60 ton tanks or sink a destroyer. Although rocket armament was used in World War I, it became a practical weapon in the Second War. From there, it has become a highly refined piece of equipment, some of them as complex and expensive as an entire fighter plane of the 1920's.

The development of radar added a second crewman to the fighter and secured his position as a technician responsible for the complex new weapons. The modern jet fighter has been refined to such a degree that it can nearly operate itself, but the pilot and radar operator are still the most important pieces of equipment on board. This has been proven again and again in actual combat.

Fighter design is still progressing. With speeds up to three-times that of sound easily attained, radical concepts in propulsion are being devised to enable the modern fighter to stand still in the air as well. Air combat of the future could extend from a tennis court-size field to the fringes of space. American technology is trying to assure that wherever a fighting aircraft is needed, an American fighter will be available to fulfill the requirements.

ACKNOWLEDGEMENT

Credit for this history must be distributed among many individuals who provided much valuable material and information and assisted in countless ways. My most sincere appreciation is given to these people:

Gordon S. Williams, Boeing; Harry Gann, Douglas; Roy Dwyer, Sr.; Lou Casey, Smithsonian Institution; Robert D. Archer; Jack Leynnwood; Alan Hess; Dustin W. Carter; Dave Wright and Gene Boswell, Rockwell Int.; Al Clare and Fred Bettinger, General Dynamics; Joan Osako, U. S. Air Force; Royal D. Frey, Air Force Museum; Bill Schultz, Rick DeMeis and Andre Hubbard, Grumman; Ted and Greg Krasel; N. Gordon Le Bert, McDonnell Douglas; Bob Ferguson, Lockheed California; Donald J. Norton, Bell Aerospace Co.; George L. Salem and Gus Morfis, Northrop; Roy E. Wendell, Fairchild Republic; and the countless others who have contributed to this effort.

And my special thanks to Gordy Williams, who generously provided so many of these photos from his personal collection, and to my wife, Peggy, for her untiring help in compiling this history.

PHOTO CREDIT

Photo credits are noted on every photo in this volume. To conserve space in the captions, the following Corporate names were abbreviated:

ABBREVIATIONS	COMPLETE NAMES
(1) Bell	Textron Bell Aerospace Division
(2) Convair	Convair Division, General Dynamics Corp.
(3) General Dynamics	General Dynamics Corp.
(4) Grumman	Grumman Aerospace Corp.
(5) LTV	Ling-Temco-Vought
(6) North American (Rockwell)	North American (Rockwell International)
(7) Republic	Fairchild Republic Co.

The Curtiss PW-8 from which the Hawk series was developed   *Air Force Museum*

The Curtiss P-1, though not an entirely new design, was the first fighter to be designated under the simplified system adopted by the Army in 1924. The P-1 was the production version of the XPW-8B, winner of the fly-off with the Boeing XPW-9 in July 1924.

A contract for ten P-1's was received by Curtiss on March 7, 1925, and deliveries began with the XP-1, Air Corps Serial 25-410, on August 17, 1925. The remaining nine P-1's were delivered in the following months and were assigned to the 27th and 94th Pursuit Squadrons where they were operational for five years. In 1926, 25 improved P-1A's were received by the Army.

The P-1 airframe was a versatile structure and the original design was the basis of many subsequent pursuit designations and subtypes. Power was provided by a twelve-cylinder Curtiss V-1150 engine which was rated at 435 hp on the early P-1 types. The first variation in the P-1 series was the P-1B, but the changes were minor—mainly up-rated engines and larger wheels. Twenty-five of this version were followed by 33 P-1C's with wheel brakes. In 1929, 52 similar Hawk AT-4 and AT-5 trainers were converted to P-1D, E, and F fighters; and, with the reversion of four P-2's to P-1's, a total of 149 P-1's were produced.

The P1-B was a single-bay biplane with a wingspan of 31 feet 6 inches and an area of 252 square feet. Length was 22 feet 11 inches and it stood 8 feet 10¾ inches high.

Two machine guns were mounted in the nose above the engine, a .30 and .50 cal., synchronized to fire through the propeller. Internal fuel capacity was 50 gallons and an external tank could carry another 50 gallons to provide a range of 342 miles.

Maximum speed of the P-1B was 165 mph, stalling speed being 58 mph. This version of the Hawk could climb at the rate of 1,600 fpm and had a service ceiling of 21,000 ft. Empty and loaded weights were 2,041 lbs. and 2,841 lbs.

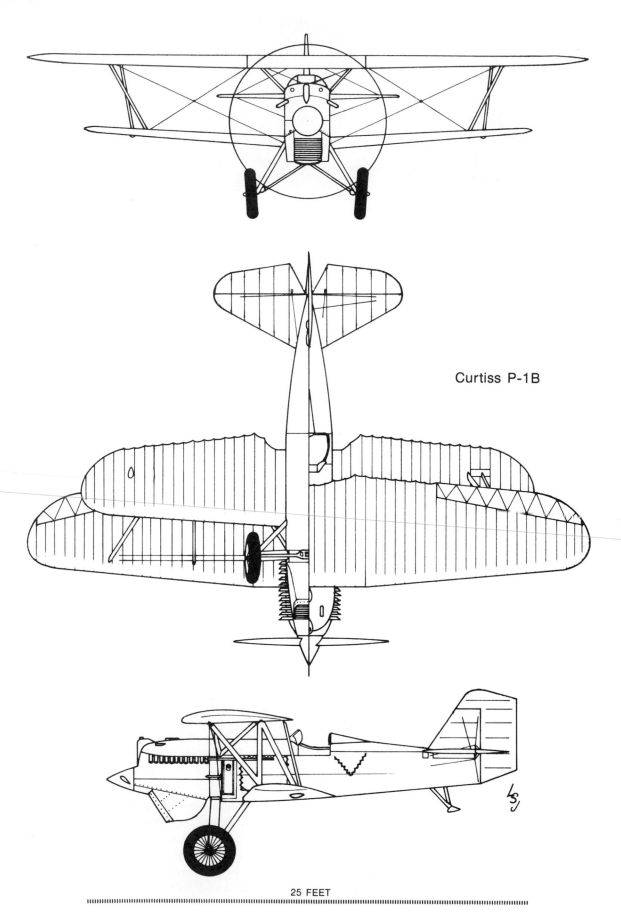

Curtiss P-1B

25 FEET

One of the 25 P-1B's showing the characteristics of the design.   Gordon S. Williams

Note the added mud guard on this P-1C.   Gordon S. Williams

The P-1 was the first of the taper-wing Hawks. This P-1D is from the 43rd School Squadron, Kelly Field, Texas.
                    Gordon Williams

CURTISS
P-2 HAWK

The first P-2. This aircraft was later fitted with a turbo-supercharger. Designation was changed to XP-2.
Gordon S. Williams

Along with the original contract for 10 P-1's, the March 7, 1925, order included five models of the Hawk with a Curtiss V-1400 engine. These planes (S.N. 25-420 to 424) were completed in January 1926. The first P-2 was modified to carry a supercharger and a ground-adjustable Hamilton propeller, and was designated XP-2. The exhaust driven turbo-supercharger increased the horsepower of the V-1400 from 510 to 600. During flight testing, Curtiss called the XP-2 the fastest plane of its type in the world with a speed of 180 mph at 20,000 feet.

The supercharger was mounted on the right side of the fuselage nose with the engine exhaust ducted through the turbine. The turbine drove a compressor which then forced air into the carburetor. However, the V-1400 engine was not satisfactory and only

the XP-2 was fitted with the supercharger.

The remaining P-2's had been put into squadron service, but with the failure of the V-1400 engine, they received new powerplants a year after their delivery. Three of the P-2's received Curtiss V-1150 engines and were redesignated P-1's. The fourth P-2, 25-423, became the XP-6 when a Curtiss V-1550 Conqueror engine was installed.

The XP-2 had a span of 31 feet 7 inches, a length of 22 feet 10 inches, and was 8 feet 7 inches high. Wing area was 252 square feet. Service ceiling was 22,950 feet, but a maximum 24,000 feet could be reached. Initial climb rate was 2170 fpm.

Weights were 2,081 pounds empty and 2,869 pounds loaded. Fuel capacity was 50 gallons; and with a 50 gallon external tank, range was 400 miles.

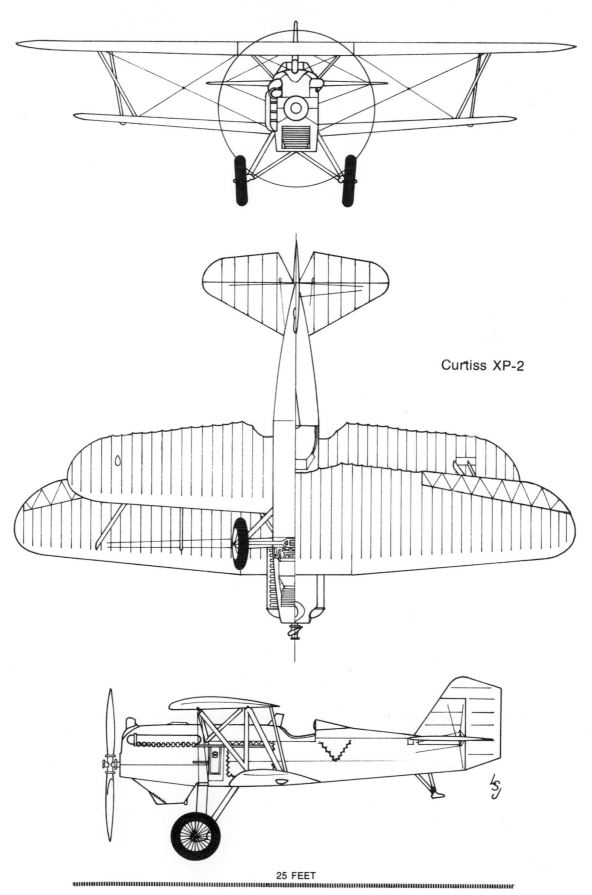

Curtiss XP-2

25 FEET

An interesting feature in this view of the P-2 is the early instrumentation boom on the left wing strut.

Gordon S. Williams

This view shows the P-3A with the Townend ring cowling. The XP-21's were identical with the exception of the engines, which were Wasp Jrs. of 300 hp. Gordon S. Williams

The six P-3's, while still retaining the basic Hawk airframe, differed in the fact that they were powered by a 410 hp Pratt & Whitney R-1340-3 Wasp radial engine. The XP-3 was actually the last production P-1A, S.N. 26-300, and was to receive a Curtiss R-1454 air-cooled engine of 390 hp. Before completion of the XP-3, it was found that the R-1454 would not be satisfactory. The Pratt & Whitney engine was substituted and the plane was designated XP-3A.

A second XP-3A (S.N. 28-189 and actually the first production P-3A) was built with a streamlined cowling and spinner for improved performance. In 1929, the Army entered this plane in the National Air Races where it placed second in the Thompson race with a speed of 186.84 mph.

The remaining four production P-3A's were delivered for service testing of the Wasp engine. The exposed engine created a great deal of drag which lessened the performance of the fighter, and the planes were fitted with Townend ring cowlings to improve the air flow. The P-3's were not popular with their pilots because the large radial engine blocked forward visibility; and the addition of the Townend ring did

more to further restrict the view than increase speed.

A continuing evaluation of the radial engine led to the mounting of a 300 hp Pratt & Whitney R-985 Wasp Jr. on both of the XP-3A's. Instead of changing the designation to P-3B, the two aircraft were somewhat deceptively labeled XP-21's. (This practice of assigning a totally different numerical designation to an airframe when the physical change was relatively minor gave the appearance of an extensive line of new aircraft. In fact, eleven of the fighters assigned "P-" designations were actually modifications of the basic airframe, primarily in the area of engine changes.)

The P-3A dimensions were: wingspan 31 feet 7 inches, length 22 feet 5 inches, height 8 feet 9 inches. Area for the top wing was 158 square feet and 94 square feet for the lower surfaces, totaling 252 square feet. Production P-3A's weighed 1,956 lbs. empty and grossed 2,788 lbs. Top speed was 153 mph, cruising at 122 mph and touching-down at 58 mph. Service ceiling was 23,000 feet.

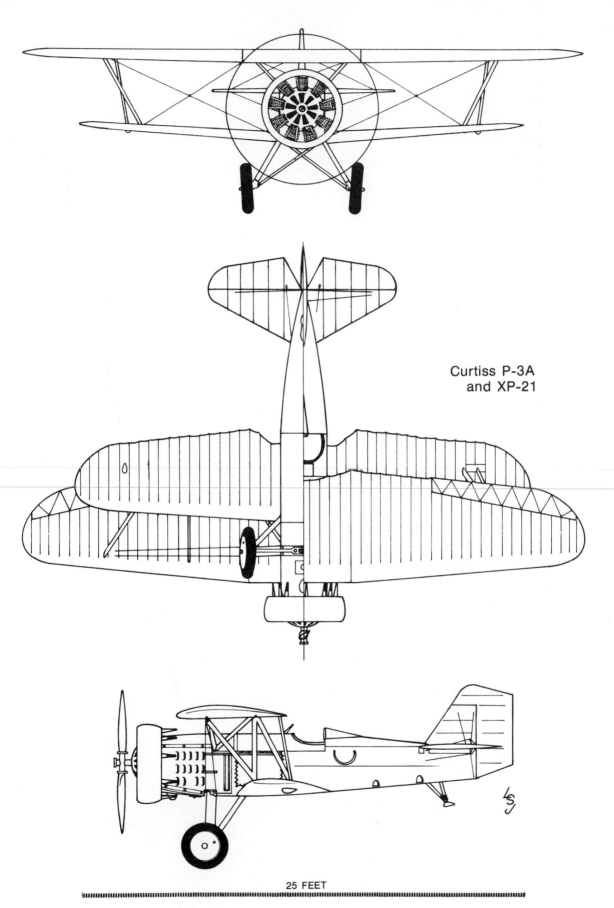

Curtiss P-3A
and XP-21

25 FEET

18

One of the six P-3's before addition of the engine cowling.   *Air Force Museum*

The completed XP-4 showing the supercharger mounting.   *Gordon S. Williams*

Prior to the adoption of the "P-" designation, Boeing had produced the PW-9 series of fighter. In 1926, the Army requested a modification to the last of these fighters as a test bed for the turbo-supercharger. A blown 510 hp Packard 1A-1500 was installed on the fighter and it was delivered as the XP-4 (25-324). The original PW-9 armament of one .30 and one .50 cal. machine guns in the nose was to be supplimented by two additional .30 cal. guns under the lower wing, firing outside the propeller arc. The added weight of these modifications led to an increase of 9½ feet to the span of the lower wing to reduce wing loading.

Flight testing proved the combination of design, weight, and powerplant were not compatible and the XP-4 was grounded after only 4½ hours.

The XP-4 carried two sets of ailerons on its 32 foot wings, and its Packard engine drove a four-bladed wooden propeller to reach a top speed of 160.9 mph. Service ceiling was 22,000 feet, and even with the supercharger, the absolute ceiling was only 850 feet higher. Range on its 100 gallons of fuel was 375 miles. The XP-4 had an empty weight of 2,783 lbs. and grossed 3,650 lbs. Length was 23 feet 11 inches and height was 8 feet 10 inches.

The PW-9 design was strongly influenced by the German Fokker D-V11 of World War I, and the inboard strut arrangement used by the XP-4 was a virtual duplication of that used on the Fokker fighter.

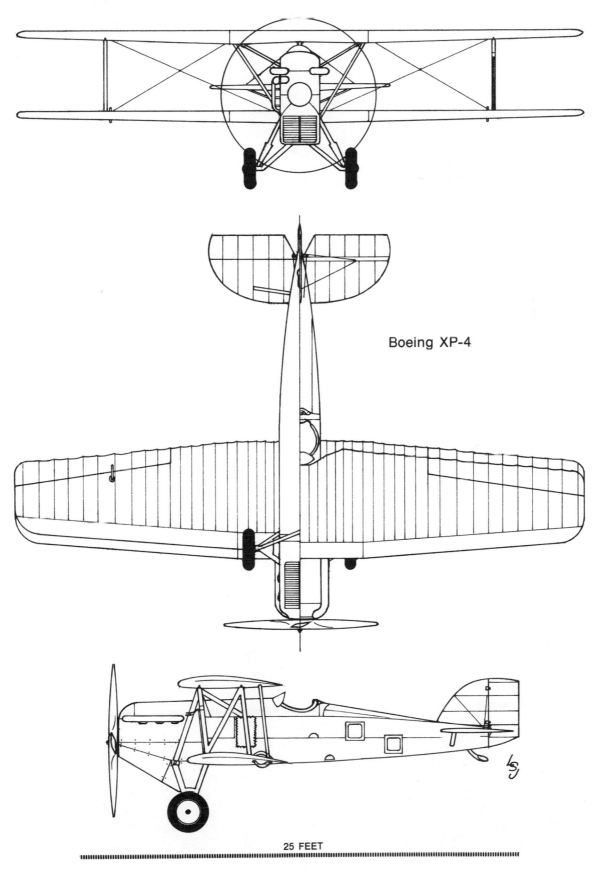

Boeing XP-4

25 FEET

Cockpit detail of the Boeing XP-4 before fuselage covering was applied. This is typical of the steel tube construction used during the 1920's.

Gordon S. Williams

CURTISS
P-5 SUPERHAWK

With the supercharged engine, the P-5 Superhawk could fly two miles higher than the P-1.
Dustin W. Carter

Still entranced with the turbo-supercharger, the Army ordered five new versions of the P-1 with Curtiss V-1150-4 supercharged engines on May 14, 1927. These planes carried the designation P-5 (S.N. 27-327 to 27-331). The first of these was delivered to Wright Field in January 1928 as the XP-5.

Flight tests again proved the value of the supercharger. The P-5 attained 173.5 mph at 25,000 feet, exceeding the P-1 by more than 8 mph; and had a service ceiling of 31,-900 feet, more than two miles higher than the P-1.

The cockpit was equipped with two oxygen bottles, and a fabric shroud was fitted around the pilot and snapped to the cockpit rim. Air was heated by passing it over the engine exhaust manifold, then ducted into the cockpit under the shroud.

At sea level the P-5 was 21 mph slower than the P-1, but within ten minutes the Superhawk could climb 20,000 feet where its supercharged engine operated more efficiently.

Two of the P-5's were lost within three months of their delivery; the last two were operated by the 94th Pursuit Squadron for four years, until April 1932.

Mounting the same wing and tail units as all the Hawk series, the P-5 had a wingspan of 31 feet 6 inches and a length of 23 feet 8 inches. Using a long landing gear and larger propeller than the P-1, the Superhawk had a height of 9 feet 3 inches. Cruising speed was 117 mph, landing speed was 62 mph. Fuel capacity was 50 gallons internally with an additional 50 gallons in an auxiliary tank giving a range of 220 miles.

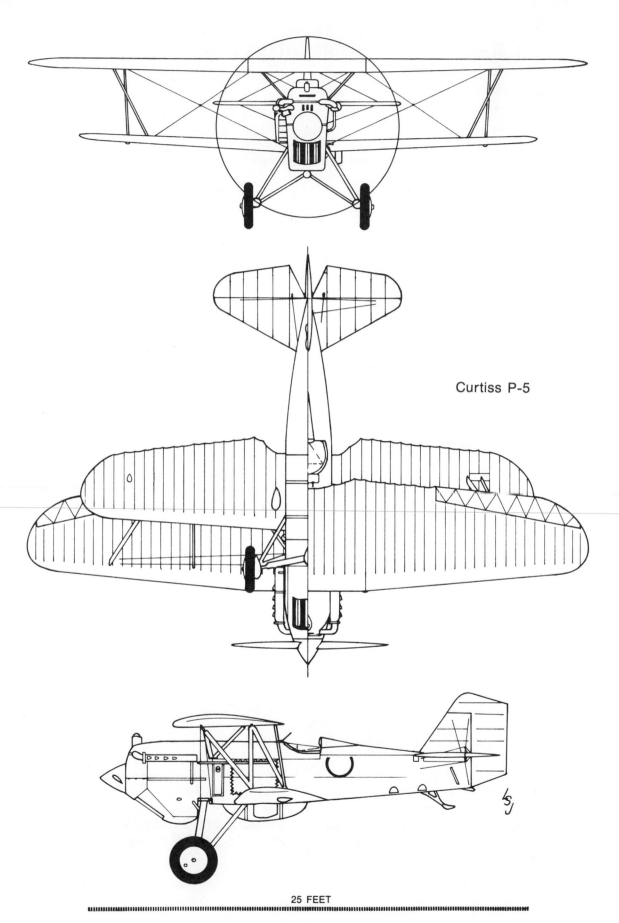

Curtiss P-5

25 FEET

The first P-5 with a supercharged V-1150-4 Curtiss D-12 engine.　　　　　*Gordon S. Williams*

The supercharged P-5 high altitude fighter. Note the shroud around the cockpit to help keep the pilot warm.
Gordon S. Williams

CURTISS
P-6 HAWK

The Conqueror engine of this P-6 and the following 8 planes were water cooled and required a large radiator system.
Gordon S. Williams

The group of Hawks carrying the P-6 label displayed more configuration changes than any other of the Hawk line. The first of the P-6's was the fourth P-2 (#25-423) with a 600 hp Curtiss V-1570 Conqueror engine. Otherwise it differed little in appearance from the P-2. The primary purpose of the installation was to provide a test bed for the new engine. In 1927, this XP-6 was entered in the National Air Races at Spokane, placing second in the unlimited class with a speed of 189.6 mph.

Winner of this race was another Hawk, actually a cross-breed between the XP-W8A and a P-1A. Carrying its P-1A serial number 26-295 but designated the XP-6A, the composite airplane presented a trim picture of speed and elegance as it won the race at a speed of 201.2 mph. The XP-6A was also Conqueror powered; but instead of

mounting a large radiator scoop under the nose, a characteristic of the Hawks, the cooling liquid was channelled through flush wing-mounted radiators. The radiators followed the contours of the 30 foot 6 inch untapered plywood-covered wings, and contributed almost no drag—suitable for a racer but too vulnerable to gunfire to be practical for a fighter. A second XP-6A was designated but this was a true P-6, S.N. 29-263, which was being used for tests and had no relationship to the racer.

The XP-6B was another P-1 (29-259) fitted with a Conqueror engine and long-range fuel tanks for a flight from New York to Nome, Alaska, in July 1929.

The initial production P-6, 29-260, was delivered in October 1929. The first of 18 P-6's, it mounted the wings and tail surfaces of its sister Hawks, but had a much fatter

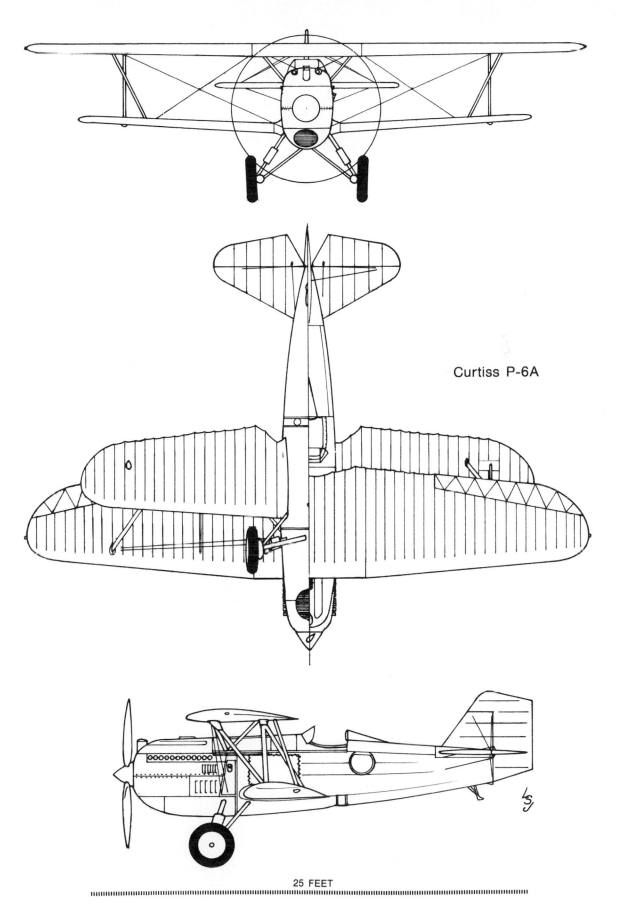

Curtiss P-6A

25 FEET

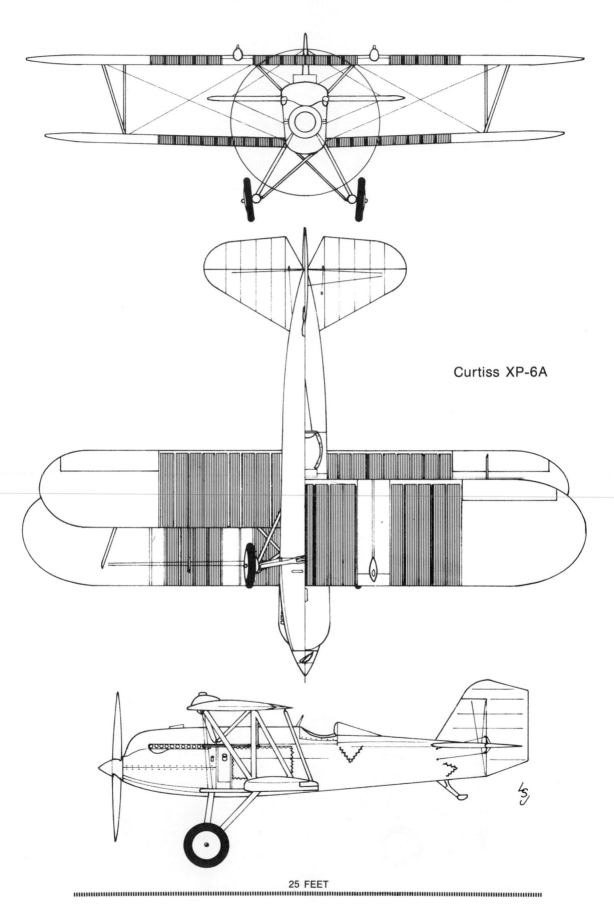

Curtiss XP-6A

25 FEET

One of the Glycol-cooled P-6A's.   Gordon S. Williams

fuselage to accommodate the large Conqueror engine. A huge radiator was faired under the engine to handle the greater cooling requirements of the big engine. The tenth P-6, and those following, were redesigned to utilize ethylene glycol for cooling, thus reducing frontal area and weight. These were identified as P-6A's.

There were many other modifications to the P-6 series, but the configuration that was produced in the largest quantity of all the biplane Hawks was the P-6E. Originally ordered as Y1P-22, 45 of the trim fighters were delivered at a cost of $12,360 per plane. The P-6E was powered by the 600 hp V-1570C Conqueror engine which provided a top speed of 197.8 mph at sea level. Service ceiling was 24,700 feet. Empty, the P-6E weighed 2,699 lbs; full, it weighed in at 3,-

392 lbs. Fuel capacity was 50 gallons internally with an additional 50 gallons in the external tank. With this fuel load, the P-6E had a range of 572 miles.

Standard armament of the P-6E was one .30 cal. and one .50 cal., or two .50 cal., machine guns in the side of the fuselage behind the engine. One version of the P-6E, the XP-6H, was tested with four additional .30's in the wings, two above and two below.

Serial numbers of the 45 P-6E's were 32-233 to 32-277. Dimensions were basically the same as the preceeding Hawks: wingspan 31 feet 6 inches, length 23 feet 2 inches, and height 8 feet 10 inches. One example of the P-6E is now part of the Air Force Museum in Dayton, Ohio.

The original XP-6A was a composite type created from a P-1 and a PW-8A for the 1927 National Air Races. It was not a true Hawk.
                                                                    Gordon S. Williams

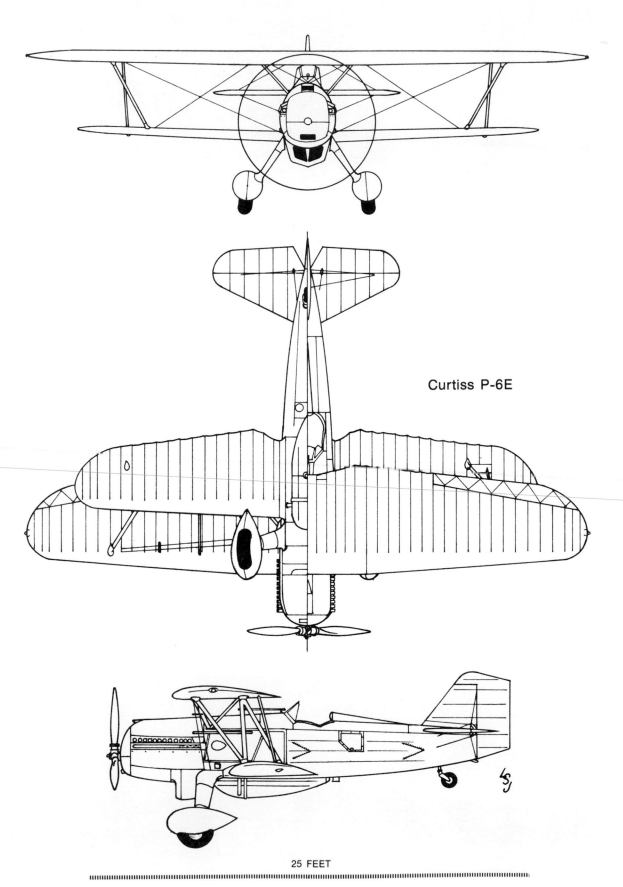

Curtiss P-6E

25 FEET

One P-6E was fitted with an enclosed cockpit and a turbo-supercharger and became the XP-6F.
Gordon S. Williams

This P-6E was used by the 33rd Pursuit Squadron.   *Gordon S. Williams*

The P-6E considered by many to be the most graceful of the Hawk fighters.   *Gordon S. Williams*

Even though the XP-7 was faster than the PW-9 from which it was built, it was at the upper limits of its design capabilities and no further models were built.
Air Force Museum

As the production of Boeing's PW-9 series was concluding, the Curtiss V-1570 Conqueror engine became available and the final PW-9D (28-41) was adapted to test this powerplant. Distinguishable from the production PW-9 by a shorter, deeper nose, the modified fighter, called XP-7, was also 73 pounds lighter and some 17 mph faster than the PW-9's.

The XP-7 was first flown in November 1928, and initial testing proved the 600 hp Curtiss engine was quite suitable for use in fighters. Because of the improved performance, it was proposed to build 4 P-7's for service evaluation—even a V-1570 powered PW-9E was suggested. But the PW-9 was already at the limit of its growth potential and the plan was abandoned in view of newer designs already being developed.

The water-cooled V-1570 provided the XP-7 with a top speed of 167.5 mph and a rate of climb of 1,867 fpm. Service ceiling was 21,120 feet. Wingspan was 32 feet, wing area was 241 square feet, length was 24 feet, and height was 9 feet. Empty weight of the XP-7 was 2,323 pounds and gross weight was 3,157 pounds. Fuel capacity was 50 gallons providing a range of 155 miles.

On completion of flight testing, the Conqueror engine was removed from the XP-7 airframe and replaced by a Curtiss D-12, converting the XP-7 back to the PW-9D. The Boeing product number for the XP-7 was Model 93.

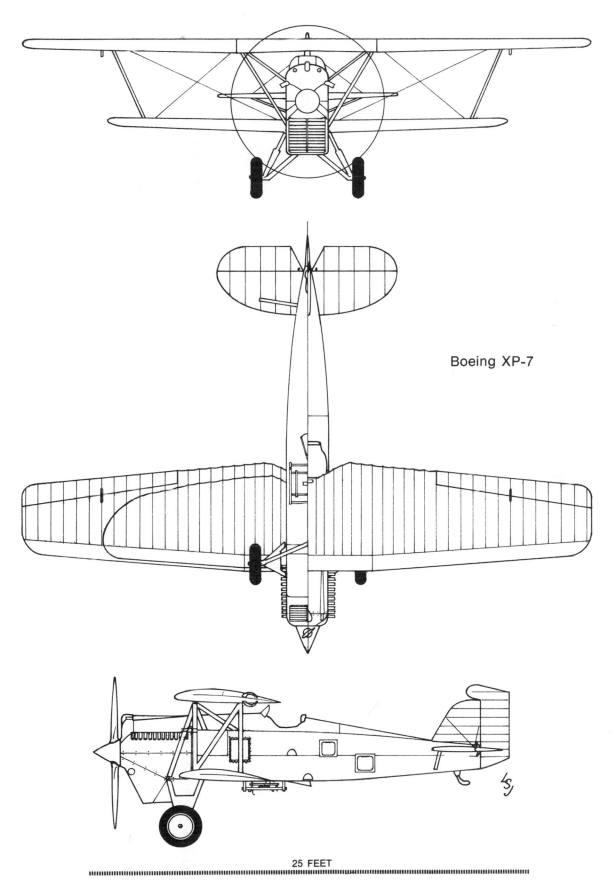

Boeing XP-7

25 FEET

BOEING
XP-8

Boeing's XP-8 featured a unique wing-root radiator for cooling its Packard engine.   Gordon S. Williams

In July 1927, Boeing delivered a new fighter to the Army for evaluation. Derived from the PW-9 series as a private venture in 1926 and designated Model 66 by Boeing, this plane was powered by an experimental Packard engine. It was unique in appearance due to the incorporation of the cooling radiator into the root of the lower wing and the slim cowling around the 600 hp engine. Wing and tail surfaces were similar to the PW-9, wing area being 4 sq. feet less than the earlier fighter.

The Army began testing the plane in January 1928, with the designation XP-8 and the serial number 28-359. Handling characteristics and design were good, but the inverted Packard 2A-1530 hindered performance to the degree that the XP-8 was rejected as a suitable fighter. The XP-8 design marked the end of the use of Packard engines in Army aircraft, and was the last

tapered-wing biplane Boeing built for the Air Corps; although, the basic XP-8 airframe was adapted successfully with an air-cooled radial engine for the Navy as the F2B.

The XP-8 had a maximum speed of 173.2 mph and cruised at 148 mph. It weighed 2,390 lbs empty and grossed 3,421 lbs. A fuel capacity of 90 gallons gave the XP-8 a range of 325 miles. Service ceiling was 20,950 feet and initial rate of climb was 1,800 fpm. Wingspan was 30 feet 1 inch, area 237 square feet, overall length 23 feet 4 inches. One .30 cal. and one .50 cal. machine gun were mounted in the nose.

The XP-8 did not meet the performance requirements for the Army's 1925 USAAC competition for which it was originally intended; but it did remain in the Air Corps until June 1929, when it was finally scrapped.

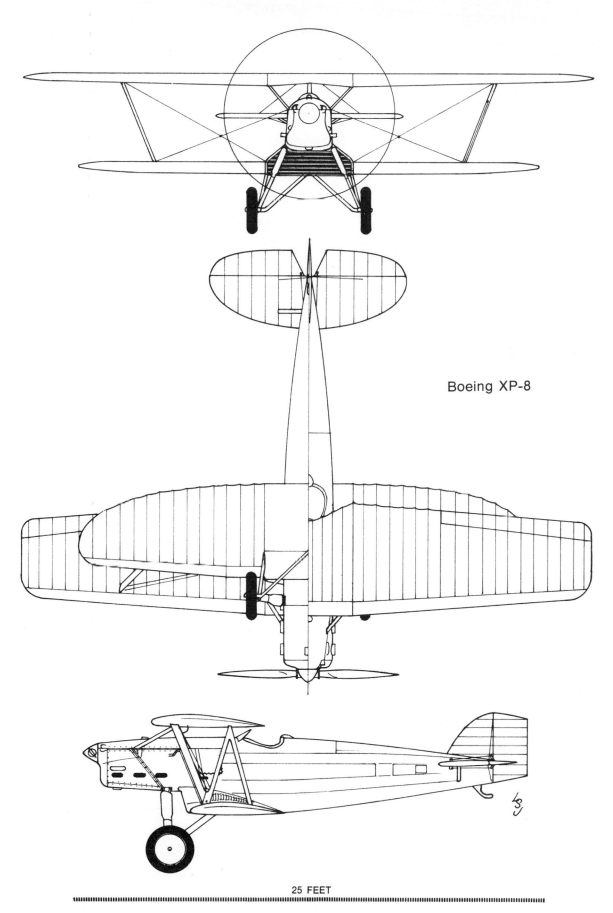

Boeing XP-8

25 FEET

BOEING
XP-9

Boeing's all metal XP-9. Though unsuccessful as a fighter, it introduced a new construction method which later became standard.   *Gordon S. Williams*

Even with the success of the biplane configuration for military aircraft, by 1928 it was apparent that the upper limits of performance for the double-wingers was soon to be reached. In 1923, the Verville-Sperry monoplane racer had reached 210 mph in tests and other single-wing designs were performing equally well. At the request of the Army, Boeing undertook the design of a monoplane fighter in 1928, to be known as the XP-9 (Boeing Model 96).

Design and development problems, as well as a low priority, delayed the delivery which had been scheduled for April 1929, until September 1930. When finally delivered, the XP-9 looked the part of a scrappy fighter. Its broad wing was mounted to the top of a stocky fuselage, but unfortunately obscuring most of the pilot's forward visibility. The reliable Curtiss V-1570-15 Conqueror engine had been chosen as the powerplant, and the usual armament of two .30 or .50 cal. machine guns could be mounted behind the engines firing through troughs at the side.

Flight testing of the XP-9, S.N. 28-386,

began on November 18, 1930; and judging from the first pilot's response, was destined to be short. Visibility was poor and the flying characteristics were no better. As the pilot put it, it was "a menace!" In its original configuration, the XP-9 mounted a small rectangular fin similar to that used on the P-12. This did not provide sufficient control and a much larger triangular surface was installed. The Conqueror engine was rated at 600 hp, but delivered only 583 hp, and pulled the XP-9 to a maximum speed of 213 mph at 12,000 feet. Service ceiling was 25,300 feet with a climb rate of 2,430 feet for the first minute. Fuel capacity was 135 gallons and the XP-9 had a range of 425 miles. The all-metal structure of the XP-9 weighed 2,669 lbs and the plane grossed 3,623 lbs. The 36 foot 7 inch wing had an area of 210 sq. feet. Length was 25 feet 1¾ inches and height was 7 feet 9 inches.

The XP-9 was not a success as a fighter but its semi-monocoque fuselage set the pace for future aircraft.

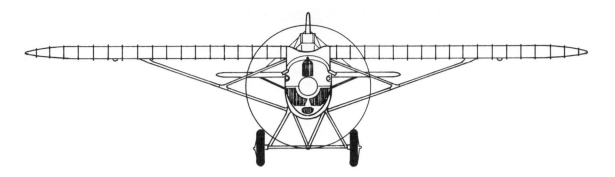

Boeing XP-9

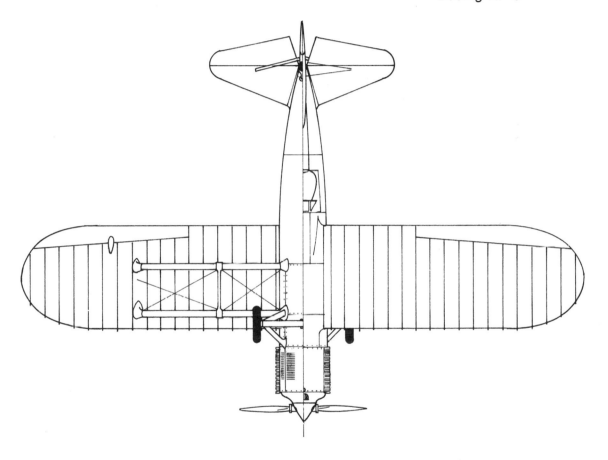

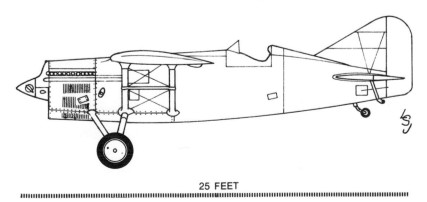

25 FEET

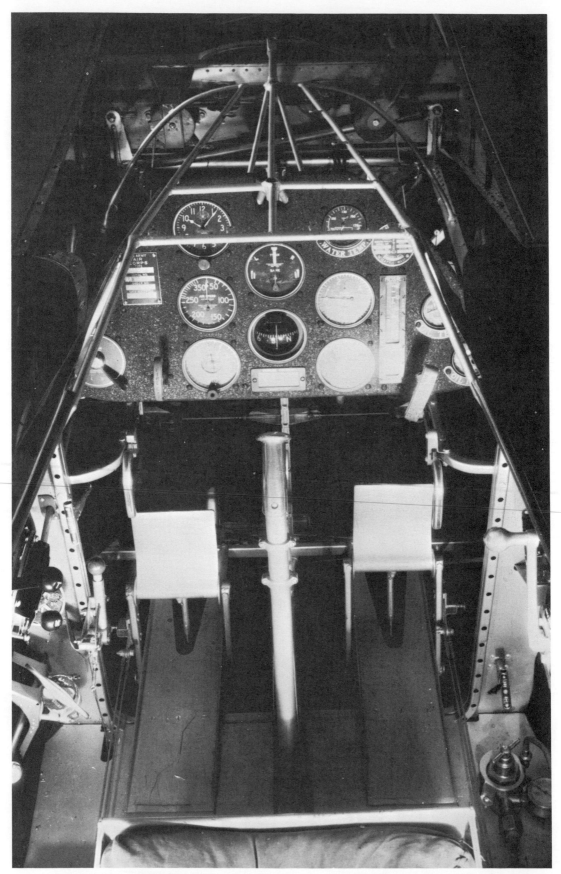

Cockpit detail of the XP-9.

Boeing

CURTISS
XP-10

The wing radiator system on the XP-10 was impractical for a combat plane due to its vulnerability to gun-fire.
Gordon S. Williams

Receiving a contract on June 18, 1928, for a fast maneuverable fighter with good pilot visibility, Curtiss designed a sleek Conqueror-powered biplane with plywood wings mounted gull-like into the fuselage. This arrangement of the wings provided excellent visibility for the pilot who had an unobstructed forward and upward view. To overcome the drag created by the characteristic radiator scoop of the water-cooled engine, the cooling system was formed of brass sheet wrapped around the upper wings. The sheeting was ribbed to form channels through which the cooling water was directed. Unfortunately, the low drag characteristics of the flush radiator were offset by the technical and mechanical problems it presented, not the least of these being its vulnerability to gunfire.

As the XP-10, the new plane received the Air Corps serial 28-387 and was delivered in August 1928. The 600 hp V-1710-15 engine provided a top speed of 173 mph, but continual problems with the plumbing of the cooling system led to the abandonment of the program. The adoption of ethylene glycol as a coolant reduced the radiator area so that it was no longer a major factor in overall drag.

The plywood-covered wings spanned 33 feet. The fuselage was made of fabric-covered steel tubing, overall length being 24½ feet. Height was 10 feet 10 inches. The XP-10 had a loaded weight of 3,700 pounds.

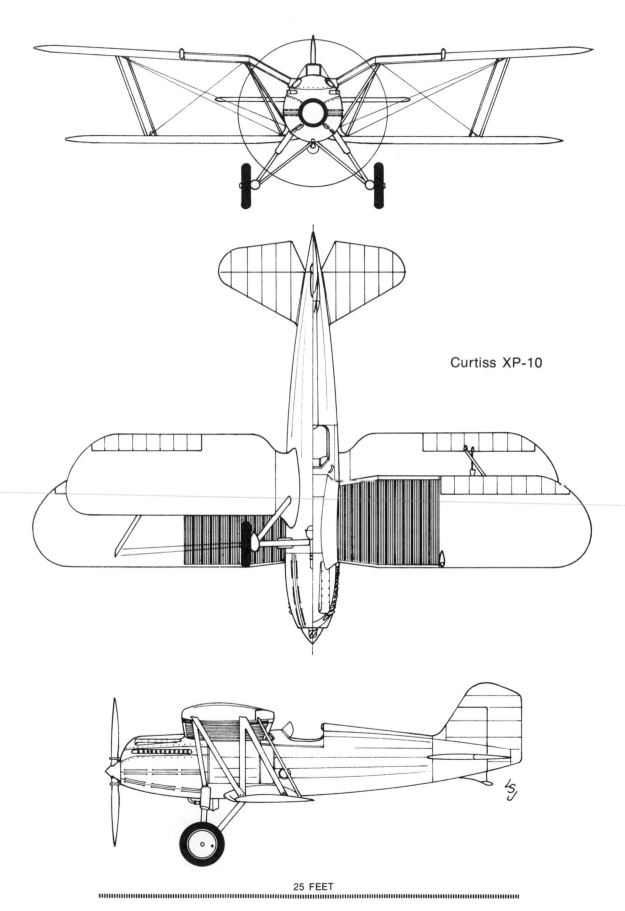

Curtiss XP-10

25 FEET

As mentioned earlier, the Hawk airframe was subjected to many modifications to improve performance and remain ahead of competing manufacturers. On October 3, 1928, three P-11's were ordered along with the initial P-6 contract. The P-11's were intended to receive the new Curtiss H-1640-1 Chieftain engine.

The Chieftain had a rather unusual configuration for an aircraft powerplant. It was a two-bank, twelve-cylinder, air-cooled, in-line radial engine rated at 600 hp. The second bank of cylinders was directly in line with the first bank and shared a common cylinder head cover. A trial installation of the Chieftain on a Curtiss XO-18 Falcon revealed serious cooling problems with the second bank of cylinders being directly inside the heat envelope of the first row. The over-heating difficulty was never overcome and all projects using the Chieftain were discontinued.

As a result of the elimination of the Chieftain engine, two of the three P-11's were completed with supercharged V-1570-23 Conqueror engines (29-367 and 68) as P-6D's. The remaining P-11, 29-374, was completed with a Wright Cyclone engine and redesignated YP-20.

Dimensions for P-11's were typical of the biplane Hawk series.

Curtiss P-11

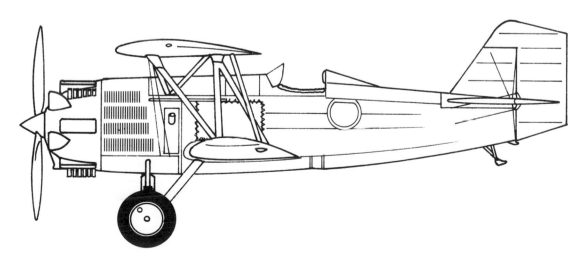

25 FEET

The third of nine Boeing P-12's.   *Gordon S. Williams*

As the production of Boeing's PW-9 series was drawing to a close in 1928, the company began development of its successor. Two prototypes of a new fighter were built as Boeing Models 83 and 89. Each of the designs was essentially the same and both were financed by the Boeing Company. Both of the planes were eventually purchased by the Navy, who designated them XF4B-1, but an Army evaluation of the Model 89 led to an order of ten aircraft as P-12's.

The first P-12, 29-353, flew on April 11, 1929, and was followed by nine more aircraft. The last of these, incorporating several improvements, became the XP-12A. As originally delivered, the P-12's Pratt & Whitney R-1340 engines were uncowled; but the XP-12A featured a long-chord NACA cowling for drag reduction plus balanced ailerons. Seven days after delivery, the XP-12A was lost in a mid-air collision, but enough information had been gained to lead to an order for 90 improved P-12B's. Although the P-12B engine remained uncowled, balanced ailerons replaced the tapered ones of the P-12. The first P-12B was fitted with a turbo-supercharger as the XP-12G, but this unit was later removed and the original designation restored.

One hundred thirty-one P-12C's, featuring ring cowlings and a spreader-bar on the landing gear, were ordered in June 1930; the last 35 of these being delivered as P-12D's. All subsequent models were built with cowled engines and the remaining P-12B's were retro-fitted with the enclosure.

The original P-12 featured untapered wings spanning 30 feet, and were constructed of wood covered by fabric. The fuselage had a square cross section made of bolted aluminum tubing. Overall length was 20 feet 1 inch. The P-12D was powered by a 525 hp Pratt & Whitney R-1340-17 which gave it a top speed of 188 mph at 7,000 feet. Service ceiling was 25,400 feet and range was 475 miles. Empty and loaded weights were 1,956 pounds and 2,648 pounds.

To help extend the service life of the P-12 series, Boeing again invested in a company-funded project to build a version of the P-12 with an all-metal fuselage. Based on the experience gained during the construction of

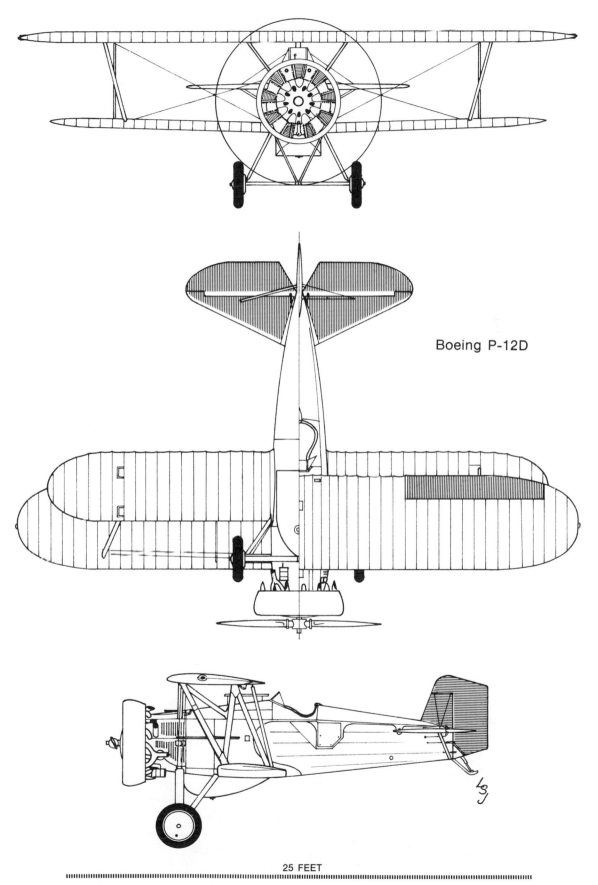

Boeing P-12D

25 FEET

This P-12D has been fitted with an "E" type tail.   *Gordon S. Williams*

The P-12E had an all-metal fuselage and a fairing behind the cockpit.   *Gordon S. Williams*

The all-metal fuselage of the P-12E was developed from the XP-9 and XP-15 monoplanes.
Gordon S. Williams

the XP-9 and XP-15 monoplanes, the Model 218 was assembled. This plane received the Air Corps designation XP-925, and flight testing led to an order for 135 examples as the P-12E. This version of the fighter had an enlarged vertical stabilizer, a feature that also found its way into the earlier P-12D's, and a headrest. Many subdesignations were assigned to the P-12E before production was completed; but the last P-12 subtype actually built on the line as such was the P-12F, 25 of which were converted from the P-12E order. These had 600 hp engines.

The P-12E wingspan was the same as the P-12D, but the overall length was 2 inches greater; wing area was 227½ square feet and maximum speed was 189 mph at 7,000 feet. Service ceiling was 26,300 feet and range was 580 miles.

The P-12 was armed with either two .30 cal. or one .30 and .50 cal. machine guns located in the nose. Additional armament, in the form of light bombs, could be mounted beneath the wings and landing gear.

A total of 366 P-12's of all subtypes was produced.

When originally delivered, the P-12B engine was uncowled.   *Gordon S. Williams*

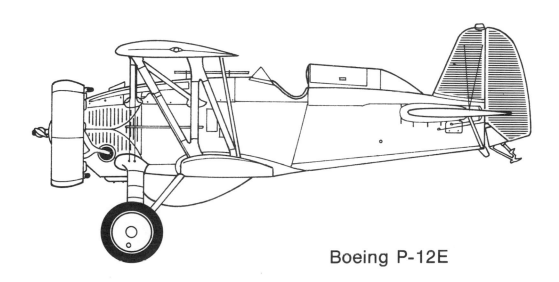

Boeing P-12E

45

THOMAS-MORSE
XP-13 VIPER, CURTISS XP-14

A complex system of baffles was installed to direct cooling air over the double bank of cylinders.

The Thomas-Morse Aircraft Corp. was one of the first American companies to become involved in fighter production after the First World War, and is probably best known for its MB-3 Scout design of 1919. A pioneer in aircraft construction techniques, Thomas-Morse built several advanced, if not attractive, designs in the hope of securing another production contract from the Army. Its final offering, though still not winning the sought-after orders, was the most successful of the lot. Given the name Viper by its builder, who also financed the project, the Thomas-Morse fighter was delivered to the Army in 1929, who purchased it in June of that year during its flight-test program. On entering the Army, it became the XP-13 with serial number 29-453.

The fuselage of the Viper was constructed of corrugated aluminum skin secured to a metal frame. The flying surfaces were also of metal frame but covered with fabric. The XP-13 had been designed to use the 600 hp Curtiss H-1640-1 Chieftain air-cooled double-row inline radial engine. Unfortunately, the Chieftain engine suffered from insurmountable cooling problems; and in September of 1930, the XP-13 received a conventional 450 hp Pratt & Whitney Wasp SR-1340C engine. With the lower rated engine, the Viper's top speed increased by 15 mph, due in part to a reduction in weight; but no production orders had been placed and Thomas-Morse was acquired by Consolidated. With the Wasp engine, the Viper became the XP-13A and flight testing continued until the plane was lost due to an in-flight fire.

The XP-13 was a single-bay biplane with a span of 28 feet and wing area of 189 square feet. Length was 23 feet 6 inches and height was 8 feet 5 inches. With the Chieftain engine, the XP-13 weighed 2,262 pounds empty and 3,225 pounds full including 80 gallons of fuel. Top speed was 173 mph with a service ceiling of 20,775 feet.

Installation of the Wasp engine reduced the weights to 2,224 lbs empty and 3,194 lbs loaded; and fuel capacity was reduced to 74 gallons. Top speed was 188.5 mph and service ceiling was raised to 24,150 feet.

A proposed version of the Viper, to be built by Curtiss, was designated XP-14.

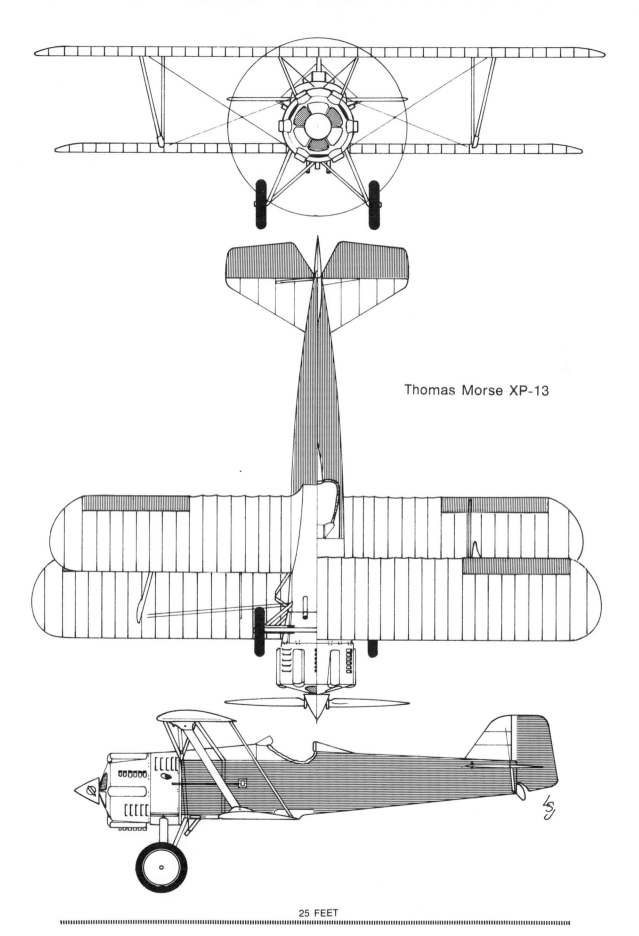

Thomas Morse XP-13

25 FEET

The XP-15 was a monoplane development of the P-12 series.   *Gordon S. Williams*

The second monoplane to bear a "Pursuit" designation was a private-venture design offered by Boeing as their Model 202. The Army accepted the plane for testing and assigned the designation XP-15 to it, but never actually purchased it and no serial number was assigned. Civil registration was X-270V.

Basically, the XP-15 was an all-metal single-wing version of the P-12. When first flown in January 1930, it mounted a P-12C type vertical stabilizer, but this did not provide enough area for the monoplane configuration and an enlarged unit was soon installed. During early testing, the 525 hp Pratt & Whitney SR-1340D was uncowled and the XP-15 reached a top speed of 178 mph. Later, with the addition of Townend ring cowling and the enlarged tail surfaces, the little monoplane was flown 185 mph at 8,000 feet.

The parasol-mounted wing had a span of 30 feet 6 inches and an area of 157.3 square feet. It had a length of 21 feet and stood 9 feet high. Weights were: empty 2,050 lbs, gross 2,790 lbs; fuel capacity was 128 gallons. Service ceiling was 26,550 feet and initial climb rate was 1,860 fpm. No armament was mounted on the XP-15, but provision was made for two .30 cal. machine guns in the fuselage.

While the XP-15 was a good performer, it did not achieve production; but its all-metal fuselage and modified tail were used to improve the P-12 series and became standard on the P-12E.

The XP-15 was lost on February 7, 1931, when a propeller blade failed during a high-speed dash and the unbalanced engine was torn from its mounts.

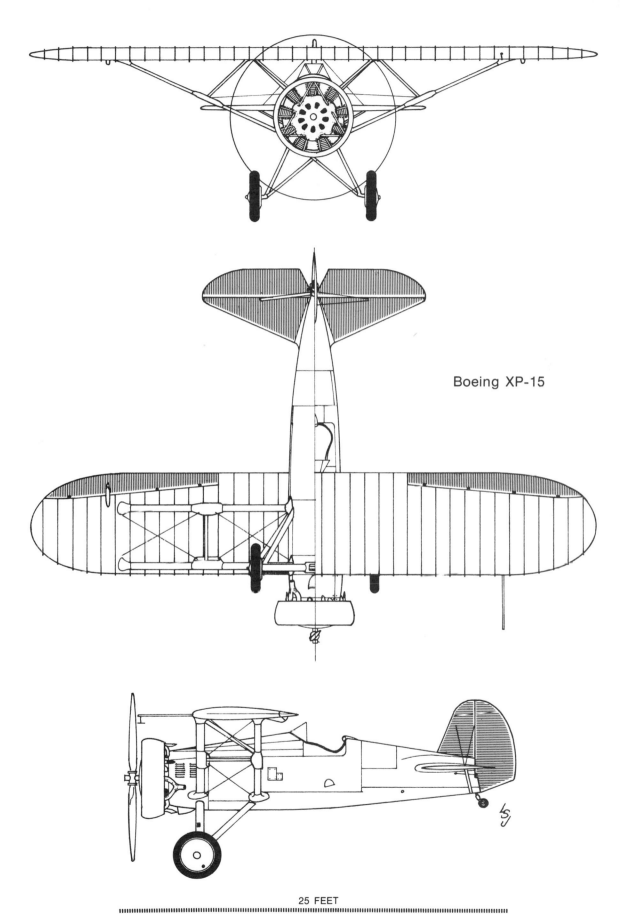

Boeing XP-15

25 FEET

The Berliner-Joyce XP-16 used a supercharged Conqueror engine but production models were not supercharged.

Rockwell Int.

In April 1929, Boeing, Curtiss, and Berliner-Joyce competed for a contract to produce a two-seat fighter. The winning proposal was submitted by Berliner-Joyce, and the first example appeared as the XP-16 in October of the same year. Two-place fighters were not new to the Air Corps, but the XP-16 was the first to appear since the unorthodox Thomas-Morse TM-24 of 1925.

The XP-16 (29-326) was a gull-winged biplane constructed of metal tubing but covered with fabric. Even the wing ribs were formed of tubing instead of being stamped from sheet metal. Power for the XP-16 was a supercharged Curtiss V-1570A Conqueror of 600 hp turning a two-bladed propeller. This engine gave the fighter a maximum speed of 186 mph at 5,000 feet and a service ceiling of 26,200 feet. The extra crewman had the duty of protecting the rear of the fighter with a single .30 cal. machine gun on a flexible mount. Forward armament installed on the production P-16's comprised two fixed .50's firing over the cowl.

After successfully passing its flight tests, the XP-16 was ordered into production and 25 Y1P-16's were built for service test and evaluation. Production aircraft were powered by a Conqueror driving a three-bladed propeller but without the supercharger. This powerplant reduced the performance and ceiling but gave a range of 650 miles.

During their service lives, the Y1P-16's were reclassified as P-16's; then, in order to distinguish them from single-place fighters, they were further classed as PB-1's (Pursuit, Biplace).

Although the P-16 carried two crewmen, it was only slightly larger and heavier than its single-seat contemporaries. Wingspan was 34 feet with an area of 279 square feet. It was 28 feet 2 inches long and stood 9 feet high. Maximum speed was 175 mph at sea level and cruising speed 151 mph. It landed at 66 mph. Internal fuel capacity was 85 gallons, and an auxiliary tank carried beneath the fuselage could carry another 75 gallons. The P-16 airframe weight 2,803 pounds empty and the plane had a loaded weight of two tons. In addition to its three machine guns, the P-16 could carry 225 lbs of bombs on external racks.

No additional orders were placed for the P-16 and the Berliner-Joyce Company was absorbed into the General Aviation Co., later to become North American.

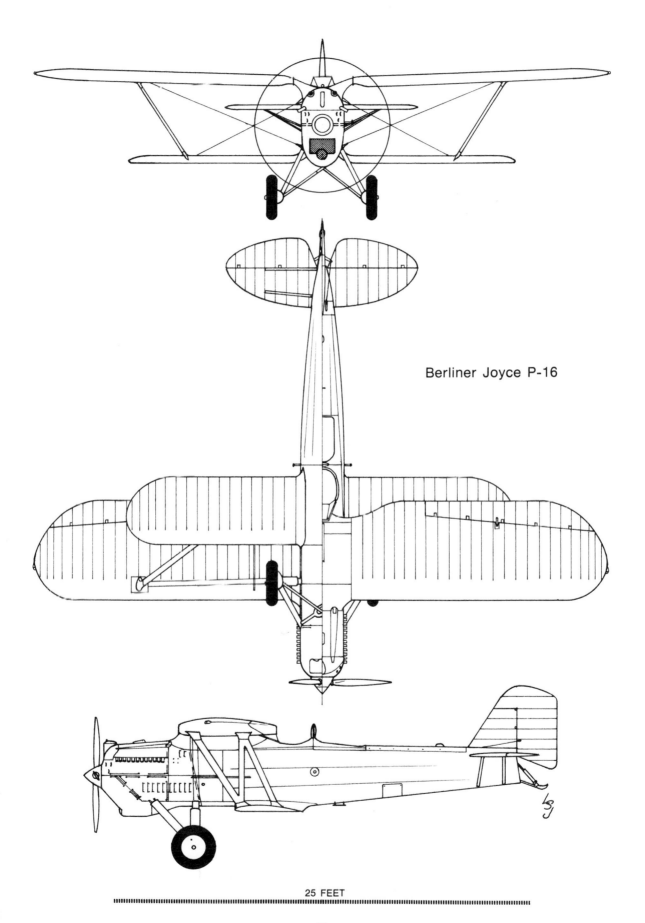

Berliner Joyce P-16

25 FEET

An operational P-16 of the 94th Pursuit Squadron.　　　　　　　*Gordon S. Williams*

The rear-facing gunner provided the P-16 with additional versatility in protecting the tail.
Gordon S. Williams

The Curtiss XP-17 was actually the first P-1 modified to test an experimental engine.   The sheet metal cowling on the XP-17 gave the aircraft a toy-like appearance.   *Gordon S. Williams*

The first P-1 Hawk, 24-410, was delivered to the Air Corps in August 1925, and began service as an engine test bed. In 1926, the original 435 hp Curtiss V-1150 D-12 engine was replaced by an air-cooled Allison-Liberty V-1410 of 420 hp. The engine was inverted and a streamlined cowl and spinner gave it a very sleek appearance. In this guise it was entered in the air races at Kansas City in 1926. Flown by Lt. W. McKierman during the Rotary Club Trophy Race to a speed of 176.18 mph, the modified fighter was in third place until the pilot was disqualified for turning inside a pylon.

In June 1930, an experimental Wright V-1460-3 engine of 480 hp was installed in the airframe and it was redesignated, at least on paper, XP-17. A simple sheet metal cowl was placed around the engine and the graceful look of the racer was replaced with a clumsy, almost toy-like, appearance. Such is the life of a test vehicle which must be adapted to take any number of fixtures that

were not around when it was on the drawing boards. One reason for the awkward appearance of the new cowling lies in the fact that the inverted engine was much wider than the P-1 fuselage. Since the airframe was totally obsolete by the time the engine was installed, there was no plan to develop the XP-17 into an operational type; and no attempt was made to blend the cowling and fuselage for better performance.

In March 1932, this airframe was finally retired and 24-410 was scrapped.

As the XP-17, dimensions were: span 31 feet 6 inches, length 22 feet 10 inches, height 8 feet 7 inches. Empty weight was 2,204 lbs and loaded the XP-17 weighed 2,994 lbs. Forty-three gallons of fuel was carried. Top speed was 165 mph at sea level. Service ceiling was 21,400 feet, and the plane could climb to 10,000 feet in 8 minutes. No armament was carried, but 200 pounds of ballast was used to balance the airframe during its testing.

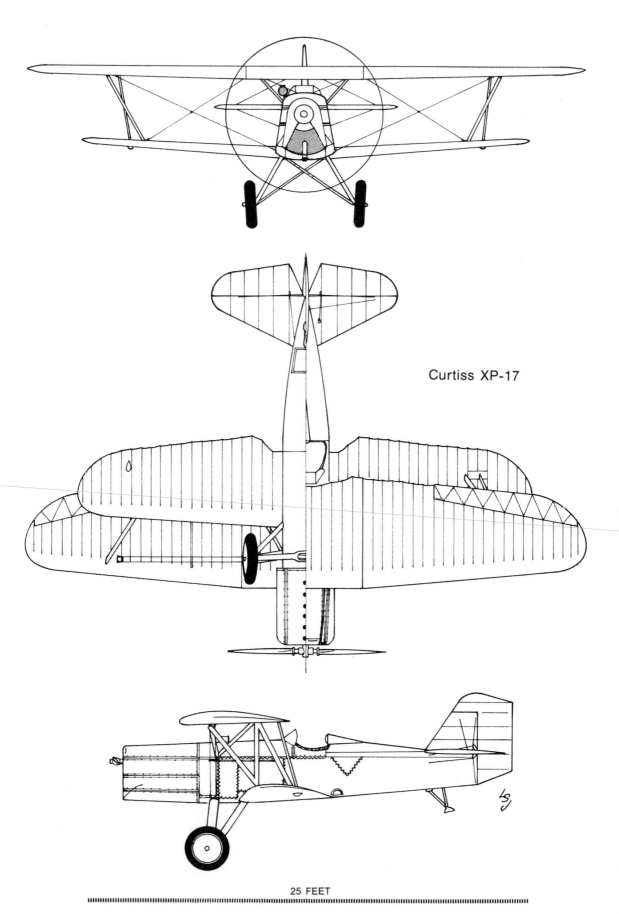

Curtiss XP-17

25 FEET

In 1930, the Army drew up specifications for two new designs which were to use a proposed Wright V-1560-1 twelve-cylinder air-cooled engine of 600 hp. The Curtiss Company was requested to design two fighters using the new engine; the XP-18 to be an original biplane (not a revision of the P-1 series), and the XP-19 to be a low-wing monoplane. The engine did not materialize, and before either of the two airframe designs were drawn up, the entire project was cancelled. Other than the specified configurations, the XP-18 and XP-19 were non-existent.

The YP-20 was created when the third P-11 was fitted with an R-1820 Cyclone engine.

Gordon S. Williams

The third P-11, ordered in 1929 to evaluate the Curtiss Chieftain engine, eventually appeared with no less than four different designations during its existence. Even before completion as a P-11, it was reclassified as YP-20 when failure of the Chieftain engine led to the fitting of a Wright R-1820 Cyclone engine. With this 575 hp nine cylinder radial engine, the YP-20 could fly a maximum of 187 mph at sea level, slowing to 184 mph at 5,000 feet. Landing speed was 61 mph. In this configuration, the Hawk weighed 2,477 pounds empty and grossed 3,233 pounds with up to 103 gallons of fuel.

The Army had planned to install a Conqueror engine in the YP-20 and change the designation to XP-22 upon completion of tests with the Cyclone. This plan was dropped when the testing was prolonged, and one of the other Hawks became the XP-22.

In its original form, the YP-20 differed from the standard P-6 only in the mounting of its radial engine and the addition of a steerable tailwheel. The engine itself was enclosed in a Townend ring. As flight-testing progressed, a crankcase cover was added and the landing gear was streamlined by installing strut fairings and wheel pants. The area of the vertical fin was increased by moving the fin-rudder dividing point up half a rib space. As the YP-20, the Hawk had an overall length of 23 feet 9 inches.

Although the YP-20 did not in fact become the XP-22, it did receive the entire front end of the latter aircraft when tests with the XP-22 design were completed. With its new nose, the YP-20 became the XP-6E—taking a numerical step backward. Before this airframe was retired, it was again the subject of a major alteration when an enclosed cockpit and engine supercharger were mounted. This version of the plane was known as the XP-6F.

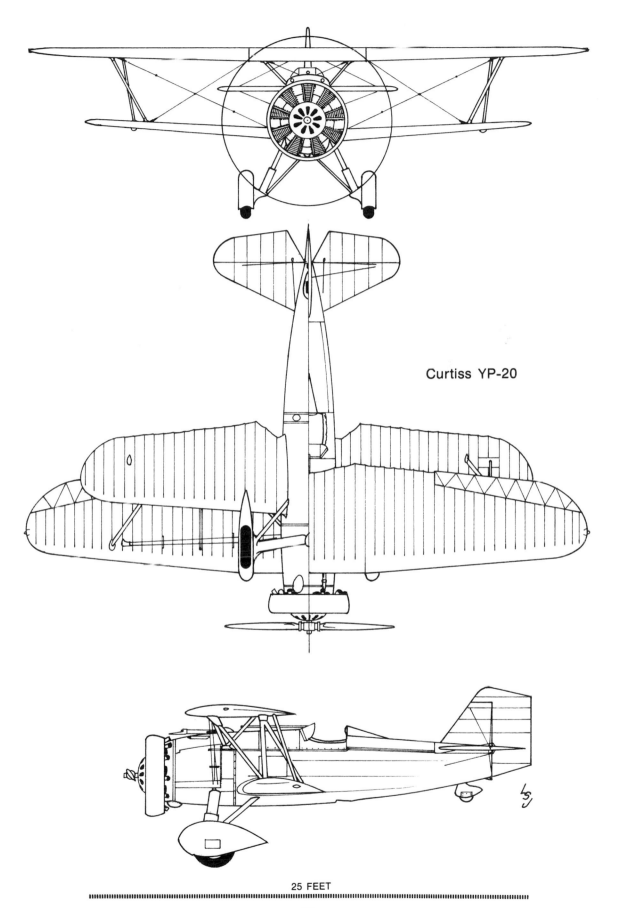

Curtiss YP-20

25 FEET

The configuration of the P-6E is visible in this view of the XP-22.   *Gordon S. Williams*

The XP-22 designation was assigned to the third production P-6A (29-262) when availability of the XP-20 was delayed by additional testing of the Cyclone radial engine. The airplane was returned to Curtiss for the requested changes, which included a relocation of the cooling radiator further back from the nose, enlarging the fin as used on the YP-20, and an experimental cowling around the 700 hp Conqueror engine. When the various Hawk conversions were performed by the Curtiss Company, the Army was charged only a token fee of $1 each.

The XP-22 underwent several changes during its testing period. The three-strut landing gear was replaced by a single streamlined strut, and the original oval cowl ring was changed to a circular one which contained the radiator. Large fillets were placed over the wing struts where they mated with the wings. During this stage, the fin-rudder ratio was restored to the original P-6 standard, but this was only temporary.

Still more changes to the XP-22 removed the external "radial" cowlings and enlarged fillets, and the radiator was moved back between the gear struts. Flight testing at this stage gave a top speed of 202 mph, a milestone for an Army combat plane.

In June of 1931, an Air Corps evaluation group met to compare the best features of their latest types: the P-6, P-12, YP-20, and XP-22. All things considered, speed seemed to be the deciding factor; and the XP-22's top speed of 202 mph won a production contract for Curtiss for 45 of the type, to be designated Y1P-22.

At this time, the nose and landing gear assembly of the XP-22 were installed on the YP-20, which then became the XP-6E. The 45 production planes were then built as P-6E's.

The XP-22 weighed 2,597 lbs and grossed out at 3,354 lbs. It had a service ceiling of 26,500 feet and could climb to 10,000 feet in 5.2 minutes. Dimensions were: Span—31 feet six inches, length—23 feet 7 inches, height—8 feet 9 inches. Fuel capacity was 50 gallons plus an additional 50 gallons in an external tank.

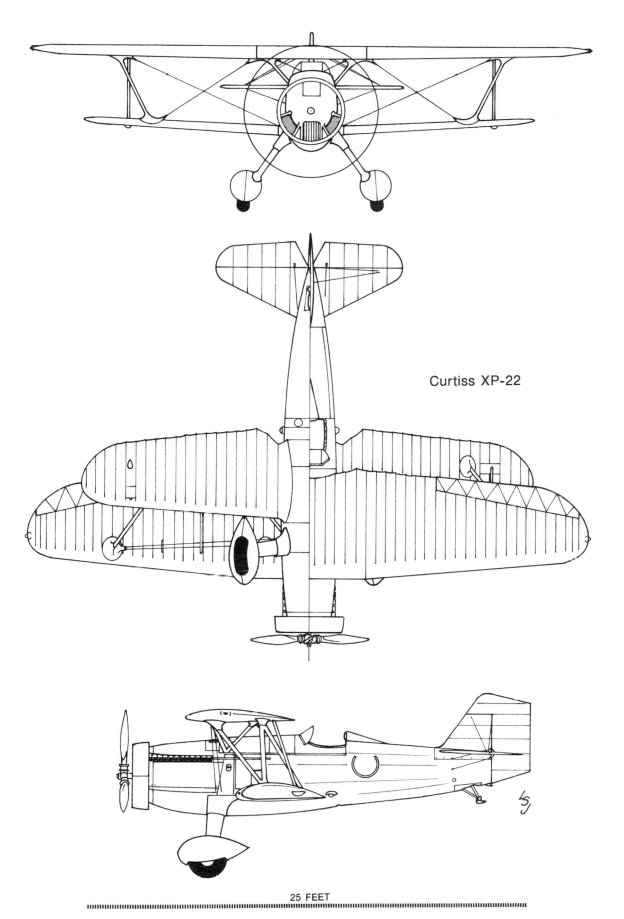

Curtiss XP-22

25 FEET

Unquestionably the most graceful of the biplane Hawks, was the sleek XP-23. Note the new vertical stabilizer
which was similar to the Condor transport.   *Gordon S. Williams*

The Curtiss XP-23, last of the Army's biplane fighters was also the most attractive in appearance, retaining only the shape of the familiar Hawk wing. Even the structure of the wing differed from the earlier Hawks. The spars and ribs of the XP-23 were constructed of metal instead of wood. A new all-metal monocoque fuselage faired smoothly around a geared 600 hp supercharged G1V-1570C Conqueror engine. The wheels were spatted for further streamlining, but were also reinforced by a spreader-bar. The distinctive angular Hawk rudder was replaced by one of a new design, one which was to become equally distinctive on such Curtiss aircraft as the T-32 Condor transport and the SOC Seagull.

The sleek new fighter could reach a speed of 223 mph at 15,000 feet, making it the fastest biplane yet offered to the Army. Unfortunately, as advanced as the XP-23 was, it was no more than an attempt to prolong the life of the biplane fighter—a cause that had already been lost to the Boeing P-26 monoplane.

The XP-23 was ordered on the same contract that provided the Army with 45 P-6E's and was assigned serial number 32-278. It was delivered on April 16, 1932, with the supercharged engine driving a three-bladed propeller. During tests, the XP-23 showed poor low-level performance, being capable of only 178 mph until it reached an altitude where its supercharged engine became more efficient. Part of its problems lay in its excessive weight of 4,124 pounds gross, making it the heaviest of the Army's biplane Hawks. Even its empty weight of 3,274 pounds was more than the loaded weight of many of the earlier Hawks.

With continual overheating and other problems associated with the turbo-supercharger, the blower was removed and the plane redesignated YP-23 indicating a service test status. In this form, the engine was equipped with a two-bladed propeller.

The XP-23 was designed to carry one .50 cal. and two .30 cal. machine guns plus 488 pounds of bombs. Fuel capacity was 78 gallons which gave the XP-23 a range of

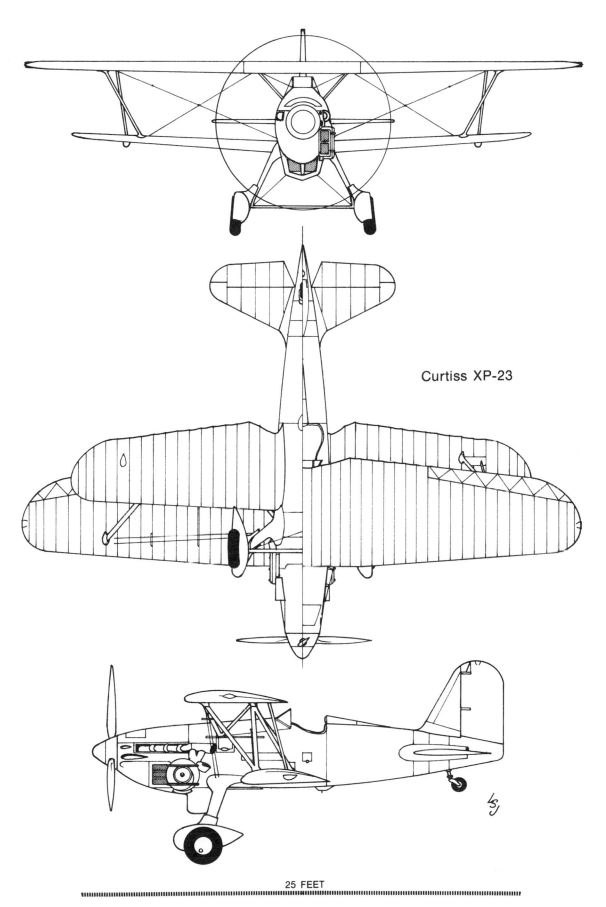

Curtiss XP-23

25 FEET

435 miles. Wingspan was 31½ feet, length 23 feet 10 inches, height was 9½ feet.

The final chapter on the Army's last biplane fighter was written when the YP-23 was returned to Curtiss for dismanteling and its wings consigned to the Navy's new XF11C-1 carrier fighter.

When the supercharger was removed, the designation was changed to YP-23, the last of the biplane fighters.
Gordon S. Williams

DETROIT-LOCKHEED
YP-24

Lockheed's monoplane YP-24 could outrun the Army's newest operational fighters.   *Lockheed*

The beginning of the monoplane generation of Army fighters was heralded by the Detroit-Lockheed YP-24; the first fighter-type to be built by this company, and the last involving the Detroit division.

The Lockheed Company was famous for its wooden monoplane airliners such as the Vega and Orion, the latter featuring a low wing with retractable landing gear. Although the company had never built a fighter before, the Air Corps was willing to gamble on a design combining the proven Lockheed wing with a new all-metal fuselage. When delivered to the Army on September 29, 1931, the plane bore the designation XP-900. Intended as a possible replacement for the Berliner-Joyce P-16, the Lockheed fighter was also two-place with a .30 cal. machine gun mounted in the rear cockpit. The .30/.50 cal. combination was located in the nose, firing through the three-bladed propeller. A fully retractable landing gear and an enclosed cockpit completed the list of features displayed by the new fighter, which was purchased by the Army as the YP-24 (32-320).

Testing of the YP-24 proved the Air Corps faith in the concept to be justified, as it could outrun any production fighter in

the sky. Its top speed was 214.5 mph, 20 mph faster than the P-6E and nearly 40 mph faster than the P-16. The YP-24's powerplant was a 600 hp Curtiss V-1570-23 Conqueror engine. The plane had an overall length of 28 feet 9 inches and a 292 square foot wing spanning 42 feet 9¼ inches. Height was 8 feet 2 inches. The composite wood-metal airframe weighed 3,010 pounds empty and grossed 4,360 pounds. The YP-24 carried 75 gallons of fuel, which gave it a range of 556 miles. Service ceiling was 26,400 feet.

On October 19, 1931, during an evaluation flight, the landing gear extension system failed with the gear partly lowered. Through a series of violent maneuvers, the pilot succeeded in retracting the gear again and attempted a belly landing; but on orders from authorities on the ground, he was compelled to bail out and the YP-24 was destroyed in the ensuing crash.

The Army was pleased with the performance turned in by the YP-24 and ordered five Y1P-24's and an additional five to be built as YA-9 attack bombers. But the Detroit-Lockheed Company was in financial difficulties and defaulted on the contracts leaving the YP-24 the sole example of its type.

63

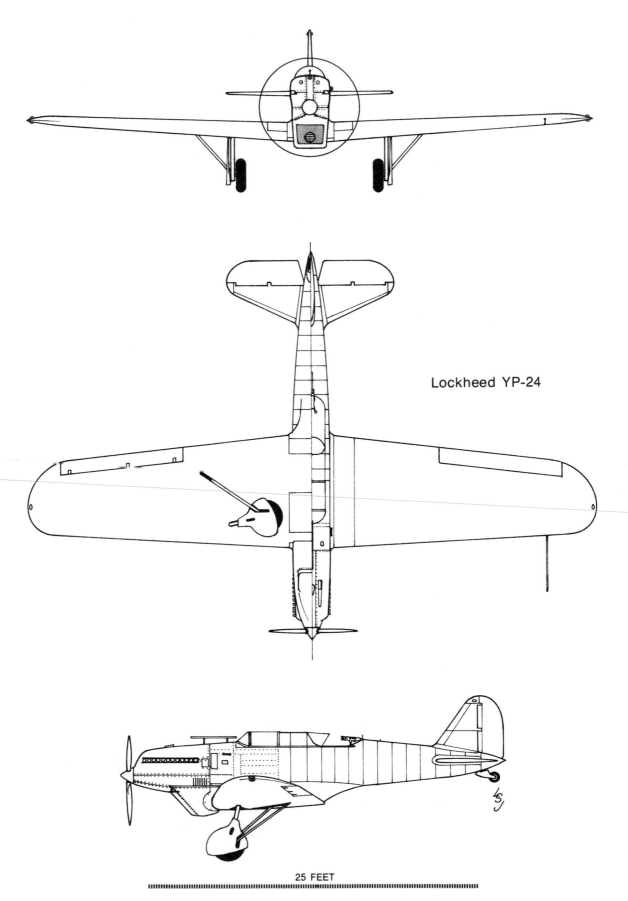

Lockheed YP-24

25 FEET

CONSOLIDATED
Y1P-25, YP-27 and YP-28

Consolidated's Y1P-25 was a development of the Lockheed P-24 design with the addition of a turbo-supercharger.
Convair

Following the financial failure of the Detroit-Lockheed Company, its designers and engineers found jobs with Bell Aircraft and Consolidated. Soon, Consolidated rolled out a new two-place fighter whose lines were based on the ill-fated YP-24. Generally more streamlined and using an all-metal wing instead of the plywood wing of the YP-24, the Consolidated fighter was designated Y1P-25 (S.N. 32-321), two of which had been ordered by the Army in 1932. Only the first airframe became a P-25, however; the second was delivered as the Y1A-11.

Powered by the same type engine as the YP-24, a 600 hp Conqueror, the Consolidated version had the added boost of a turbo-supercharger giving it a top speed of 247 mph at 15,000 feet. Again the destiny of this design was marred by crashes as the Y1P-25 was destroyed on January 13, 1933, followed a week later by the Y1A-11. The

accidents were not considered to be a reflection on the design, however, and an order was placed with Consolidated for a very successful version of the plane as the P-30.

The Y1P-25 was slightly larger than the YP-24, having a wingspan of 43 feet 10 inches, a length of 29 feet 4 inches, and a height of 8 feet 7 inches. Weight also was greater than the earlier fighter; empty, it was 3,887 lbs while it grossed at 5,110 lbs.

In May 1932, a proposal was made to construct two versions of the Y1P-25 with air-cooled engines. One of these planes was given the Army designation Y1P-27, with a 550 hp Pratt & Whitney R-1340-21 Wasp. The second, Y1P-28, to be powered by a 600 hp P & W R-1340-19 Wasp. The anticipated performance of these two designs was not considered justification for their development and the projects were cancelled.

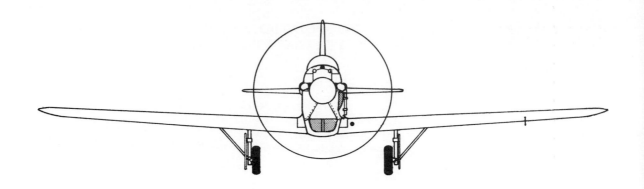

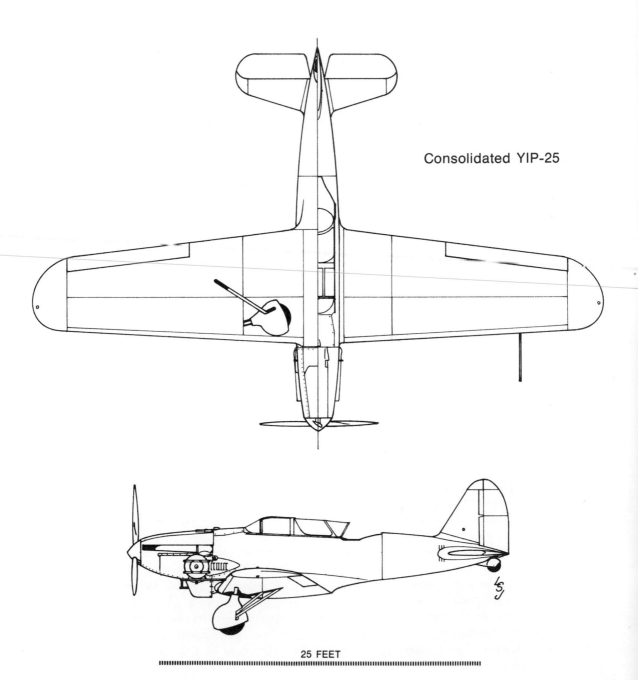

Consolidated YIP-25

25 FEET

The second P-25 ordered was completed as the un-supercharged Y1A-11. However, the data block under the cockpit reads U. S. Army Y1P-25, Serial No. 32-322. Note the clipped rudder.   *Gordon S. Williams*

Consolidated P-27/P-28

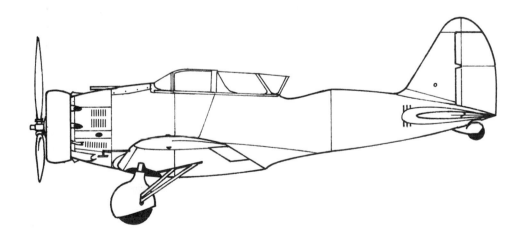

The third XP-936 prototype during flight testing. The low headrest was replaced on production models of the P-26.
Gordon S. Williams

The next fighter to fill the ranks of the Army's pursuit squadrons was Boeing's nimble P-26, affectionately referred to as the little "Peashooter". Begun in January 1932, at Boeing's expense as Model 248, three prototypes of the proposed design were built. The first of these took to the air on March 20, 1932, as the XP-936. It was constructed entirely of metal covered with thin aluminum skin. Although a second wing and its attendant struts were absent, the monoplane wing was braced with a series of wires intended to eliminate any tendency it might have to collapse under high "G" conditions. This was the last time external bracing wires appeared on a U. S. Army fighter.

The success of the flight tests led to an order of 111 of the fighters as P-26A's, followed closely by an additional order for 2 P-26B's and 23 P-26C's. The first P-26A, powered by a 550 hp Pratt & Whitney R-1340-27 Wasp, took off on January 10, 1934. At 7,500 feet, it could fly at 234 mph and had a cruising speed of 210 mph. Service ceiling was 27,400 feet.

Two significant changes took place early in the service life of the P-26. When first delivered, the P-26A had a low streamlined headrest aft of the cockpit. One of these planes overturned during a landing on soft ground; and, though damage to the plane was slight, the pilot was killed. As a result, the headrest was raised eight inches higher. Being a fighter, the P-26 was naturally designed for high speed, but unfortunately, the small 149.5 square foot wing also required a high landing speed. The touch-down speed of 82.5 mph was of great concern to the Army pilots, and one P-26A was fitted with a pair of landing flaps which reduced the speed to an acceptable 73 mph. These flaps then became standard equipment on all P-26's.

The 112th and 113th P-26's were delivered to the Army on June 20 and 21, 1934, with fuel-injected Wasp 600 hp R-1340-33 engines. These were the first P-26B's. The remaining twenty-three planes were completed as P-26C's, but were virtually identical to the "A's". The fuel-injection system on the P-26B's proved satisfactory for service, and the P-26C's were then modified into P-26B's with the

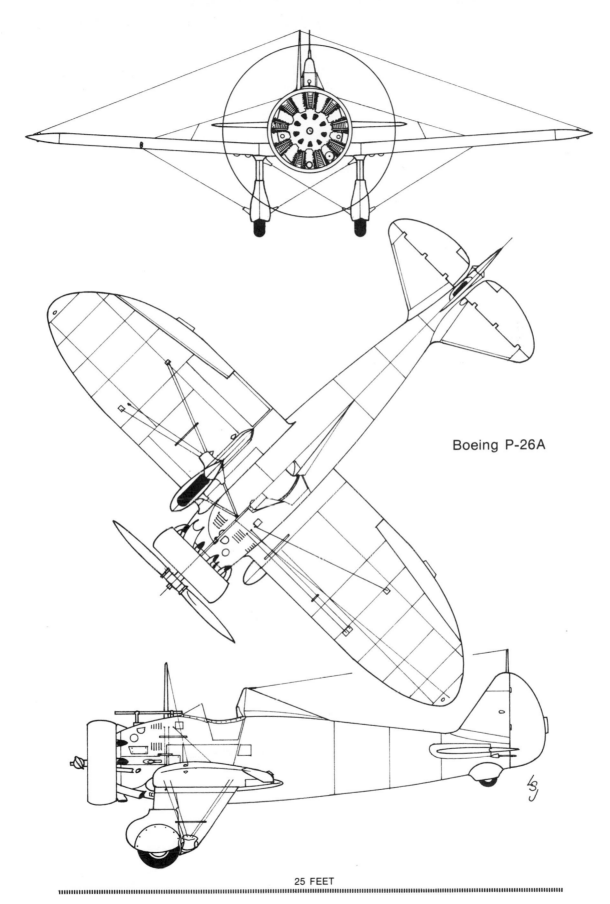

Boeing P-26A

25 FEET

injected engines.

P-26's were armed with two .30 cal. machine guns or one each .30 cal. and .50 cal. gun located in the fuselage and firing between the cylinders. Two 100 pound bombs or five 30 pound bombs could be fitted to racks under the wings and fuselage. The P-26A wingspan was 27 feet 11½ inches, it was 23 feet 10 inches long, and stood 10 feet 5 inches high. Empty weight was 2,196 lbs, gross weight was 2,955 lbs. Up to 107 gallons of fuel could be carried to provide a maximum range of 745 miles.

The P-26's still in service at the outbreak of World War II were relegated to training and secondary duties; but one squadron based in the Philippines engaged invading Japanese bombers, and one of the P-26A's is credited with destroying a bomber. Guatemala was operating several P-26's as late as 1957. Two of these planes have survived to become museum displays in the United States.

A formation of the classic Peashooters.   *Boeing*

The YP-29 was an attempt to improve the performance of the P-26.   Gordon S. Williams

The open cockpit, wire wing braces, and fixed landing gear used on the P-26 created speed-reducing drag which Boeing engineers sought to eliminate with their Model 264, or XP-940. Using the same 550 hp Pratt & Whitney R-1340 Wasp engine as the P-26, the first of three P-29 types flew on January 20, 1934, and tests showed a maximum speed of 220 mph at 10,000 feet. The semi-retractable landing gear was tucked rearward into the fully cantilevered wing, and the cockpit canopy faired straight into the rudder. The Army was not satisfied with the canopy arrangement and the plane was returned to Boeing for conversion to an open cockpit to become the YP-29A.

In the meantime, the second plane, designated YP-29, was delivered with an enlarged greenhouse-type canopy affording greater visibility than the original model. This version also included landing flaps, not present on the first XP-940. The YP-29 reached a top speed of 244 mph at 10,000

feet. The third plane was the YP-29B which duplicated the altered YP-29A, with the exception of one degree more dihedral in the wings and the addition of a one-piece landing flap.

The three P-29's were heavier than the P-26 and did not show a great improvement over the latter's performance; therefore no further examples were built and the program was abandoned.

The YP-29 weighed 2,573 lbs empty and 3,572 lbs loaded; its 177 square foot wing spanned 29 feet 4½ inches. Overall length was 25 feet, and it was 7 feet 8 inches high. Service ceiling was 24,200 feet. The YP-29 could carry 110 gallons of fuel with a range of 520 miles. The usual two-gun armament was included in the design, and 327 pounds of bombs could be carried.

A more powerful version using the same airframe with a 700 hp twin-row Pratt & Whitney R-1535-1 was proposed and the number XP-32 was assigned, but did not materialize.

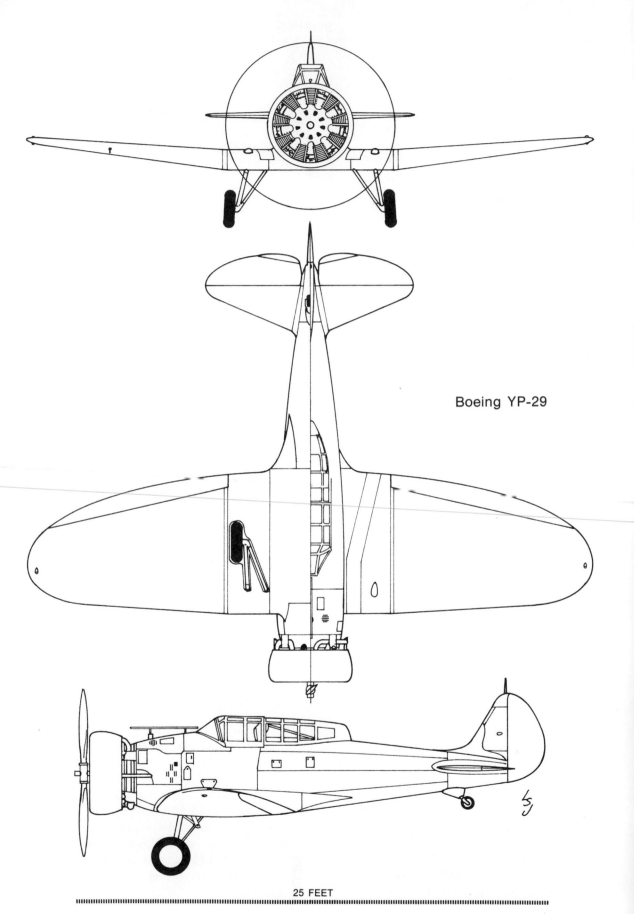

Boeing YP-29

25 FEET

The Army did not like the enclosed canopy of the first P-29. Upon its removal, the plane was redesignated YP-29A.
Gordon S. Williams

73

CONSOLIDATED
P-30, P-33

Many new features were introduced as standard equipment on the P-30's such as controllable-pitch propellers, retracting landing gear and cockpit heating.
Gordon S. Williams

Consolidated's P-30 represented a bold step forward for the Air Corps. Here was the first American fighter ordered into production with many of the features that had for years been just beyond the grasp of success. Standard equipment on the P-30 were fully retractable landing gear, enclosed heated cockpit (for the pilot at any rate), exhaust-driven turbo-supercharger, and a fully cantilever wing.

Following the crash of the Y1P-25, the Army ordered four refined examples of the two-place fighter, calling them P-30's (33-204 to 33-207), for service evaluation. At the same time, four similar but un-supercharged A-11's were ordered but this branch of the design did not proceed further. Testing of the P-30's in 1934 resulted in some complaints by the pilots regarding the value of a tail gunner during maneuvers. Their location in the rear of the plane invariably caused them to black-out during sharp turns or dive recovery. Despite these complaints, the Army was pleased with the airplane and on December 6, 1934, Consolidated received an order for 50 P-

30A's, these being assigned serial numbers 35-1 to 35-50. Delivery had just begun when the Army decided to identify them as Bi-place pursuits and they were reclassed as PB-2A's.

The production models were fitted with Curtiss Electric Constant Speed propellers driven by a Curtiss V-1570-61 Conqueror of 700 hp with the G. E. Supercharger. The landing gear was retracted by means of a hand-wound crank in the cockpit; and a certain degree of skill was required for a pilot to maintain formation while pulling up the gear. The P-30A/PB-2A had a service ceiling of 28,000 feet, and the crew was provided with oxygen via a converter which changed liquid oxygen to gas that was inhaled through a rubber hose. High altitude flights were seldom performed, though, because of the expense, inconvenience, and discomfort to the crewmen in their bulky flying suits. At 25,000 feet, the P-30A achieved a speed of 274.5 mph. At 15,000 feet, a more reasonable operating altitude, the plane had a top speed of 255.5 mph and cruised at 215 mph.

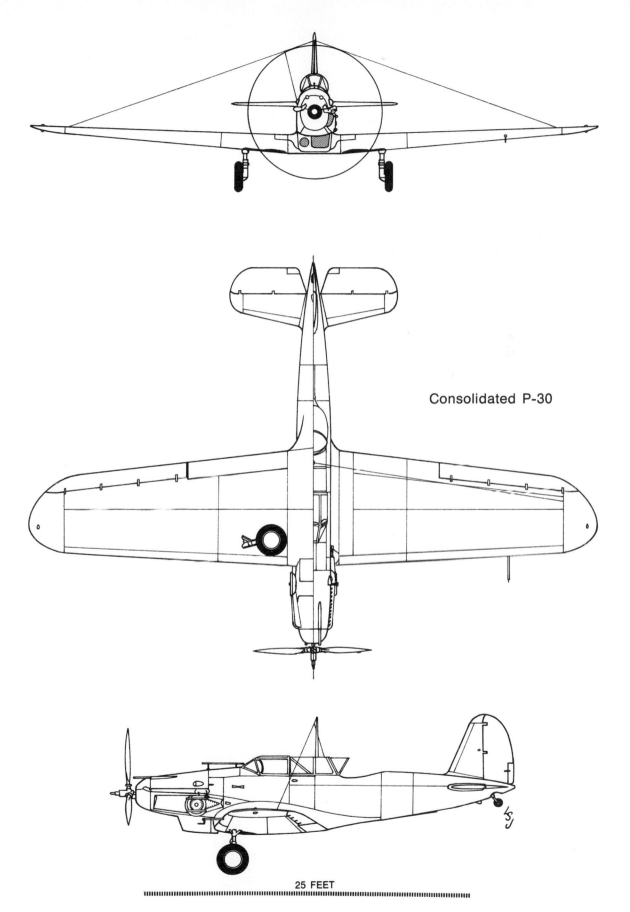

Consolidated P-30

25 FEET

One P-30A was evaluated as a single seater with the canopy blending into the tail with a metal fairing. In 1936, it was an unsuccessful entry in an Army competition for single-seat fighters.

The P-30A was constructed entirely of metal with a wingspan of 43 feet 11 inches, area of 297 square feet, length of 30 feet, and height of 8 feet 3 inches. The rearward-firing .30 cal. machine gun was supplimented by two more .30's in the nose. Empty weight was 4,306 pounds and the P-30A grossed 5,643 pounds. Range was 508 miles on 180 gallons of fuel.

A proposal to mount an 800 hp fourteen cylinder Pratt & Whitney R-1830-1 Twin Wasp led to the designation P-33; but this project was cancelled as the two-place concept of the P-30 proved, in the long run, to be impractical. The concessions to performance caused by the use of a second man solely as a gunner was not justified, a fact that was more than proven by the British Boulton Paul Defiant of World War II. The place for the second man in a fighter was yet to come.

The value of the rear gunner was dubious as they often blacked out during high "G" maneuvers. Convair

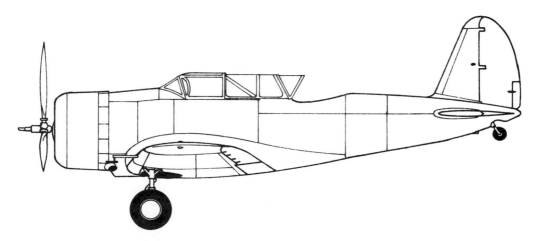

Consolidated P-33

76

CURTISS
XP-31 SWIFT

The full length leading edge slats and the landing flaps are apparent in this view of the XP-31.
Gordon S. Williams

The first Curtiss monoplane fighter to be built was offered to the Army in 1932 as competition for the Boeing P-26. A low wing monoplane, it was generally similar to the Boeing fighter with fixed landing gear supporting wing struts and powered by a 700 hp Wright Cyclone. As the XP-934, the Swift was first flown in July 1932. Performance with the radial engine was so poor it was replaced with a V-1570 Conqueror of 600 hp and delivered to the Army on March 1, 1933. The Conqueror installation improved both performance and appearance of the little fighter, but it was all academic as the Army had ordered the Boeing P-26 into production a few days earlier.

The Swift, officially designated XP-31 and given the serial number 33-178, was of all-metal construction. It was the first single-place fighter in the Air Corps designed with an enclosed cockpit, chronologically preceding the Boeing YP-29, but fixed landing gear and wing struts were the last seen on a U. S. Army fighter. Other advanced features displayed by the XP-31 were retractable slots along the entire leading edge of the wing and large trailing-edge flaps. It is interesting to note again the appearance of the Condor transport tail design, first seen on the XP-23.

As small as the XP-31 was, it was also quite heavy with an empty weight of 3,334 lbs and grossing 4,143 lbs. Dimensions were: 36 foot wingspan with 203 square feet of area, 26 foot 3 inch length, and 7 foot 9 inch height. The excessive weight of the XP-31 was reflected in its performance. Its maximum speed was 208 mph—26 mph slower than the P-26. Service ceiling was 24,400 feet, and range on 125 gallons of fuel was 370 miles. Armament consisted of two cowl-mounted .30 cal. machine guns and two more mounted in blisters beside the cockpit.

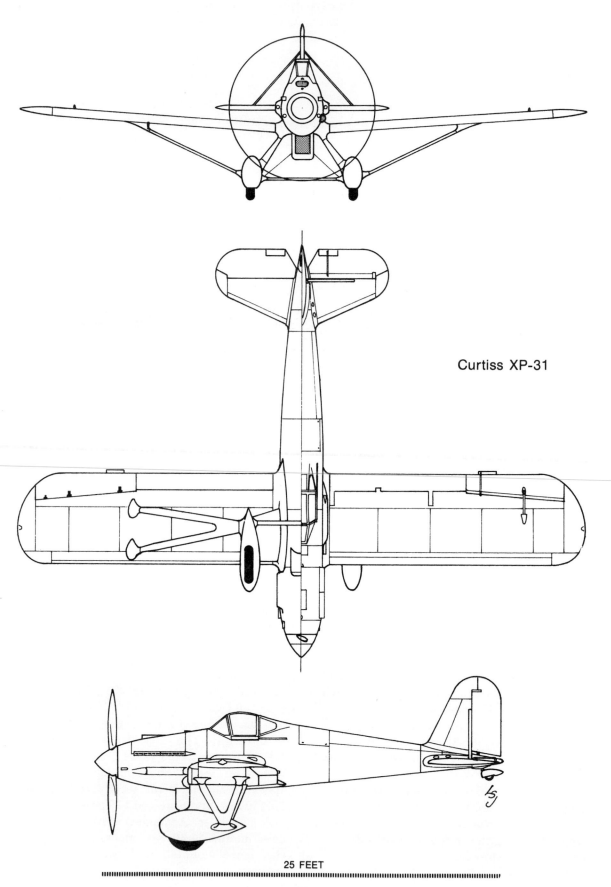

Curtiss XP-31

25 FEET

The name "Swift" given to this fighter seemed to be wishful thinking as its excessive weight made it twenty-six miles an hour slower than the Boeing P-26.   Gordon S. Williams

The XP-31 underwent several changes during its evaluation. This view shows revised wheel pants, engine exhaust and fuselage gun blister.   Gordon S. Williams

Since the concept of the fighter plane included the ability to travel at a high rate of speed, combined with maneuverability, it was reasoned that they would also perform well as racing planes. Several fighter types flown by Army pilots turned in notable performances at the National Air Races; some incorporating advanced design features which eventually became operational on military planes.

As a result of the Army's interest in racing planes, the Wedell-Williams Co., one of the most noted race plane designers of its day, asked if the Air Corps might be interested in a fighter developed from their racer. In response, they Army indicated they felt the racer was not heavy enough to serve in the combat role; but on May 6, 1935, a proposal for such a design was accepted. A design study contract was awarded on October 1, 1935, for an XP-34 to be powered by a Pratt & Whitney R-1535 Twin Wasp Jr. radial engine of 700 hp. The XP-34 was

to have a speed of 286 mph at 10,000 feet and, in appearance, the design resembled the Wedell-Williams "44" racer. The huge double-row engine dominated the airframe and contributed greatly to its gross weight of 4,250 pounds.

Before construction was begun on the XP-34, the results of the April 1936, fly-off competition indicated its proposed performance had already been exceeded by the types then flying. Therefore, the design was revised to incorporate a 900 hp Pratt & Whitney XR-1830-C Twin Wasp. With the new engine, the XP-34 was intended to reach a speed of 308 mph, but the project was abandoned before the airplane materialized.

The XP-34 proposal had a wingspan of 27 feet 8½ inches, a length of 23 feet 6 inches, and a height of 10 feet 9 inches. Construction was of metal with fabric covering the aft part of the fuselage and the control surfaces.

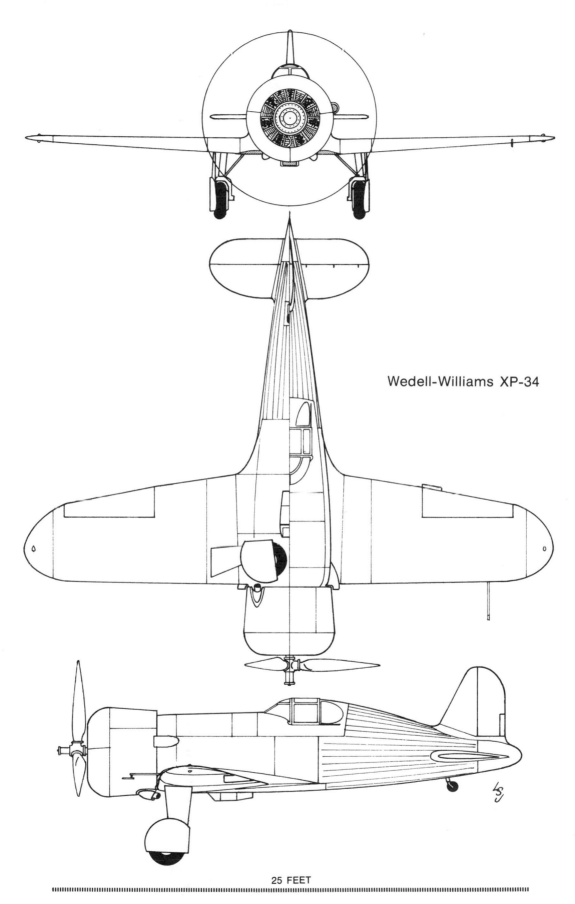

Wedell-Williams XP-34

25 FEET

The Eagle emblem of the 27th Pursuit Squadron adorns the side of this P-35.   *Gordon S. Williams*

With the purchase of 77 Seversky P-35's on June 16, 1936, the Army Air Corps began the next generation of fighters. Retractable landing gear, all-metal construction, enclosed cockpit canopy—all were standard on fighters now, and the new designs displayed an aesthetic elegance as they flashed through the sky.

The Seversky Sev-1 was declared the winner of a hotly contested competition with the Curtiss Model 75 in April 1936. Engine troubles plagued both competitors during the evaluation. The Seversky plane could not reach the guaranteed 300 mph speed with its 850 hp Wright XR-1820-39 Cyclone engine so an 850 hp Pratt & Whitney R-1830 Twin Wasp was mounted in its place. The top speed dropped even more as the new engine actually developed only 740 hp. Despite the engine problems, the Army accepted the Seversky contender and began receiving the first of 76 Twin Wasp powered P-35's in July 1937. (36-354 to 36-429)

The landing gear of the P-35 retracted straight back and remained partially exposed. A streamlined fairing smoothed the airflow around the tire to reduce drag. Armament was two nose-mounted machine guns,

one .30 cal. and one .50 cal., totally inadequate by now but stubbornly adhered to by the Air Corps. Ten 30 pound bombs could be carried externally. Fuel capacity was 200 gallons providing a range of 1,000 miles at 200 mph.

Seversky began taking orders for an export version of the P-35 as the EP-1, and a contract for 120 planes was received from Sweden. Half of the order had been delivered to Sweden when war broke out and the deliveries ceased. The U. S. Army purchased the remaining 60 EP-1's as P-35A's. By this time, Seversky had become the Republic Company and subsequent fighters of this type bore the Republic name.

The P-35A was a greatly improved plane with a 1,050 hp Twin Wasp finally delivering the elusive 300 mph speed—it could reach 305 mph at 12,000 feet. The P-35A also carried increased armament in the form of two .30's and two .50's, the bigger guns in the nose and the .30's mounted in the wing roots.

Wingspan of the P-35's was 36 feet, length was 25 feet 2 inches, and height was 12 feet 5 inches. Wing area was 220 square feet. Empty and gross weights were 6,373 lbs and 6,723 lbs respectively for the P-35A.

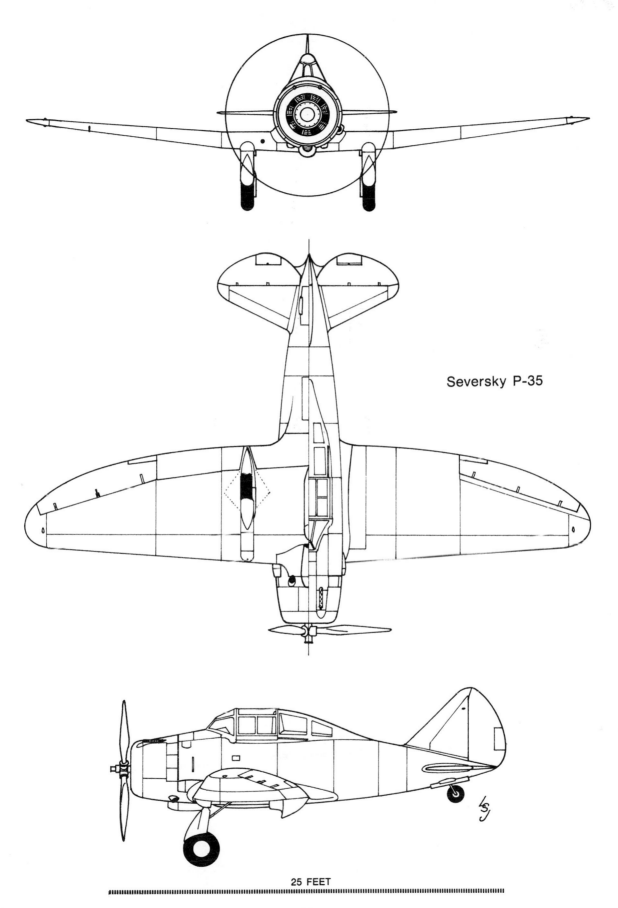

Seversky P-35

25 FEET

This is one of the sixty P-35A's from the Swedish contract. The P-35A carried two wing-mounted machine guns.   *Republic*

A P-35A carrying camouflaged paint after the outbreak of World War II.   *Gordon S. Williams*

CURTISS
P-36 HAWK

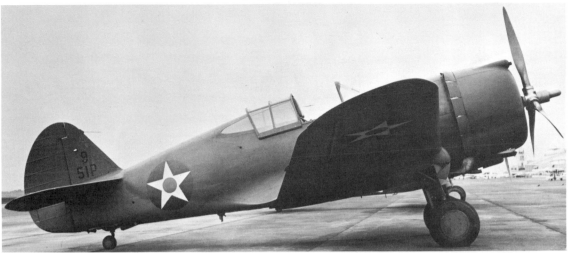

A new generation of Hawks began with the P-36 such as this "A" model. Gordon S. Williams

A new family of Hawks began with the Curtiss Model 75. Runner-up in the 1936 fighter competition, the Model 75 nevertheless merited a contract for 3 service test examples (37-68 to 70), and was designated Y1P-36. The planes were delivered to the Army in February 1937, with refinements which improved the fighter's performance. Power was provided by a Pratt & Whitney R-1830-13 Twin Wasp delivering 1,050 hp for take-off and 900 hp at 12,000 feet.

In May 1937, one of the Y1P-36's was entered in a fighter competition at Wright Field, and this time the new Hawk won an order for 210 aircraft—the Army's largest fighter contract in nineteen years. Deliveries of the P-36A began in April 1938. After 177 of the "A" models were completed, a 1,200 hp Twin Wasp and two .30 cal. wing-mounted machine guns (supplementing the two cowl guns) were introduced on the line, and the remaining planes were finished as "C" models.

Like the biplane Hawks, the P-36 was subjected to many modifications. The P-36B (38-20) was a one-off model with a 1,-100 hp R-1830-25 engine which reached a speed of 313 mph at 10,000 feet. The XP-36D was tested with two cowl-mounted .50 cal. guns and four wing-mounted .30's. The XP-36E, also an armament test vehicle, carried eight .30's in the wings and one .50 in the nose. The XP-36F had two under-wing 23 mm Madsen cannon in addition to one .30 and one .50 in its nose.

The landing gear of the P-36 was fully retractable, the main units rotating 90 degrees as they folded aft to lay flush in the wing. Streamlined fairings covered the struts and produced the characteristic knuckle at the front of the wings. The P-36 was a classic example of simplicity in fighter design. It was popular with its pilots and was considered one of the best fighters of its day.

By 1941, export versions of the monoplane Hawk had experienced a great deal of actual combat experience; particularly in France where they were outnumbered 3 to 1 and officially credited with 311 kills to a loss of only 29 Hawks. When the Japanese attacked Pearl Harbor, P-36's based in Hawaii became the first American fighters used in World War II. This Hawk can also claim the distinction of meeting its own kind in combat when several were captured and turned against the Allies.

The dimensions of the P-36C were: wingspan of 37 feet 4 inches, length of 28 feet 6 inches, height 12 feet 2 inches, and wing area of 235 square feet. Empty weight of the all-metal airframe was 4,620 pounds with a gross weight of 5,734 pounds. Top speed was 311 mph at 10,000 feet. Service ceiling was 32,000 feet. Range on 162 gallons of fuel was 820 miles.

An example of this aviation classic is displayed at the Air Force Museum near Dayton, Ohio.

85

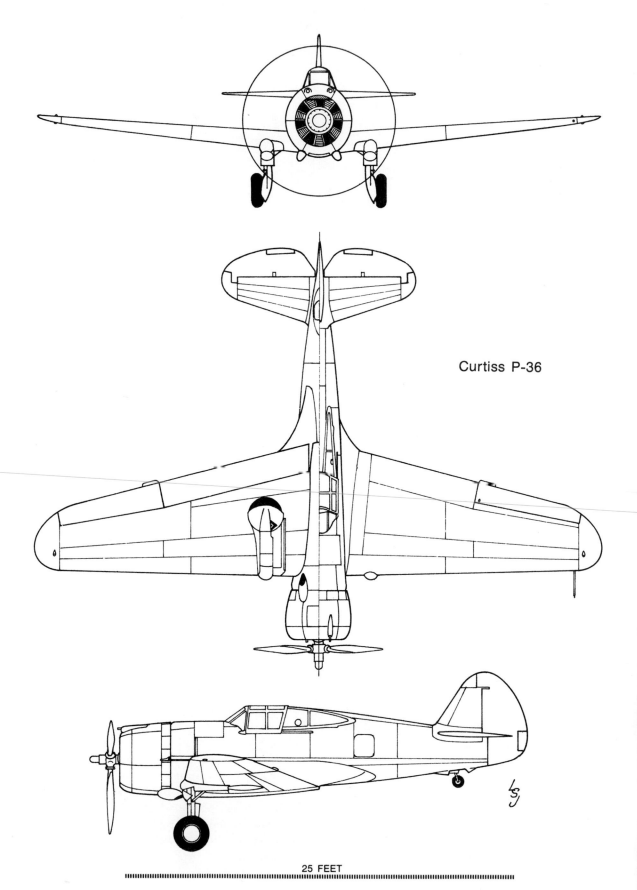

Curtiss P-36

25 FEET

A P-36A of the 79th Pursuit Squadron running-up.   Gordon S. Williams

The 27th Pursuit Squadron participated in the 1939 War Games with their planes decorated in gaudy camouflage patterns such as shown on this P-36C.   Gordon S. Williams

A hastily applied camouflage job is apparent on this P-36C.   Gordon S. Williams

The YP-37, 22 inches longer than the XP-37, looked more like a racer than a fighter. Pilots complained about the location of the cockpit. *Gordon S. Williams*

The development of aircraft powerplants was moving at a pace equal to the refinements in airframe design. The P-36 was proving itself insofar as maneuverability was concerned, but its contemporaries were outperforming it with their higher speeds. The latest foreign-built fighters were powered with slim inline engines and were reaching speeds well over 300 mph. The U. S. Army's interest in developing a suitable inline engine for its fighters is indicated by the fact that they invested $500,-000 into the engineering of the Allison V-1710 engine.

Attempting to keep their foot in the door for the next round of fighter contracts, Curtiss constructed the XP-37, adapting the P-36 airframe to the Allison engine. Its long, pointed fuselage with the cockpit just ahead of the tail fin gave the XP-37 a futuristic look. The radiator for cooling the Prestone was located behind the supercharged Allison V-1710-11, necessitating the relocation of the cockpit to the rear. This arrangement was very unpopular with the pilots because of the poor visibility over the long nose. Performance of the turbo-supercharger was also unsatisfactory, although the plane did achieve a guaranteed 340 mph at 20,000 feet when all systems were functioning.

Despite the shortcomings of the XP-37, the Army ordered 13 YP-37's for service tests. The YP-37's were some 450 pounds heavier than their progenitor and fell short of the 340 mph top speed by 9 mph. The YP-37 fuselages were 22 inches longer than the "X" model, the cockpit was moved forward a bit, and the radiator and supercharger were modified; but the P-37 was not the answer to the Army's need for an inline engine fighter.

The YP-37's (38-472 to 38-484) had the same 37 foot 4 inch wings as the P-36. Overall length was 32 feet 10 inches and height was 9½ feet. Armament was still one .30 cal. and one .50 cal. gun in the nose. Service ceiling was 34,000 feet and range was 870 miles. Empty, each YP-37 weighed 5,-723 pounds; and loaded, including 164 gallons of fuel, weight was 6,890 pounds.

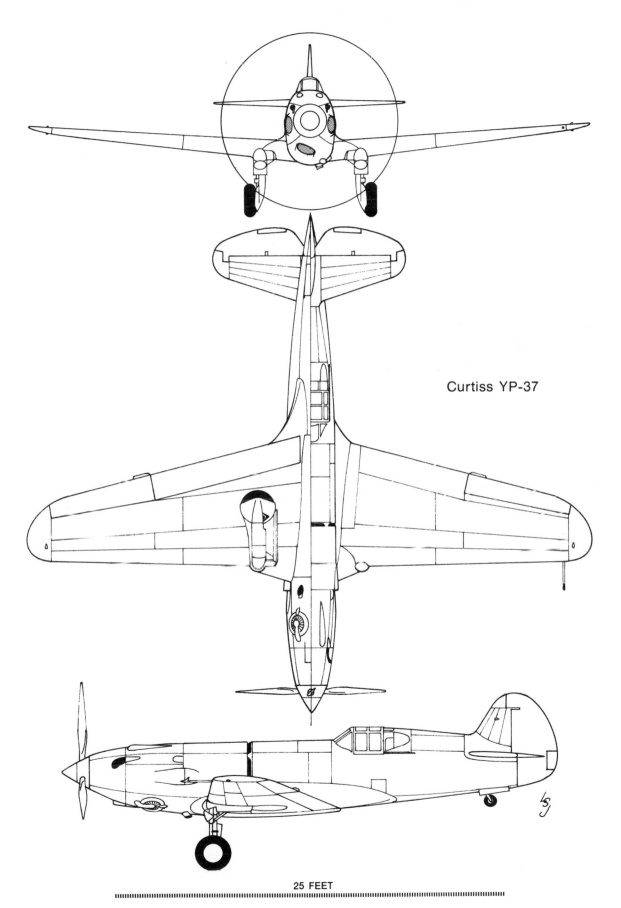

Curtiss YP-37

25 FEET

With the Allison-powered XP-37 Curtiss hoped to make the P-36 design more competitive with European fighters.
Gordon S. Williams

LOCKHEED
P-38 LIGHTNING

The XP-38 introduced a new dimension to American fighters—a second engine.   *Lockheed*

The Lightning represented one of the most radical departures from tradition in American fighter development. It was a complete break-away from conventional airframe design, power, and at long last, armament. Not only did it have twice the power and almost twice the size of its predecessors, but with no less than four .50 cal. machine guns plus a 20 mm cannon, the P-38 had enough firepower to sink a ship—and sometimes did. Concentrated in the central fuselage pod, the guns fired parallel and no propeller synchronizer was needed.

The Lightning's tricycle landing gear and twin-boom configuration completed the list of major deviations from what might be considered conventional Army fighters. In this respect, it was very unusual that the Lightning design progressed beyond the testing stage; such radical concepts seldom achieved production status. But the simple fact was that the P-38 design worked and the Army seemed to have found its dream plane in this 400 mph fighter.

The XP-38, 37-457, was built under tight secrecy and made its maiden flight on January 27, 1939. Its performance justified

Lockheed's investment of nearly $600,000 of its own funds to complete the prototype. The Army was so delighted with the big new fighter, it lifted the wraps of secrecy from the plane for a transcontinental speed dash on February 11, 1939. This event was marred by a crash when the XP-38 undershot the runway at Mitchel Field, N.Y. The airplane was written off, but Lockheed received a contract for 13 YP-38's along with the usual list of improvements.

The XP-38 had been powered by two Allison V-1710 engines turning 11½ foot Curtiss Electric propellers rotating inward. With the YP-38's and all subsequent Lightnings, the propellers rotated outward negating torque when both engines were operating. One XP-38A was built with a pressurized cabin. Armament on the YP-'s was altered by replacement of two of the .50's with .30's, and the 20 mm cannon gave way to a 37 mm. But even before the YP-38's were completed, the original machine gun arrangement was standardized for production types. The first production order was 35 P-38D's, followed by 210 P-38E's which reverted back to the 20 mm

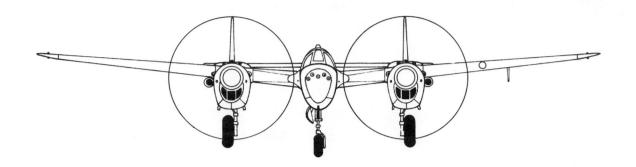

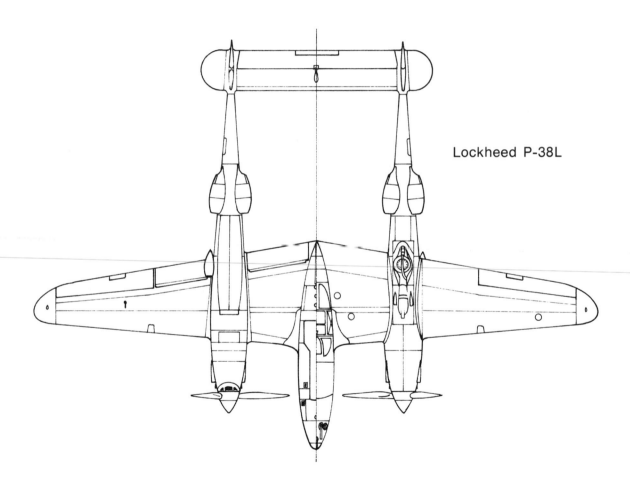

Lockheed P-38L

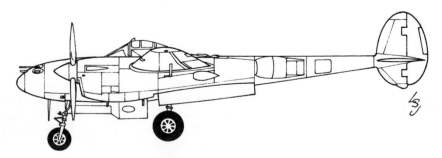

25 FEET

cannon. These planes began to arrive in October 1941, just before America entered World War II. With the P-38D came self-sealing fuel tanks and armor protection for the pilot. The Lightning was ready for war!

The only major external change in the P-38 during its production life took place with the P-38J when the intakes under the engines were enlarged to house core-type intercoolers, the curved windscreen was replaced by a flat panel, and the boom-mounted radiators were enlarged.

The Lightning's turbo-supercharged engines gave the big fighter a top speed of 414 mph at 25,000 feet and service ceiling of over eight miles. The balky superchargers had at last been tamed and delivered the anticipated power increases at altitude. When the U. S. entered World War II, the P-38 was the Army's fastest and most heavily armed fighter. The concentration of firepower in the Lightning's nose was so effective that a one-second burst could destroy an enemy plane.

The fastest of the Lightnings was the P-38J with a top speed of 420 mph, and the version produced in the greatest quantity was the "L", of which 3,735 were built by Lockheed and 113 by Vultee. The P-38L was powered by two 1,475 hp Allison V-1710-111 engines.

As with any long-term production aircraft, the P-38 underwent many modifications. Some were fitted with bombardier-type noses, and were used to lead formations of bomb-laden P-38's to their targets. The P-38M was a two-seat radar-equipped night fighter, a few of which had become operational before the war ended. One interesting variation had an elevated tail assembly on upswept booms; another one had an elongated center pod and was used for airfoil evaluation.

The dimensions of the P-38 remained the same throughout production, its wing spanning 52 feet with an area of 328 square feet. Overall length was 37 feet 10 inches; height was 12 feet 10 inches. The P-38L weighed 12,800 pounds empty and 17,500 pounds gross. Thus, the P-38 was the largest, heaviest, and fastest "P" type to date. An internal fuel capacity of 410 gallons could be increased to 1,010 gallons with two external drop tanks and gave the Lightning a range of 450 miles, making it the first fighter suitable as a long-range bomber excort.

In addition to its devastating nose armament, the P-38 could carry up to 4,000 pounds of external weapons including bombs and rockets.

This P-38E was fitted with a raised tail to overcome flutter problems. Unfortunately, the tail broke away during flight tests and the aircraft was destroyed.
Lockheed

The "Swordfish" was a P-38 modified for use in evaluating airfoils.   *Lockheed*

The P-38L could carry up to fourteen rockets to supplement its nose armament.   *Lockheed*

The nickname "Droop Snoot" was given to Lightnings which had bombardier-type noses. These planes carried Norden bomb sights and guided fleets of bomb laden P-38's to their targets. P-38L's were converted to this role.   *Lockheed*

BELL
P-39, P-45, P-76 AIRACOBRA

Cooling and carburetor air was fed to the engine of the XP-39 from side-mounted air scoops. The rear-mounted engine and long drive shaft proved extremely reliable in service.   Bell

When the Detroit Aircraft Company was absorbed by Consolidated, some of its designers joined the newly-formed Bell Aircraft Corp. and remained in New York. Less than 3 years after the formation of the company, Bell unveiled their initial pursuit design when the XP-39 made its first flight on April 6, 1938. The influence of the earlier YP-24 was readily apparent in the wing shape of the new fighter. The overall appearance of the XP-39 was one of simplicity, its graceful lines due to the unique location of the 1,150 hp Allison V-1710 engine behind the cockpit.

Ideally, the best placement for an aircraft engine is on the airplane's center of gravity. This allows a slimmer nose and excellent maneuverability; but it also presents the problem of delivering the power to the propeller, which is usually located at an extreme end of the fuselage. In the case of the Airacobra, as the P-39 was called, the propeller was driven by an 8 foot extension shaft passing under the cockpit to a gearbox in the nose. Air to cool the engine was taken in through scoops in the fuselage sides. Later, these were moved to the wing leading edge.

The first flight testing was done with a supercharged engine, and the XP-39 could reach 390 mph at 20,000 feet. These tests showed the necessity for some revisions and the plane was returned to Bell for modification. Meanwhile, a contract for 12 service test YP-39's and one YP-39A was awarded, but these planes were to be without superchargers—an unfortunate decision that actually changed the operational future of the Airacobra. With the lower rated engine and a higher gross weight brought about by the requested modifications, the top speed fell to 368 mph at 13,600 feet. The YP-39's were armed with two .30 cal. and two .50 cal. machine guns in the nose. A 37 mm cannon occupied the space usually taken by a forward mounted engine and fired through a hollow propeller spinner.

On August 10, 1939, the Army placed an order for 80 Bell P-45 Airacobras, but the designation was soon changed to P-39C. These planes were equipped with bulletproof windshields and self-sealing fuel tanks. As production orders increased, so did the Airacobra's weight. Without the extra power of the supercharged engine, the performance of the P-39 began to fall rapid-

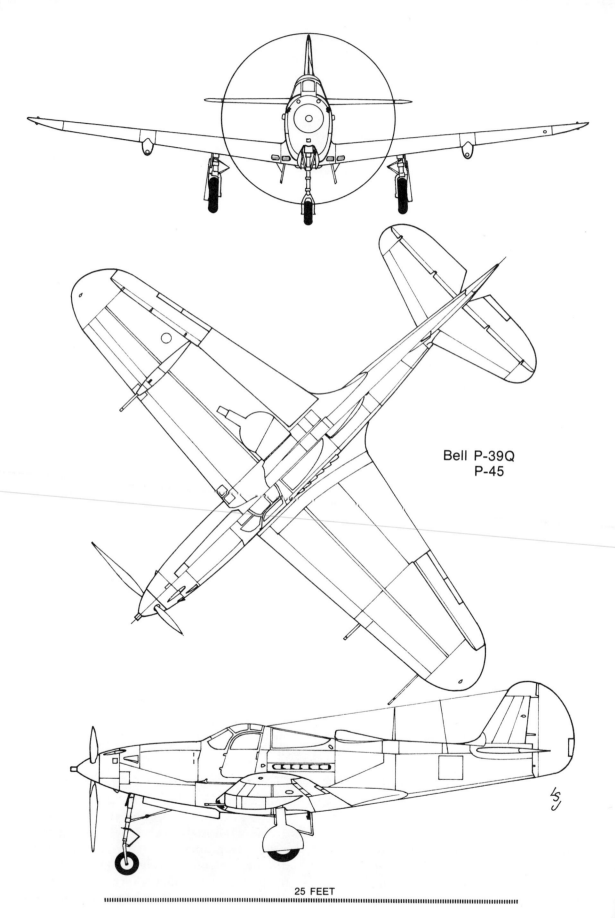

Bell P-39Q
P-45

25 FEET

ly. It could no longer be considered suitable as an interceptor or effectively engage in dog fights since it was outclassed by the lighter, more maneuverable fighters used by the enemy. The Allison V-1710-35 gave its best performance below 10,000 feet. As a result, when the P-39D version was delivered in April 1941, the fighter was reclassed in the ground-attack role. The P-39D was armed with four .30 cal. machine guns in the wings, two .50 cal. guns in the nose, and the 37 mm cannon. The subtypes from the P-39D to "M" differed mainly in engine power ratings and armament changes.

The major production variant of the P-39 was the "Q" model, of which 4,905 were built. The P-39Q carried the same nose armament as the earlier models, but the four .30 cal. machine guns in the wings were replaced by two .50 cal. types mounted in underwing pods.

Four thousand examples of the Airacobra were ordered on February 24, 1942, as the P-76. It was virtually identical to the P-39M, differing only in minor detail. This order was cancelled on May 20, 1942, to permit the use of the construction plant for the assembly of B-29 bombers.

The placement of the engine drive shaft under the cockpit was a source of apprehen-

sion among pilots when the Airacobra was first introduced. It did not take much to imagine the extent of damage that could be caused by a broken shaft whipping around the cockpit. In fact, any such fear was unfounded and the system proved quite safe even in crash landings.

Characteristics of the P-39Q were typical of the Airacobra series. The 213 square foot wing spanned 34 feet, overall length was 30 feet 2 inches, and height was 11 feet 10 inches. Weighing 5,645 pounds empty, the P-39Q was almost 100 pounds heavier than the gross weight of the XP-39. This fact, no doubt, contributed to the P-39Q's poorer performance, since it had only 13 sq. feet more wing area to lift an all-up weight of 7,700 gross pounds. Fuel capacity of the "Q" ranged from 104 gallons to 295 gallons, depending on the weight of the armor in the particular airplane. The P-39Q-21 and later models had four-bladed propellers instead of the three-blader used on the rest of the series.

Airacobra production was completed with the 9,558th plane. Half of these planes were sent to Russia under our Lend-Lease program where their effectiveness in the ground-attack role made it very popular with the Soviet Union.

The P-39C was originally designated P-45 for a short while.   *Bell*

CURTISS
P-40 WARHAWK

This P-40 formed a part of the 55th Pursuit Squadron. This aircraft, one of 200 P-40's, is physically similar to the P-40B & P-40C types which followed in production.

Gordon S. Williams

While Lockheed and Bell were refining their new Allison-powered P-38 and P-39 designs for production, Curtiss was ready with an interim version of their P-36 Hawk. Converting a P-36 airframe to mount an Allison engine gave the Army a fighter with performance similar to that of the Messerschmitt and Hurricane. Though not as advanced as the P-38 and P-39, the XP-40 (as the new Hawk was designated) was on hand when it was needed.

The XP-40 was developed from the tenth P-36A, and was first flown on October 14, 1938. In its original form, the Prestone-cooling radiator was located behind the wing. Strangely enough, the engineers were asked by the Curtiss-Wright Sales Department to move the radiator forward under the engine, and the characteristic P-40 nose was born. (The rear-mounted radiator would become the trade mark of another famous fighter.)

The first P-40 contract was awarded on April 26, 1939, for 524 planes. Only 200 had been delivered to the Army when production was deferred to permit construction of 142 export model 81-A's ordered by France, but ultimately taken over by Britain

as Tomahawks. From the next batch, built specifically for Britain, would come the planes which became famous as the Flying Tigers. Following these were 131 P-40B's and 193 similar P-40C's to complete the original Army contract.

When America became embroiled in the Second World War, the P-40 formed the backbone of the Army's fighter squadrons.

The P-40 underwent many obvious physical changes during its production run. The original P-40 types mounted a single .30 cal. and .50 cal. machine gun astride the nose, firing through the propeller arc via a synchronizer. The first change came about when a 1,150 hp Allison V-1710-39 engine was mounted on a modified export model H-87A airframe. Called the Kittyhawk by the British, the nose guns were deleted and four .50 cal. machine guns were mounted in the wings outside of the propeller radius. The U. S. Army ordered 22 of these as the P-40D. The "D" had a larger spinner and a bolder cooling radiator in addition to some refinements to the cockpit area. A six-gun version of this type became the P-40E, of which 2,322 were built—many going to the R.A.F. Top speed was 354 mph at 15,000 feet.

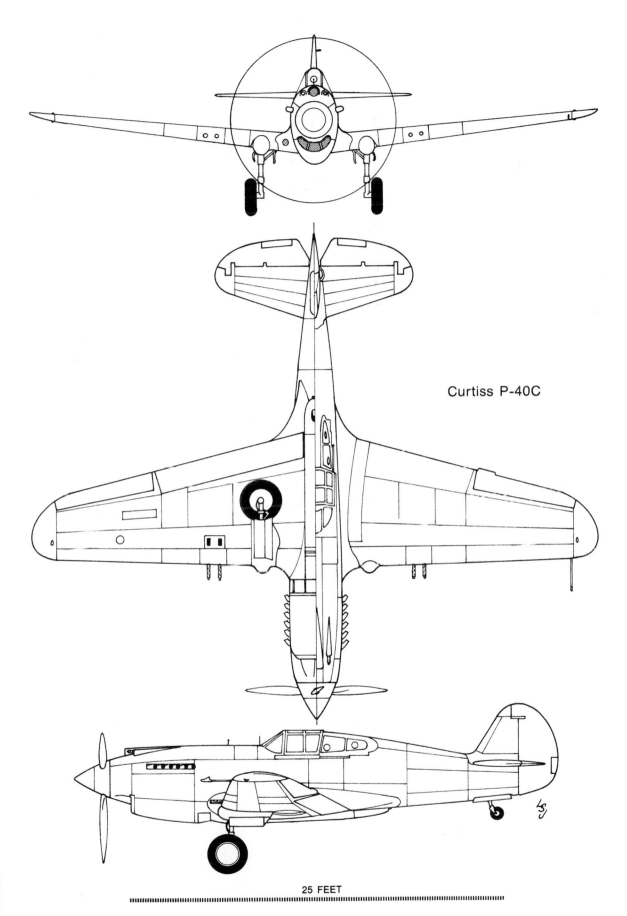

Curtiss P-40C

25 FEET

With the P-40F, an entirely new powerplant was installed on the P-40 airframe—the Rolls Royce Merlin. As the XP-40F, the first Merlin-powered Warhawk could reach 373 mph. A production order led to 1,311 P-40F's, distinguished by the absence of the carburetor air intake above the Packard-built Merlin engine. The demand for the Merlin in the P-51 superseded the P-40 requirements, however, and the Allison again became the standard engine on later P-40 types.

Some problems with lateral stability became apparent as the P-40 airframe was developed and the vertical fin was enlarged as a corrective measure. This was not adequate so the fuselage was extended 19 inches, moving the vertical stabilizer rearward. This change was made during the production of the P-40F; this type, therefore, having both short and long fuselages.

The P-40N was the type built in the largest numbers—over 5,000 being completed. The "N" utilized the long fuselage introduced on the "F" and added a distinctive new canopy. The familiar side windows for rearward visibility, first used on the P-36, were replaced by a cut-down panel and the canopy itself extended back. The P-40N was lightened by the use of aluminum in the radiators and oil coolers, spoked wheels, and, in the first models, only four machine guns. They were the fastest of the entire Warhawk line with a top speed of 378 mph at 10,500 feet.

The lightweight P-40N-1 weighed 6,000 pounds empty and grossed 6,400 pounds as compared to 6,350 pounds and 6,900 pounds for the P-40E. All the Warhawks used the same 236 sq. foot wing spanning 37 feet 4 inches. Those with the short fuselage measured 31 feet 9 inches, and the extended ones were 33 feet 4 inches. All versions were 12 feet 4 inches high. The P-40N had a fuel capacity of 292 gallons and a range of 240 miles.

For most of its service life, the P-40 was outclassed by more advanced types. A last-ditch attempt to extend its production life came in 1944 in the form of the P-40Q. A much cleaner airplane, it sported a full bubble canopy, smaller cooling radiator, and clipped wings. Still powered by an Allison V-1710, it could turn out a good speed, topping 422 mph, but that was in an age when fighters were nearing 500 mph. The P-40Q made a good racer but it could not match its contemporaries in combat.

Curtiss P-40's were operated by many nations during WW II. This P-40E belonged to the Royal Canadian Air Force.
Gordon S. Williams

Over 5,000 P-40N's of this type were built making it the major P-40 sub-type.   Dustin W. Carter

The XP-40Q was the last of the line and ended its days as a race plane.   Dustin W. Carter

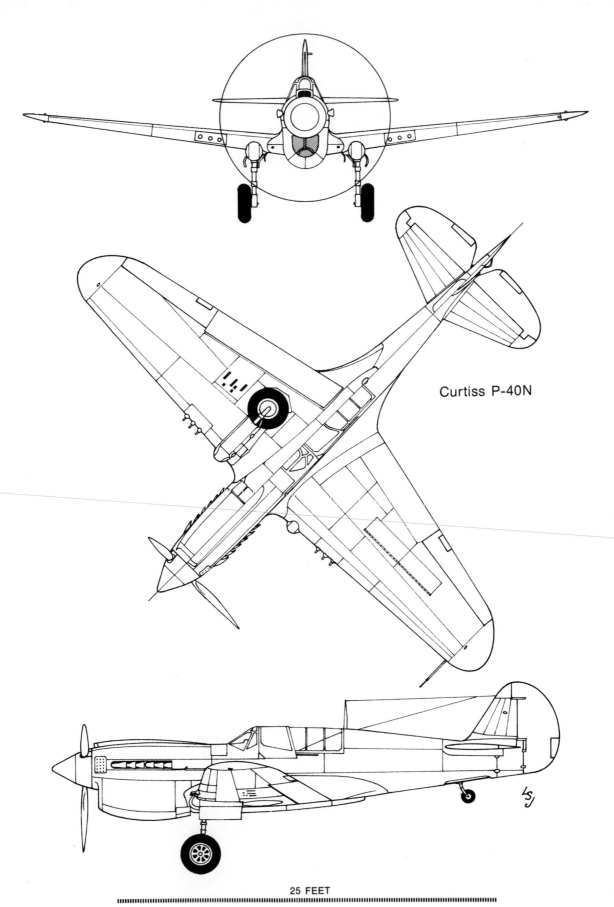

Curtiss P-40N

25 FEET

The XP-41 was the last Seversky-built plane delivered to the Army. It was the final P-35 with the addition of a turbo-supercharger and inward retracting landing gear. Republic

Included as part of the contract for the first Seversky P-35's was the XP-41. Strongly resembling the P-35, it was different in many respects; some facets of its design foretelling the future configuration of the P-47. The XP-41 first flew in March 1939.

The bulky half-retracted landing gear of the P-35 was replaced by a fully-retractable system folding inwards. The dihedral on the wing was unbroken from the tip to the fuselage and the cockpit greenhouse was much lower, the framing having some of the appearance of the future Thunderbolt. Using the same Pratt & Whitney R-1830 Twin Wasp engine as the P-35, the XP-41 had a horsepower from 950 to 1,200. This gave

supercharger to increase the available the plane a maximum velocity of 323 mph at 15,000 feet. The supercharger was a two-stage two-speed type located in the lower fuselage behind the wing, air being fed through a scoop in the left wing root.

Armament for the XP-41 was one .30 cal. machine gun with 500 rounds and one .50 cal. machine gun with 200 rounds—the typical fighter complement for the 1930's. The XP-41, being the last P-35 (S.N. 36-430), had the same wingspan of 36 feet, but with a length of 27 feet was 22 inches longer than the P-35. Height was 12 feet 6 inches. The empty airframe weighed 5,390 pounds and the XP-41's gross weight was 6,600 pounds.

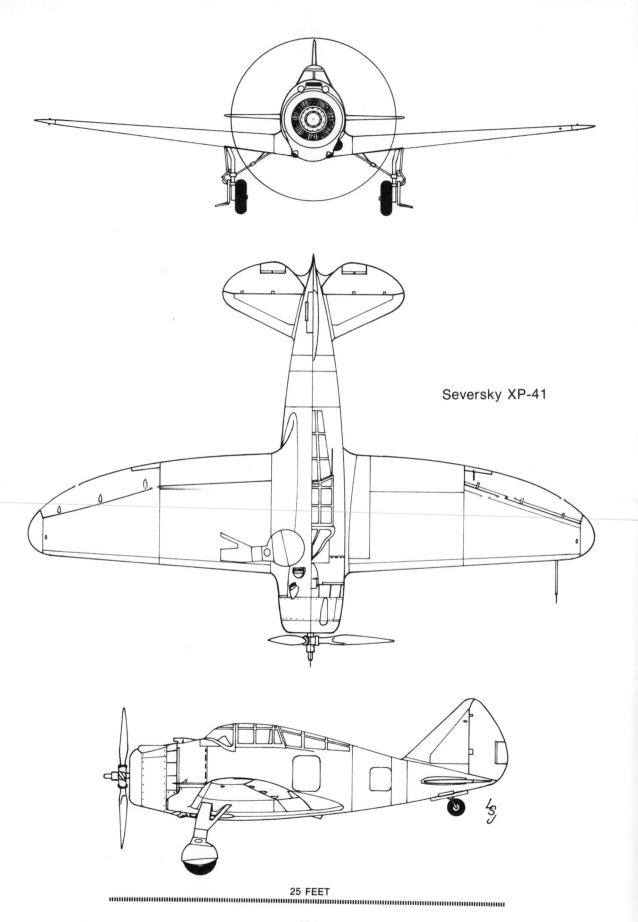

Seversky XP-41

25 FEET

With its bullet nose, the XP-42 appeared to be much faster than it actually was. Gordon S. Williams

The fourth P-36A Hawk (38-004) was used extensively for the evaluation of long-chord cowlings on radial engines. As a test vehicle, it was designated XP-42 and was delivered to Wright Field in March 1939, to begin tests.

The object of these tests was to determine the feasibility of streamlining an air-cooled radial engine to obtain inline engine performance. With the military concentrating on radial engines in the late thirties, development of the inline types was lagging. Overseas, the Spitfire, Hurricane, and Messerschmitt Bf 109 fighters, powered with inline engines, were exceeding the performance of the latest American fighters. Although the radial engines could develop as much power as the inline ones, their bulk created enough drag to reduce performance drastically. With the XP-42, an attempt was made to design the drag away aerodynamically.

In its original form, the XP-42 engine, a Pratt & Whitney R-1830-31 Twin Wasp, was fitted with an extension shaft which located the propeller well forward of the P-36 placement. The sheet-metal of the cowling wrapped tightly around the engine and tapered to the front to terminate in a sharply-pointed spinner. A large scoop under the engine admitted cooling air while two small scoops above the engine fed air to the carburetor. The XP-42 was immediately beset with cooling problems and drag reduction was hardly noticeable. Nearly a dozen cowling/prop/spinner configurations were tested, and the highest speed attained was 344 mph at 14,500 feet. While this was faster than the 313 mph of the standard P-36, it was slower than the Allison-powered P-40, which was capable of 347 mph under the same conditions. Eventually the cowling was shortened until its original length was reached.

In 1942, an all-flying stabilizer was installed on the XP-42, similar to the stabilator used on supersonic jets. The flights were limited to a maximum speed of 260 mph but much valuable data was obtained from these tests.

In its original form, the XP-42 was 30 feet 3 inches long with a wingspan of 37 feet 4 inches. Height was 12 feet. Empty weight was 4,818 pounds and gross weight was 5,920 pounds. No armament was installed.

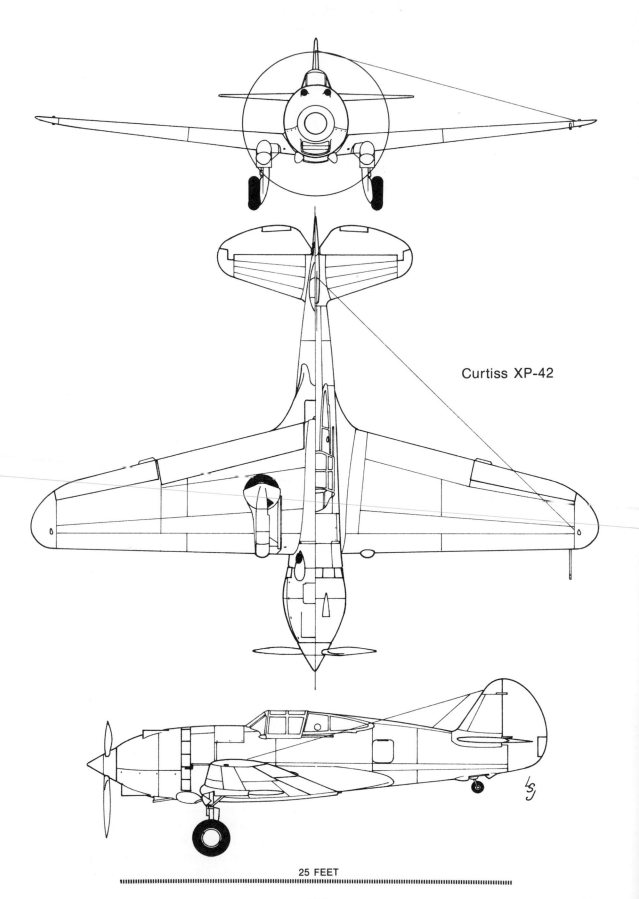

Curtiss XP-42

25 FEET

In this view of the P-43, the rear-mounted supercharger can be seen.   *Air Force Museum*

Development of the successor to Republic's P-35 began with the supercharged XP-41. Although the XP-41 was not placed into production, many of its features were incorporated into a parallel but similar design which did achieve production status as the P-43 Lancer. Originally developed under the company designation AP-4, the plane first appeared with a close-fitting cowling that blended into a huge, pointed spinner. This attempt at streamlining the big air-cooled radial engine was accompanied by the same overheating problems found in the Curtiss XP-42 test program, and was soon replaced by a conventional cowling. The engine supercharger developed in the XP-41 was included in the AP-4, as was the inward-retracting landing gear and the 1,200 hp R-1830 Pratt & Whitney engine.

On May 12, 1939, thirteen YP-43's were ordered for service evaluation; the first of these was to be delivered one year later. The YP-43 differed from the AP-4 in having a lower cockpit profile, extended tail wheel strut and relocated supercharger intake.

On the basis of reports from Europe, which was in the first stages of World War II, the YP-43 was already obsolete. On September 13, 1939, the Army placed an order for 80 AP-4J's, a progressive development of the AP-4 design, as P-44-1's with 1,400 hp Pratt & Whitney R-2180-1 engines. Named Rocket, the P-44 differed little in appearance from the P-43 but had prospects of greater performance, including a top speed of 386 mph.

Construction began on the first of the 80 Rockets while engineering design was undertaken on an even more promising version of the AP-4 series, the AP-4L. As the P-44-2, this model would use the 2,000 hp Pratt & Whitney R-2800-7 engine which would increase the Rocket's maximum speed to 406 mph. On July 12, 1940, the Army ordered 225 of the newer Rocket design and on September 9, 1940, this order was increased to a total of 827 copies of the P-44-2.

By mid-1940, the evidence from Europe clearly indicated that even the P-44 designs would be outdated by the time the first one flew, let alone reached production status. By

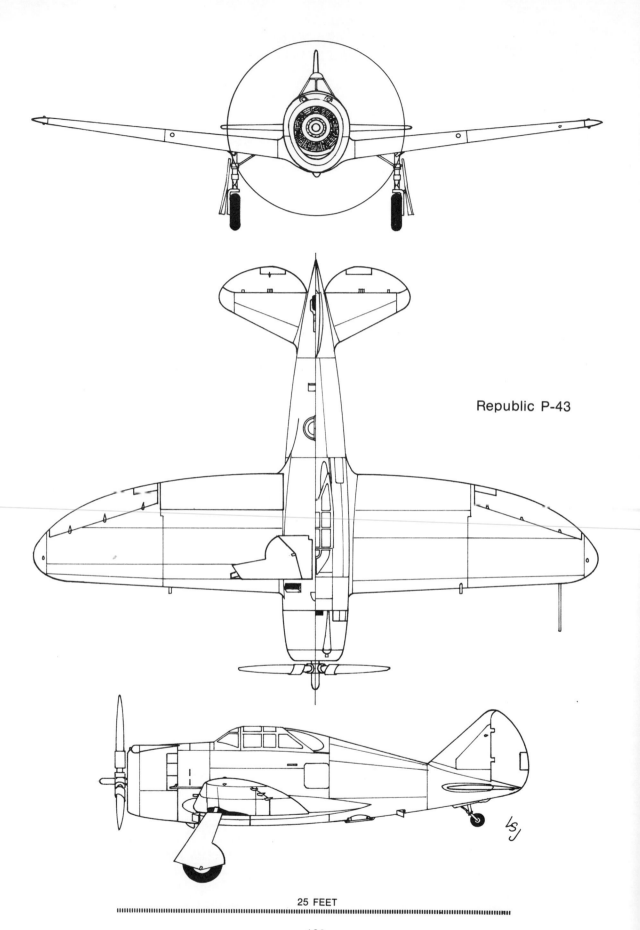

Republic P-43

25 FEET

This is an artist's concept of the XP-44 Rocket.   *Republic*

this time Republic engineers had devised a replacement that would reflect the requirements of actual combat based on the European reports. This design, which was to become the famous Thunderbolt, had been approved by the Army on September 6, 1940; and on September 13, four days after the P-44 order had been increased, all Rocket contracts were cancelled.

In order to maintain production at the Republic plant while the Thunderbolt design was under development, the Army ordered the P-44's under construction to be completed as P-43's. Initially 54 Lancers were ordered, these being powered by Pratt & Whitney R-1830-35 engines of 1,200 hp with turbo-supercharging. These planes had a top speed of 351 mph and were armed with two .30 cal. machine guns in the nose with 500 rounds each, and one .50 cal. gun in each wing with 200 rpg. Additional production orders for P-43's followed, bringing the total to 272 planes. Later

models were powered by the R-1830-47 or -57 engine. This engine increased the Lancer's maximum speed to 356 mph at 20,000 feet.

All the P-43's had been delivered before the United States entered into World War II, and most of those remaining in the U. S. Army were converted for use as photo-reconnaissance planes. These models were designated P-43B and C. No American Lancers were used in combat, but the Chinese Air Force used export models of the P-43 in their fight against the Japanese.

The P-43A had a wingspan of 36 feet, length of 28 feet 6 inches, and the Lancer stood 14 feet high. Wing area was 224 square feet. Empty weight was 5,730 pounds with a gross of 7,300 pounds. In addition to its four machine guns, the P-43 could carry either six 20 lb. bombs or two 200 lb. bombs. Fuel capacity was 218 gallons, giving a range of 800 miles at 280 mph.

The XP-46 showed promise on paper but was a disappointment in the air.   *Air Force Museum*

With the P-40 series well in production, Curtiss turned to the development of a potential successor. By the end of 1939, the new generation of European warplanes were exposing their strengths and weaknesses. Reports of combat situations were being evaluated by American plane builders and the U. S. Army.

The XP-46 was an attempt to design a fighter incorporating those features felt most desirable from actual pilot experience in Europe. Curtiss proposed the new design to the Army, who then drew up a requirement around the proposal. On September 29, 1939, a contract for two prototypes was given to Curtiss, one XP-46 fully equipped and an XP-46A without armament to expedite the testing program.

Power for the two XP-46's was the new Allison V-1710-39 with 1,150 hp and it was hoped that a speed of 410 mph at 15,000 feet could be attained. In spite of Curtiss' intention that the new fighter be light-weight, within a month of issuing the contract, the Army added self-sealing fuel tanks and 65 pounds of armor plating. However, the adverse effect on the performance caused by the added weight was academic because the

Army had decided to replace the XP-46's with V-1710-39-powered P-40D's before the two prototypes were completed.

The first XP-46 to fly was actually the second airframe completed. The XP-46A, 40-3054, took to the air on February 15, 1941. Although smaller in proportion and lighter in weight than the P-40, the XP-46 displayed disappointing performance characteristics. Maximum speed was 355 mph at 12,200 feet, it could climb 12,200 feet in 5 minutes, and had a service ceiling of 29,500 feet. With 156 gallons of fuel, the XP-46 had a range of 325 miles. In addition, much of the equipment and accessories were inaccessible, making maintenance difficult.

Some of the features adopted for the XP-46 as a result of the evaluation of European fighting were automatic leading-edge slats similar to those on the Messerschmitt Bf 109 and up to eight wing-mounted .30 cal. machine guns in addition to the two nose-mounted .50's.

Dimensions of the XP-46 were: wingspan of 34 feet 4 inches, length of 30 feet 2 inches, height of 13 feet. Wing area was 208 square feet. Empty weight was 5,625 lbs. gross weight was 6,750 lbs.

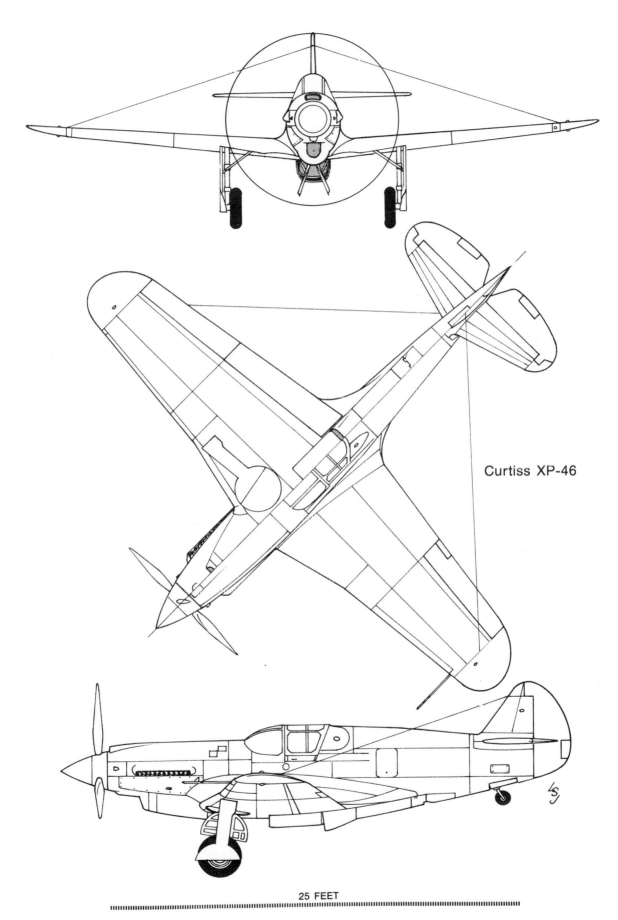

Curtiss XP-46

25 FEET

This is the XP-46A, second of the two planes built. The armament was not installed to expedite testing.

Gordon S. Williams

The front view of the XP-46 shows its relationship to the P-40.

Air Force Museum

REPUBLIC
XP-47, P-47 THUNDERBOLT

A P-47D-20. The aft positioning of the supercharging outlet is apparent in this view, as is the characteristic razor-back spine.   Republic

On August 1, 1939, Republic proposed development of a light-weight fighter, similar in many respects to the ill-fated Curtiss XP-46. With a gross weight of only 4,900 pounds, the proposed AP-10 was to be powered by an Allison V-1710-39 liquid-cooled engine of 1,150 hp. Armament was to consist of two .50 cal. machine guns and wing area was 115 square feet. The proposal in this form was rejected, but an enlarged version with four .30 cal. guns in the wings and a gross weight of 6,150 pounds was ordered as the XP-47 in November 1939. A second model, stripped of combat equipment, was also ordered as the XP-47A. The estimated performance of the XP-47 was 400 mph at 15,000 feet, and it should reach that altitude in 4.8 minutes.

Wingspan of the proposed XP-47 was 30 feet with an area of 165 sq. feet. Overall length was 27 feet 6 inches with a height of 12 feet. Empty weight was to be 4,790 pounds. The Allison engine turned a 10 foot constant speed Curtiss propeller. The two .50 cal. guns in the nose were to each have 200 rounds with 500 rounds each being provided for the eight wing guns.

Before construction could begin on the lightweight fighter, combat reports from Europe again indicated the design was deficient and the Republic design team, under Alexander Kartveli, proposed a new radial-engined design with eight .50 cal. guns and a weight nearly twice that of the XP-47.

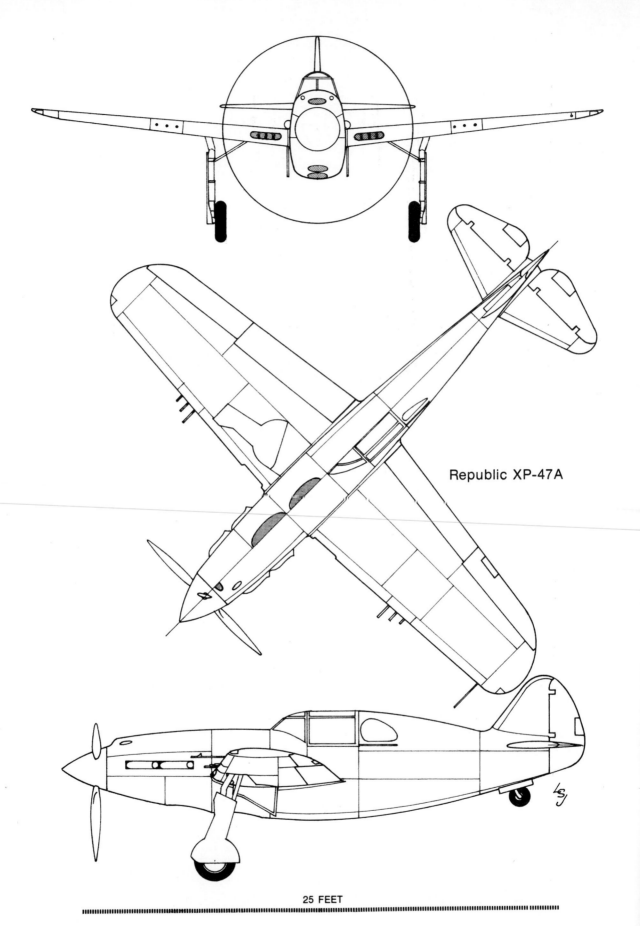

Republic XP-47A

25 FEET

This lightweight Thunderbolt, XP-47J, was the first piston-powered plane to exceed 500 mph in level flight. Notice the attempt to improve rearward cockpit visibility.   *Republic*

Following Alexander Kartveli's proposal on June 12, 1940, for an 11,500 pound, eight gun fighter, the Army issued a revision to its XP-47 contract ordering 171 P-47B and 602 P-47C fighters.

Republic assembly lines turned out P-43 Lancers in order to keep the plant operating while the P-47's were designed and the new Pratt & Whitney R-2800 Double Wasp engines were being assembled. The supercharging system for the big fighter created many problems during the design stage. Because of the importance of a smooth airflow between the supercharger and the engine, this portion of the P-47 was actually designed first, the rest of the plane fitting around it. Despite the fact that the supercharger was in the tail and the engine in the nose, the system proved quite successful and did not even suffer greatly from battle damage.

In keeping with the gigantic proportions of the fighter, the engine turned over a twelve-foot propeller. In order to mount the landing gear in the wing and have room for the eight machine guns, yet still provide ground clearance for the propeller, the designers used a telescoping strut which lengthened the gear 9 inches when it was lowered.

On May 6, 1941, the XP-47B made its first flight. Weighing twice as much as its contemporaries, the P-47 was the largest, heaviest, single-engine single-seat fighter to reach the production stage. Nearly two years of testing and refining were required before the huge fighter, now called Thunderbolt, was ready for combat. When it did arrive, it was met with mixed emotions. Experienced fighter pilots used to the trim lines and light weight of the P-39, P-40, and Spitfire looked at this new monster with some misgivings. It became the butt of many jokes, few of them intended to glorify the big plane. But time was to prove the wisdom of Kartveli's design and the Thunderbolt became one of aviation's classics.

The first P-47 combat missions were flown in April 1943; and Thunderbolt pilots found they could out-dive anything in the skies, thus breaking off combat at will. This is a definite advantage, as any fighter pilot will tell you.

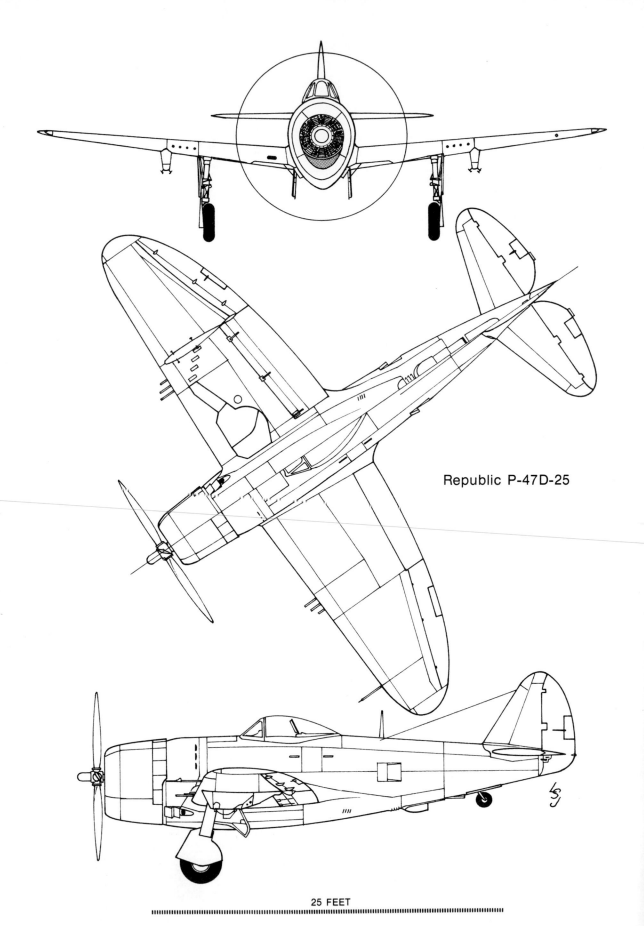

Republic P-47D-25

25 FEET

116

On October 13, 1941, the improved P-47D was ordered. In appearance, the first P-47D's were similar to the "B" and "C" versions with the cockpit blending into the tail via a razorback spine. This spine, although aerodynamically efficient, created a 20 degree blind spot behind the tail which could drastically reduce a pilot's life expectancy in combat. To eliminate this blind area, one P-47 was fitted with a bubble canopy from a British Typhoon. Designated XP-47K, it proved the value of the increased visibility, and bubble canopies were introduced on the production line with the P-47D-25. The cut-down fuselage created some yaw problems which were corrected by the addition of a dorsal fin on later "D's" and subsequent models. A total of 12,602 P-47D's were built.

The P-47 airframe provided the basic structure for several test beds, some even receiving new fighter designations. Among these was the XP-47H, a grotesque-looking machine adapted to test the 2,300 hp Chrysler XIV-2220-1 sixteen-cylinder inverted Vee liquid-cooled engine. This version, two of which were converted from P-47D's, reached a level speed of 490 mph. The P-47H was not developed because the Chrysler engine failed to reach production.

The XP-47J, nicknamed Superman, was the fastest of all the Thunderbolts. This model was the result of a study in simplifying the P-47 design. Nearly 200 pounds were pared from the airframe by reducing the eight-gun armament to six and other design refinements. A Pratt & Whitney R-2800-57 engine was closely cowled and force-cooled by a fan. This plane also had a larger supercharger and reached a level-flight speed of 504 mph to become the first piston powered fighter to exceed 500 mph! Production plans for the XP-47J were shelved in favor of another P-47 development, the XP-72.

One hundred sixty (160) P-47M's, using the same engine and supercharger as the XP-47J, were built and sent to Europe to chase down the V-1 Buzz Bomb. These planes carried air brakes under the wings for rapid deceleration after diving on their targets. The P-47M's reached 470 miles per hour.

The final Thunderbolt model built was the long-winged P-47N, specifically conceived for the long-range missions in the Pacific war.

At the conclusion of production, 15,677 Thunderbolts had been assembled—the greatest quantity of any American fighter built. Of this total, Curtiss built 354 P-47G's Republic-built P-47D-10 types.

The P-47D-25 is typical of the Thunderbolt series. It had a wingspan of 40 feet 9 inches, a length of 36 feet 2 inches, and was 14 feet 2 inches high. Wing area was 300 square feet. Maximum speed was 429 mph at 20,000 feet. Service ceiling was 40,000 feet. Fuel capacity was 370 gallons internally, but with external tanks, a total of 1,080 gallons could be carried. Armament consisted of either six .50 cal. machine guns with 1,602 rounds total or eight .50's with a total of 2,136 rounds. Empty weight was 10,700 lbs., and the P-47D grossed 17,500 pounds.

The durability and strength of the P-47 led to the nickname "Juggernaut" by its pilots, or more affectionately, just "Jug." Many times, the big planes returned from missions with great quantities of daylight showing through the airframe; and even with portions of the engine blown away, the venerable, durable "Jug" brought its pilot home safely.

The ungainly-looking XP-47H with the Chrysler 16 cylinder engine which reached a speed of 490 miles per hour.
                                                                                    Republic

A colorful red and white striped P-47D-30 of the 526th FS, 86th FG, Pisa, Italy. Wing racks contain napalm tanks.
                                          Harvey Lippencott, Connecticut Aeronautical Historical Association

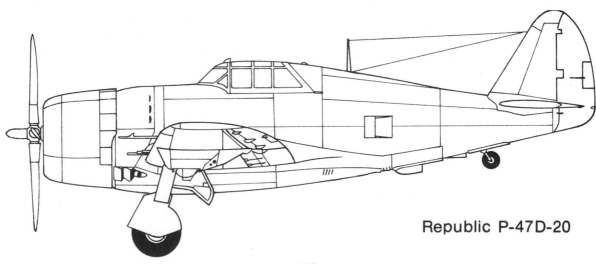

Republic P-47D-20

DOUGLAS
XP-48

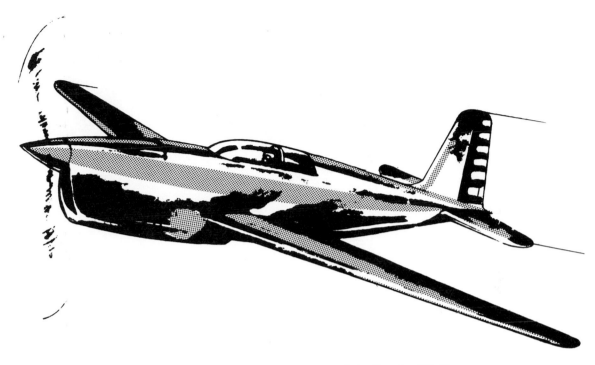

This drawing is an engineering impression of the Douglas XP-48.

In 1939, Douglas Aircraft Company offered a small, lightweight, high altitude fighter to the Army—their Model 312. Power was to be supplied by a twelve-cylinder inverted Vee Ranger SGV-770 engine with a two-stage supercharger, turning a relatively large nine-and-a-half foot three-bladed propeller. This combination was to provide 525 hp for the little fighter, but no estimated performance figures were released. Apparently the manufacturer's estimate of performance was a bit optimistic; as one official Army document states, "Performance with proposed engine installation not considered feasible. Contract cancelled."

The XP-48 design had a high aspect ratio wing spanning 32 feet with a mean chord of 35.64 inches. Wing area was 92 square feet. Overall length was 21 feet 9 inches. Height was 9 feet. Armament was one .30 cal. machine gun with 500 rpg and one .50 cal. gun with 200 rpg. Empty weight of the XP-48 was to be 2,675 pounds with a useful load of 725 lbs., making the gross weight 3,400 pounds. Fuel capacity was 50 gallons.

The tricycle landing gear retracted rearwards, the nose gear rotating 90 degrees and the main gear folding into the fuselage sides in a manner similar to that used on the later XB-42 and A3D bombers.

119

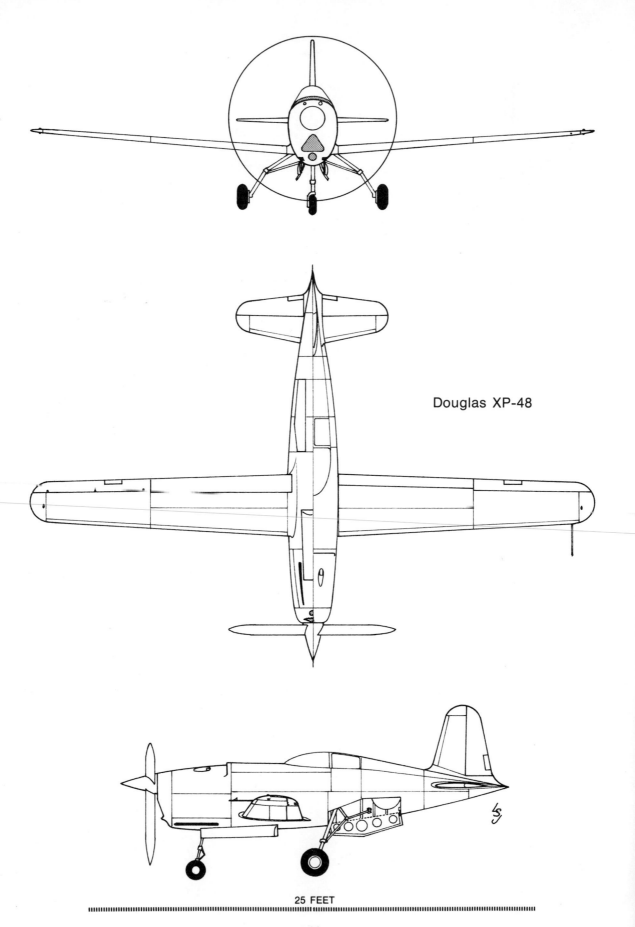

Douglas XP-48

25 FEET

The lighter engines required lengthening the nacelles. Note the additional stripes when the extra height was added to the rudder.
Lockheed

In answer to a U.S.A.A.C. Circular Proposal for a new fighter design, Lockheed submitted their Model 222 (later changed to 522) to the competition. On August 3, 1939, the Lockheed design was awarded the most points among four offers; the Grumman G-46 winning second place. It was felt that both planes should be developed further and contracts were placed for one example of each. The Lockheed plane became the XP-49 (S.N. 40-3055).

Originally conceived by the Lockheed design team as a possible replacement of the P-38 Lightning, the XP-49 was actually a further development of the P-38 intended to use the new Pratt & Whitney twenty-four cylinder X-1800 engines. Lockheed received the order for the XP-49 in October 1939, and a contract was signed on January 8, 1940. Two months later it became apparent the X-1800 engines would not be available and two Continental XI-1430-1 engines were substituted. The 1,600 hp Continental engines provided considerably less power than the 2,300 hp Pratt & Whitneys. Therefore, the estimated maximum speed of 473 mph was substantially reduced to 406

mph at 15,000 feet.

The XP-49 design included several advanced features for fighter aircraft: a pressurized cabin, two 20 mm cannon, heated gun compartments using prestone. Ninety-round ammunition drums were developed for the 20 mm cannon which became Air Corps standard equipment despite the fact no armament was actually installed in the XP-49.

Because of difficulty in obtaining armor plate, dummy armor was installed to avoid a delay in completing the prototype. On November 11, 1942, the XP-49 lifted from the runway at Burbank, California for its first flight. Handling was generally good but an increase in vertical fin area was required. This added area on the twin fins led to an unusual tail marking. The official rudder markings on U. S. Army planes consisted of 13 horizontal stripes. When the extra area was added to the XP-49's tail, the painters simply added two more stripes rather than repaint the entire surfaces.

A few days after flight testing had begun, the original engines were replaced and new fuel tanks were installed. On one test flight,

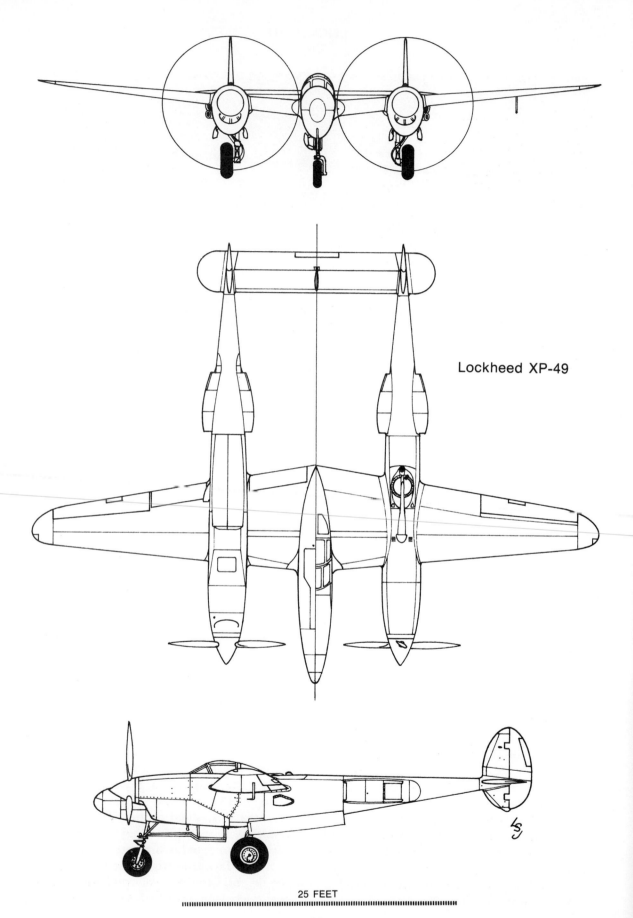

Lockheed XP-49

25 FEET

The engines on the P-49 rotated outward to counteract torque as seen in this photo.   Lockheed

a hydraulic failure led to a crash-landing, but the damage, while serious, did not necessitate termination of the program. A month-and-a-half later testing resumed; but the XP-49 did not display any notable advantages over the P-38, so plans for production were discarded.

On June 25, 1943, the XP-49 was flown to Wright Field for further evaluation. Here, modifications were made to the fuel tanks in an attempt to eliminate a leakage problem which had plagued the fighter. But the leakage continued, and, as other minor problems manifested themselves, the program was abandoned and the XP-49 was scrapped.

The XP-49 was proportionately similar to the P-38 with a wingspan of 52 feet and an area of 327½ sq. feet. Its overall length of 40 feet 1 inch was slightly greater than the Lightning's. The XP-49 was 9 feet 9½ inches high. A top speed of 406 mph was reached at 15,000 feet, and the XP-49 had an initial climb rate of 3,300 fpm. Internal fuel capacity was 300 gallons, but up to 725 gallons could be carried with external tanks. The XP-49 weighed 15,475 pounds empty and 18,750 pounds loaded. Like the planned pressurized cabin, the proposed armament of two 20 mm cannons and four .50 cal. machine guns was not installed.

The Grumman fighter offered excellent pilot visibility as can be seen by the high mounting of the cockpit.

Grumman

Runner-up in the 1939 U.S.A.A.C.'s Circular Proposal 39-775, in which the Lockheed XP-49 was winner, the Grumman Model G-46 received a development contract on November 25, 1939. Like the Lockheed design, the Grumman fighter was also based on an existing airframe; in this case, the Navy XF5F-1 carrier fighter.

Grumman's fighter, designated XP-50, was given the serial number 40-3057. In appearance, it was quite similar to the Navy fighter, the main difference being in the extension of the nose to house the forward member of the tricycle landing gear. Power was obtained from two supercharged Wright R-1820-67/69 nine cylinder radial engines of 1,200 hp each, geared to rotate in opposite directions.

Following an investment of $353,828, the prototype XP-50 was readied for its initial flight from Grumman's facilities on Long Island, New York. On Wednesday, May 14, 1941, the XP-50 took to the air for its maiden flight. Shortly after take-off, the XP-50 was shaken by an explosion in one of the turbo-superchargers and the affected engine burst into flames. The pilot successfully abandoned the stricken plane, but the XP-50 was destroyed as it plunged into the ocean.

As a result of the crash, no performance figures for the XP-50 were actually obtained. However, the proposed maximum speed was 424 mph at 25,000 feet. Service ceiling was to be 40,000 feet. The XP-50 had an empty weight of 8,307 pounds and grossed 10,558 pounds with 217 gallons of fuel. Range was to be 585 miles at 317 mph at an altitude of 10,000 feet. The wings spanned 42 feet and the XP-50 was 32 feet long and 12 feet high.

During the construction of the XP-50, Grumman had begun design studies for a more advanced twin-engine fighter, the G-51. Due to the crash of the prototype and the new design study, further development of the XP-50 was terminated.

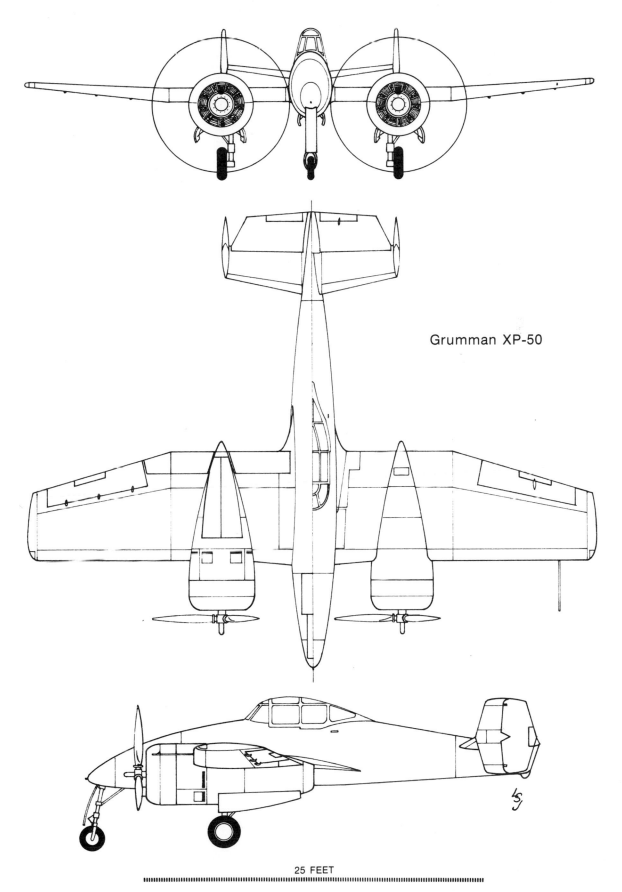

Grumman XP-50

25 FEET

Grumman's XP-50 runs up its engines prior to its fateful maiden flight.

Grumman

*Here is the prototype Mustang, the NA-73, being readied for a test flight. Note the absence of all markings ex-
cept the rudder stripes, which is unusual as the plane was ordered by the British.*   North American

In late 1939, with the likelihood of full-
scale war in Europe a major concern, the
British Royal Air Force was looking
seriously at methods of quickly increasing
its fighter strength. In April 1940, the
British Air Purchasing Commission ap-
proached North American Aviation with
the intent of having them build Curtiss P-
40's for the R.A.F. Instead, North American
offered to build an entirely new fighter using the same Allison V-1710-39 engine as
the P-40. The British agreed only on the
stipulation that a prototype be on hand
within 120 days. North American designers
Raymond Rice and Edgar Schmued immediately set about meeting the requirements. Schmued had been a part of
Willy Messerschmitt's design group in Germany; no doubt the somewhat angular lines
of the new fighter came from this
relationship.

The Allison-powered prototype NA-73
was assembled within the specified period,
but the engine was not yet ready, causing a
delay of some six weeks before the NA-73
could fly. In the meantime, on May 4, 1940,
the U. S. Army released the design for ex-

port sales with the condition that two of the
planes be delivered to them for evaluation.
At this time the NA-73 was assigned the
XP-51 designation. The first and tenth airframes were sent to the Army for testing;
these were given the serial numbers 41-38
and -39. An order for 150 P-51's followed.
These planes were named "Apache" for a
short time, but later the name "Mustang"
was adopted for the P-51.

The P-51 was an immediate success. It
outperformed even the Spitfire, but the
Allison engine placed limitations on the
performance. In England, a mock-up was
devised to use the Rolls Royce Merlin in the
P-51 airframe. One concept was to locate
the new engine behind the cockpit, but this
idea was rejected and the Merlin was
mounted in the conventional position in the
nose. Four airframes were adapted in
England to take the Merlin engine. These
planes had deep intakes below the engine
for carburetor air. In the meantime, North
American had undertaken a similar conversion project and was building two Packard
Merlin-powered Mustangs. The results of
the British tests were passed on to North

127

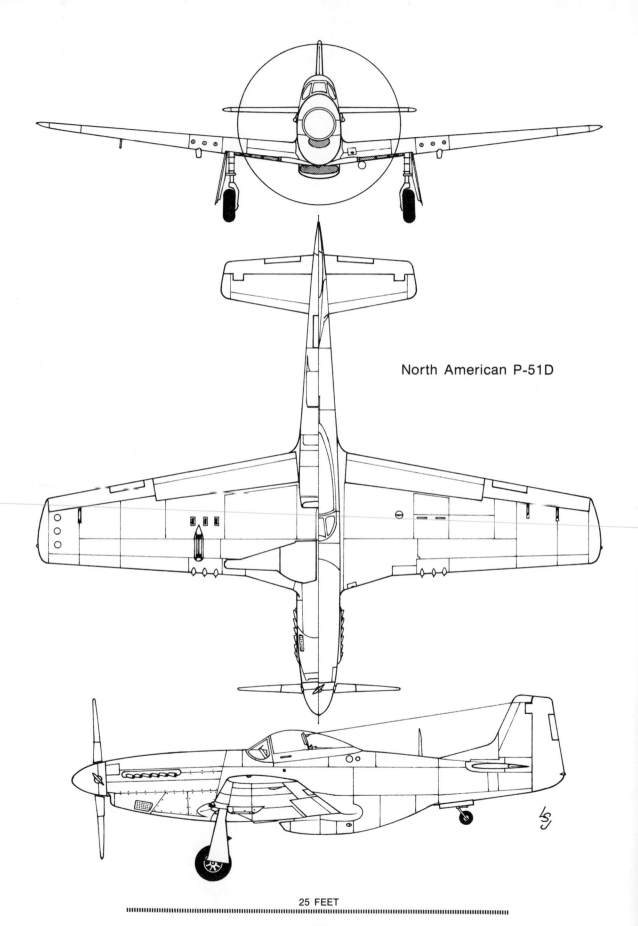

North American P-51D

25 FEET

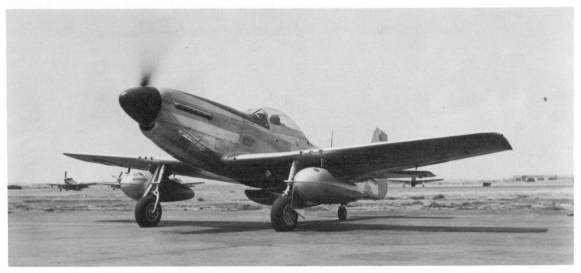

A new bubble-topped P-51D begins its delivery flight to a combat unit.   *North American*

The addition of the Merlin engine, as installed in this P-51B, improved the performance of the Mustang.
North American

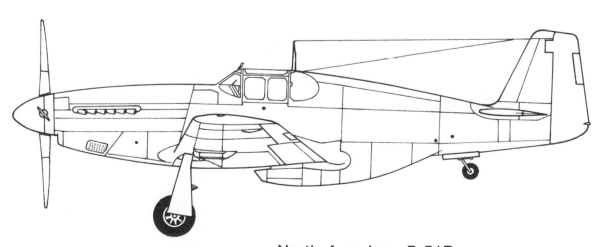

North American P-51B

American; and even before the Army's Merlin-powered Mustangs had flown, the U. S. Army ordered 2,200 of the more powerful fighters. For a short time, this model was designated P-78, then reclassed as P-51B.

To say the Merlin Mustangs were successful would be an understatment. The P-51 became one of the aviation world's elite. The total number of 14,819 Mustangs of all types were built for the Army. American Mustangs destroyed 4,950 enemy aircraft in Europe to make them the highest scoring U. S. fighter in the theatre. They were used as dive-bombers, bomber escorts, ground-attackers, interceptors, for photo-recon missions, trainers, transports (with a jump-seat), and after the war, high-performance racers.

The Merlin-powered P-51B and its Dallas-built twin, the P-51C, began operations in December 1943. A further improvement to the Mustang was introduced when a graceful teardrop canopy was installed to eliminate the dangerous blind area created by the faired cockpit. First tested on two P-51B's, they became standard on the P-51D and all later models. The P-51D became the version produced in the greatest quantities, 7,954 being completed. The "D" model carried six .50 cal. machine guns instead of the four mounted in the "B's"; and other refinements, such as

moving the wing forward slightly and providing for rocket launchers, were included. The first "D" types were delivered without dorsal fins but this feature was added to compensate for keel-loss when the bubble canopy was adopted.

Later developments to the P-51 series included the final production type, the P-51H with several changes which made it the fastest production variant with a maximum speed of 487 mph at 25,000 feet. Five hundred fifty-five P-51H's were delivered before VJ Day led to cancellation of the P-51 production program.

The P-51D represents the typical Mustang configuration. It had a 37-foot wingspan with an area of 233 square feet and was 32 feet 3 inches long. Height was 13 feet 8 inches. The Packard-built Merlin V-1650-7 was capable of delivering 1,695 hp which provided a speed of 437 mph at 25,000 feet. Weights were 7,125 lbs. empty and 10,100 lbs. normal gross, but an additional 2,000 lbs. could be carried. Internal fuel capacity was 105 gallons, giving a range of 950 miles at 362 miles per hour at 25,000 feet. Armament was six .50 cal. wing-mounted machine guns with 1,880 total rounds.

The P-51 was one of the first fighters to use a laminar-flow airfoil, a high-speed shape which became standard on most later high performance fighters.

The oft photographed "Millie G" shows the characteristic lines of the classic Mustang.

General Edward Giller

As World War II burst forth in Europe, the U. S. Army was seeking advanced fighter designs in preparation for future involvement. First of these unique designs was Bell's Model 16. A twin-boom pusher configuration, to be powered by a 1,250 hp Continental XIV-1430-5 inverted Vee. double-bank, twelve cylinder liquid-cooled engine, the XP-52 was the first pusher to receive a "P" designation. Cooling air for the radiator was to be ducted through an intake in the nose. The power was to be delivered to a pair of nine foot contra-rotating Hamilton Standard propellers. This arrangement was to provide a maximum speed of 425 mph at 19,500 feet. Time to 20,000 feet was to be 6.3 minutes. Service ceiling was 40,000 feet.

The unbuilt XP-52 was to be armed with six 50 cal. guns, three in the front of each boom and provided with 3,000 rounds of ammunition. Additionally, two 20 mm cannons were to be located in the central pod, each of these having 100 rounds.

Specifications for the XP-52 gave a wingspan of 35 feet, a length of 34 feet, and a height of 9 feet 3 inches. Wing area was 233 square feet. Design weights were 6,480 pounds empty, 8,750 pounds gross. Fuel capacity was 120 gallons, but could be increased to 270 gallons for a range of 960 miles at a speed of 420 mph.

Further development of the design led to a new proposal for an enlarged version, designated XP-59. The XP-52 was cancelled in favor of the newer proposal on November 25, 1941.

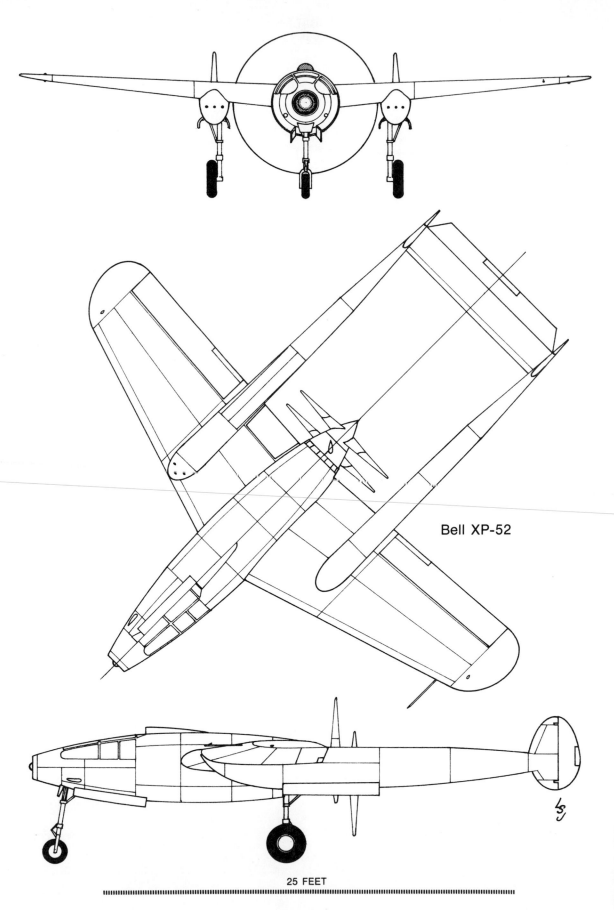

Bell XP-52

25 FEET

With the XP-53, Curtiss again attempted to provide a replacement for its P-40 series. Several concepts were offered to the Army; but one, similar in appearance to the P-40 and embodying a laminar-flow wing, was considered most practical and given the designation XP-53. Two prototypes were ordered on October 1, 1940. The two planes were to be powered by Continental's experimental XIV-1430-3 inverted Vee twelve cylinder liquid-cooled engine. With this engine, the XP-53's were expected to have a speed of 430 mph at 15,000 feet.

Six weeks after the two XP-53 prototypes were ordered, the Army notified Curtiss that it wished to acquire a fighter using a British Rolls Royce Merlin V-1650 engine with the laminar-flow wings. The original order was modified to produce the second XP-53 with these changes as the XP-60.

Assembly of the first XP-53 continued as ordered until November, 1941, when it was decided to use the airframe as a static test-bed for the planned production P-60's. The guns, bullet-proof windshield, and self-sealing fuel tanks from the XP-53 were installed in the XP-60 and, though the XP-53 was delivered, it never was flown.

That the European war influenced armament on American fighters is evidenced by the proposal to mount eight .50 cal. machine guns in the wings of the XP-53. The XP-53 had a wing spanning 41 feet 5 inches, was 35 feet 3 inches long and 12 feet 5 inches high. Wing area was 275 sq. feet. Empty weight was 7,650 lbs. with gross weight being 9,975 lbs.

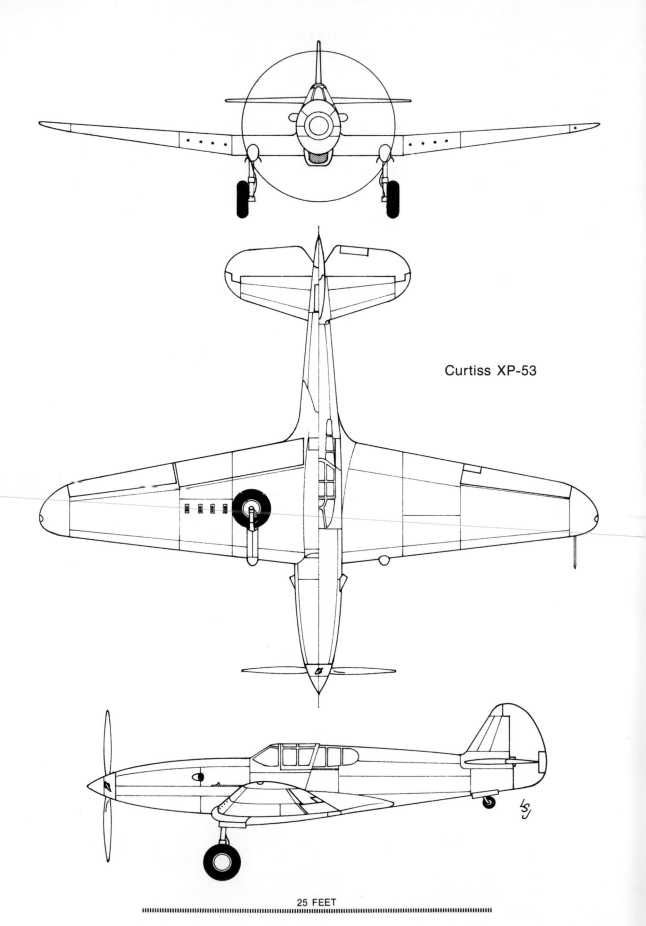

Curtiss XP-53

25 FEET

VULTEE
XP-54 SWOOSE GOOSE, XP-68
TORNADO

The second XP-54 on its only flight, from the Vultee plant to Norton AFB, in Calif. The Swoose Goose was impressive in the air.   *Dustin W. Carter*

Another of the unconventional fighter designs approved by the Army in 1941 was Vultee's Model 70. Winning the Army's R-40C Competition that would also spawn two more radical design concepts by Curtiss and Northrop, the Vultee fighter proposed the use of an experimental Pratt & Whitney X-1800-A4G engine. With an unsupercharged rating of 1,850 hp and driving contra-props, this engine could, according to Vultee, push the proposed fighter to a speed of 510 mph at 20,000 feet.

The Vultee fighter was assigned the 54th number in the series; and as the detailed design progressed, Pratt & Whitney announced they had discontinued the X-1800 engine program. In its place, a Lycoming XH-2470 of 2,200 hp was chosen. The XP-54 design was altered to accept the substitute engine, but additional problems arose when the fighter's original role as a fast-climbing interceptor was changed to bomber-destroyer. Originally six .50 cal. machine guns were to be installed, but now it was to have two .50's and two 37 mm cannons. The revised XP-54, now Vultee Model Number 84, had grown in both

dimensions and weight; but the available power had not increased proportionately, and this was reflected in the performance estimates.

By the time the first of two XP-54's was completed, it bore only a general similarity to the original design. The unique double-tapered wing, found also on the Vultee Vengeance dive bomber, provided a distinctive silhouette. Although the configuration was a major departure from the conventional fighters, it presented a pleasant appearance to the observer.

Two unusual features set the XP-54 apart from its contemporaries. The first was the articulated nose section containing the armament package. No doubt, the two 37 mm cannons could destroy a bomber, but the low muzzle velocity required that they be elevated to obtain the desired range. To achieve this, the entire nose section in front of the cockpit could be tilted upward to permit lobbing the cannon shells at the target. Meanwhile, the machine guns, with their higher muzzle velocity, were depressed at the same time.

The second novel feature of the XP-54

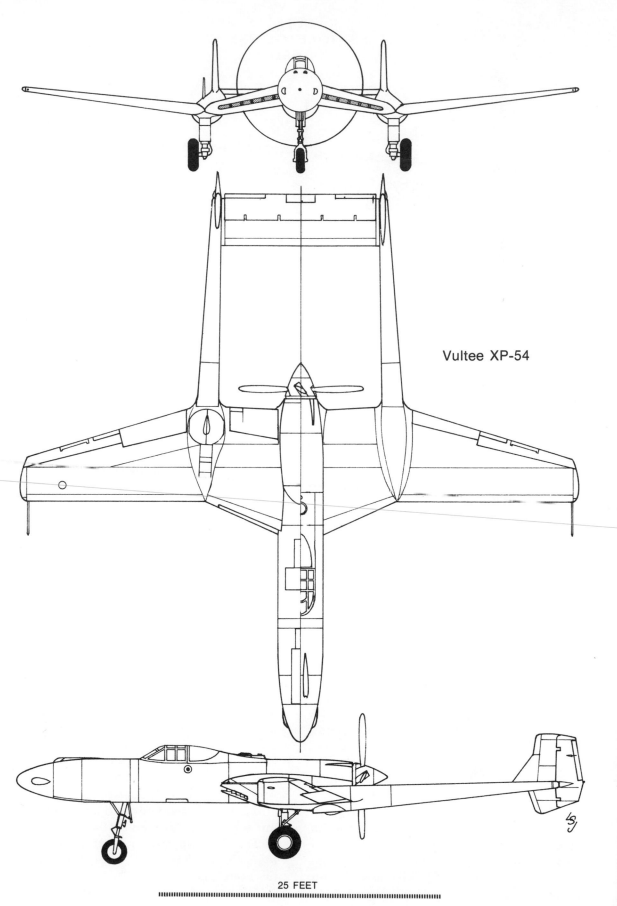

Vultee XP-54

25 FEET

This view of the XP-54 gives some impression of its large size.   U. S. Air Force

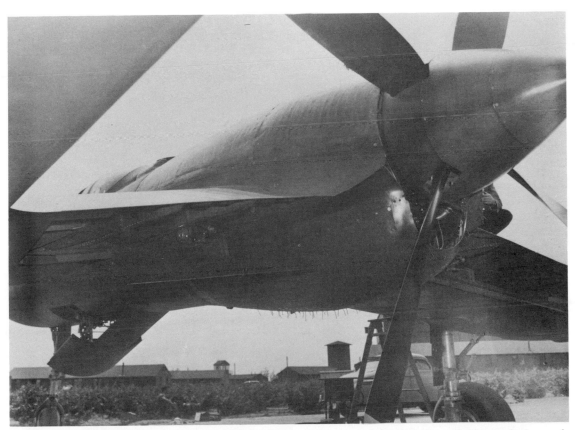

A detail view of the combined cooling and landing flap. The entrance hatch to the cockpit is in the lowered position on the left in this photo.
Dustin W. Carter

concerned the method by which the pilot entered and exited the cockpit. With the bottom of the fuselage nearly six feet off the ground, entrance to the cockpit could be difficult. An ingenius arrangement utilizing a hinged section below the cockpit dropped downward, lowering the pilot's seat with it. The pilot then simply mounted the seat and rode up into the cockpit. This also simplified the sealing of the cockpit for pressurization. In the event of an emergency bail-out, the seat slid rapidly downward as the hinged panel folded backward and the pilot was dropped safely below the propeller and stabilizer. Virtually a downward ejection seat!

Cooling air for the engine entered the wings at the root, passed over the radiators, and exited through the trailing edge of the landing flaps. A small flap was mounted on the landing flap for controlling airflow in flight.

The first XP-54 ·was flown on January 15, 1943. After 86 flights had been made, the plane was delivered to Wright Field on October 28, 1943, where engine trouble grounded the big plane. It was decided to use the first plane as a spare for the second XP-54; however, the number two plane was flown only once, from Downey, Calif. to Norton Air Corps Base, San Bernardino, where the unique tilting nose was removed and shipped to Eglin Air Base in Florida for further testing.

The XP-54 achieved a maximum speed of 381 mph at 28,500 feet. It could climb 2,300 fpm from sea level and reached 26,000 feet in 17.3 minutes. Service ceiling was 37,000 feet. Dimensions were: wingspan 53 feet 10 inches, length 54 feet 9 inches, height 13 feet, and wing area was 456 square feet. The plane weighed 15,262 lbs. unloaded and 18,233 lbs. at take-off. Fuel load was 223 gallons, giving a range of 500 miles at 328 mph.

A proposal to adapt the XP-54 to use the 42 cylinder Wright R-2160 radial engine was assigned the designation XP-68 Tornado, but neither the engine nor airplane materialized.

The XP-54 sits at Wright Field between test flights.   *Dustin W. Carter*

CURTISS
XP-55 ASCENDER

Several changes are visible on this, the second XP-55. In particular, note the swept wingtip, gun blisters and modified gear doors.
Gordon S. Williams

The tail-first Curtiss XP-55 was certainly one of the most novel American fighters to actually be constructed, although the canard configuration was far from new. It will be recalled that the Wright Flyer of 1903 was constructed in the same manner, but it was unusual to see such a design on a modern, high performance aircraft.

The XP-55, Curtiss Model 24, was the second type selected by the Army for the 1939 specifications for unorthodox designs. A request for specific engineering data was received by Curtiss on June 22, 1940. Results of wind tunnel testing did not satisfy the Army, so Curtiss constructed a full-size flying model to evaluate the radical layout. The model was successfully flown 169 times at Muroc, California. The flight tests did indicate several areas requiring improvements, mainly in vertical keel area, but the Army was satisfied with the potential of the design and approved construction of three XP-55's on July 10, 1942.

Originally intending to use the Pratt & Whitney X-1800 engine, an Allison V-1710-F16 was substituted when the P & W engine was cancelled. Because of the pusher arrangement of the engine, it was necessary to devise a means of jettisoning the

propeller in the event of an emergency bail-out.

The first XP-55, now named Ascender, was ready for flight testing on July 13, 1943. The initial take-off run was so long that the nose elevator area was increased fifteen percent for subsequent flights, and the ailerons were trimmed upward when the flaps were lowered.

On November 15, 1943, the XP-55 flipped onto its back during stall tests and attempts to recover failed. The plane stabilized in the inverted state but the engine quit and the XP-55 fell vertically 16,000 feet before the pilot decided an inverted landing would ruin his whole day and safely abandoned the stricken machine. The possibility of this condition had been predicted by the early wind-tunnel tests, and now it was necessary to correct the design. The second Ascender was nearing completion and flight testing was resumed when it was available, but stalls were restricted. The third XP-55 did incorporate the necessary revisions. These included extended wingtips with small additional "trailerons" outboard of the wing-mounted rudders, as shown in the three-view drawing.

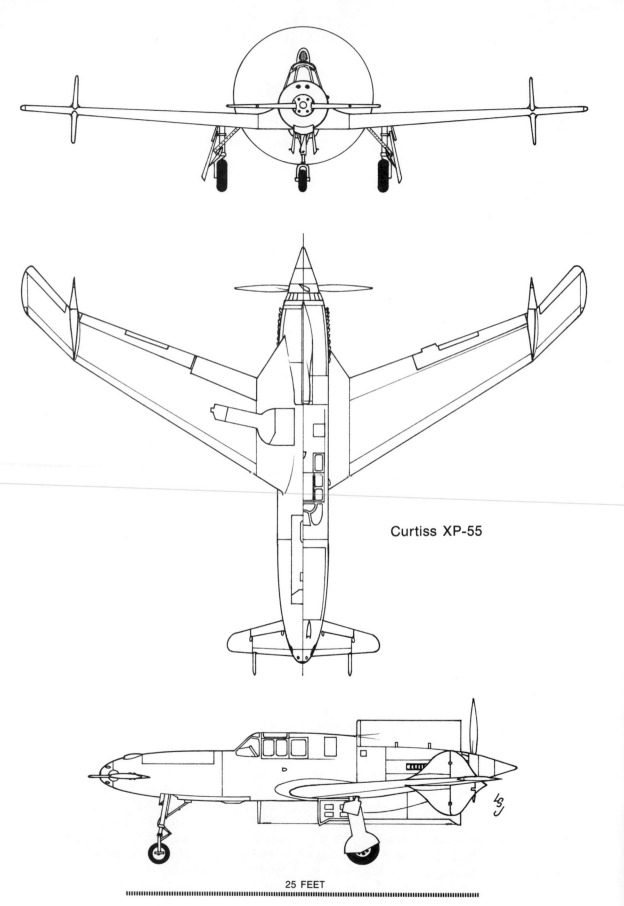

Curtiss XP-55

25 FEET

The Ascender displayed satisfactory handling characteristics during normal flight, but at low speeds, it became overly sensitive; and, even after modifications, the stall was quite an experience. Engine cooling was inadequate and some stability problems remained, when the Army decided the unorthodox little fighter would not be an effective weapon.

The XP-55 was not a true canard since it lacked a fixed forward elevator. The entire surface was movable and trailed in normal flight. In effect, it was a flying wing with a forward trimming surface.

Performance of the XP-55 was similar to many conventional fighters, having a top speed of 390 mph at 19,300 feet. Service ceiling was 34,600 feet, and it could reach 20,000 feet in 7.1 minutes. The swept-wing of the third XP-55 spanned 44 feet 6 inches, length was 29 feet 7 inches, height was 10 feet, and wing area was 235 sq. feet. Fuel capacity was 110 gallons. Empty and gross weights were 6,354 pounds and 7,330 pounds. Four .50 cal. M2 machine guns were located in the nose, each gun having 250 rounds.

An example of the XP-55 Ascender has been preserved by the Smithsonian Institution for display in the National Aerospace Museum.

This view of the Ascender shows an increase in the vertical fin area. Notice also the wing fence.

Dustin W. Carter

The first XP-55 on July 11, 1943, two days before its initial flight.

Dustin W. Carter

NORTHROP
XP-56 BLACK BULLET

The original XP-56 suffered from inadequate vertical surfaces. Yaw was created by the split flaps visible on the drooped wingtips.   *U.S. Air Force*

The third radical design resulting from the Army's proposal R-40C was Northrop's N2B tailless fighter constructed of magnesium. This plane was the only one of the trio to actually use contra-rotating propellers, a feature proposed for all three types. Like the Curtiss and Vultee designs, Northrop's original proposal envisioned the use of the Pratt & Whitney X-1800 engine, but in this case the substituted engine was the Pratt & Whitney R-2800 air-cooled radial. Northrop engineers were not entirely satisfied with the replacement, but on July 21, 1941, it was decided to modify the design to accept a 2,000 hp R-2800-29 engine. The designation XP-56 was given to the fighter. The flying-wing configuration selected for the XP-56 was similar to the all-wing N1M which had been designed and flown by Northrop in 1940. This little machine, the world's first true flying-wing, had proven the all-wing concept was practical and convinced the Army a second XP-56 prototype should be built for more extensive testing.

The first XP-56, S.N. 41-786, was completed in April 1943, and taxi tests were begun to determine the characteristics of the radical design. Initially, trouble with the brakes caused the fighter to yaw dangerously during high-speed taxi runs. New brakes were devised and installed before testing could proceed. Additional difficulties were encountered with the engine and finally, on September 30, 1943, the "Black Bullet", as it was called, finally left the ground. The first flight was made at an average altitude of five feet as the pilot gingerly tried the controls. In following flights, the altitude was gradually increased. Before the full performance of the XP-56 could be studied, the first machine suffered nose-wheel shimmy during a high-speed ground run. Collapse of the gear strut caused the blunt nose to dig into the ground and the stubby fighter tumbled over onto its back, terminating its short existence.

On March 23, 1944, the highly-modified second XP-56 (42-38553) was flown. This flight lasted only some seven minutes, however, due to excessive nose-heaviness. On later flights this undesirable characteristic vanished when the gear was retracted. Variations to the second aircraft

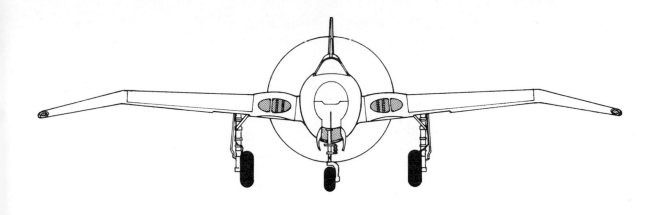

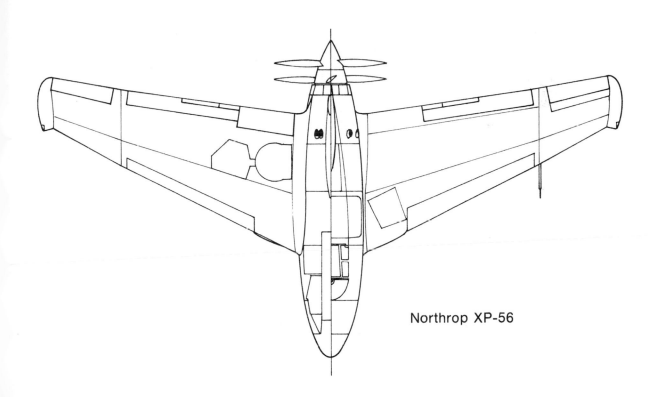

Northrop XP-56

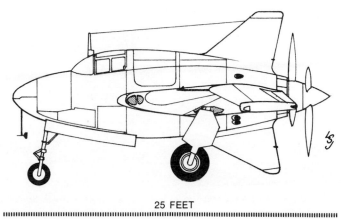

25 FEET

included an increase in vertical fin area and redesigned wingtips with novel venturi-like rudders consisting of tube-mounted valves which caused differential drag to create yaw.

Flight testing of the XP-56 proved disappointing and, in view of the success of conventional fighters, the need for information on such radical configurations was no longer important and the entire program was abolished.

The dimensions of the second XP-56 show a wingspan of 42 feet 6 inches, length of 27 feet 6 inches, and a height of 11 feet.

Wing area was 307 square feet. Empty weight was 8,700 pounds, gross weight was 11,350 pounds. Fuel capacity was 215 gallons, giving the XP-56 a range of 660 miles at 396 mph. Since the full range of performance was not achieved, the top speed is estimated at 465 mph at 25,000 feet. Service ceiling was to be 33,000 feet. Proposed armament was four .50 cal. machine guns with 400 rpg, and two 20 mm cannon with 100 rpg, all nose mounted. This second XP-56 is retained at the Smithsonian Institution's museum facilities as an example of a unique answer to an engineering challenge.

The first XP-56 "Black Bullet" being serviced before a test flight. Note the Spartan Executive in the background. U.S. Air Force

From this view, it is apparent why the all-magnesium XP-56 was named the Black Bullet. The second example, shown here, used a venturi type rudder and had an enlarged vertical fin. Northrop

In contrast to the radical shapes and heavy weights displayed by the new fighter designs of 1940, the plane proposed by the Tucker Aviation Co. of Detroit, Mich. was as simple as the others were complex. Proposed to General Hap Arnold in May 1940, the Tucker fighter was to be an extremely maneuverable, lightweight aircraft constructed of wood and metal. A development contract was awarded and the designation XP-57 was assigned to the project. Before much more than the paperwork was done, the Tucker Company found itself unable to proceed with construction due to financial problems and the XP-57 contract expired.

With a wingspan of 28 feet 5 inches, and a length of 26 feet 7 inches, the XP-57 was small indeed. It had a wing area of 120 sq. feet and stood just over 8 feet high. The fuselage was to be constructed of aluminum-covered steel tubing, but the wings were to be of plywood. A 720 hp Miller L-510-1 eight cylinder liquid-cooled engine was to be placed behind the pilot driving the eight foot propeller through an extension shaft that would pass between the pilot's legs. Proposed performance showed a maximum speed of 308 mph at sea level with a range of 960 miles at 265 mph. Fuel capacity was 125 gallons. Service ceiling was 26,000 feet. It was anticipated that the little plane would reach 18,000 feet in 11 minutes. Empty weight was 1,920 lbs., design gross was to be 3,000 lbs.

A choice of armament was offered in the XP-57 design; three .50 cal. machine guns with 498 rounds, or one .50 with 400 rounds and one 20 mm cannon with 50 rounds.

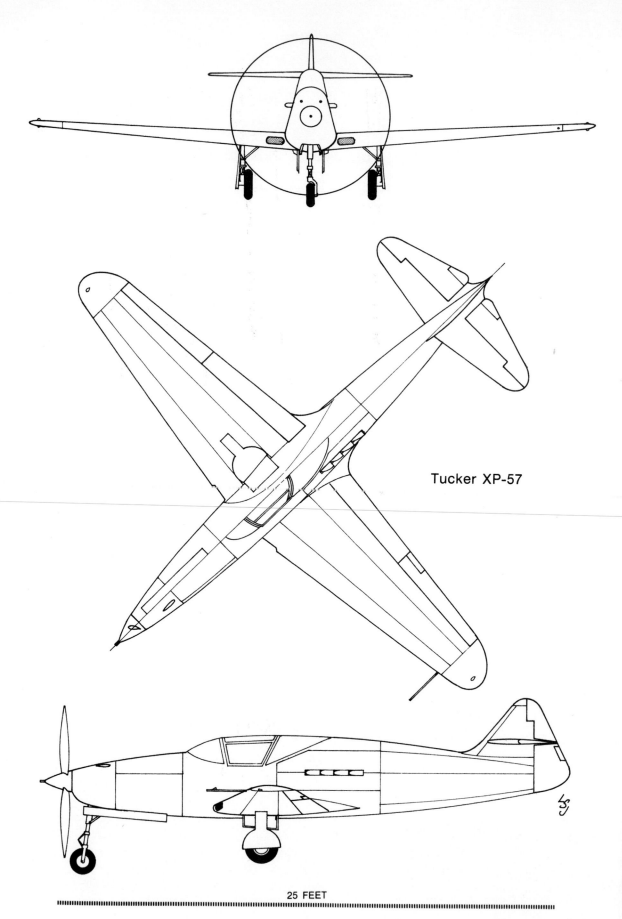

Tucker XP-57

25 FEET

LOCKHEED
XP-58 CHAIN LIGHTNING

The XP-58 making a taxi test at Burbank, California. The pilot in the cockpit gives an impression of the great size of this plane.
Lockheed

When an aircraft design proves successful, it is only natural that it become the basis of continuing development. In some instances, this can lead to superior performance and a vastly improved aircraft. In other cases, the result does not merit the effort put forth and the end product soon vanishes into obscurity. Such was the case of the huge Lockheed XP-58, called Chain Lightning.

When Lockheed was granted the right to sell the P-38 Lightning to the British, they agreed to develop, at no cost to the Army, an improved version of the P-38. A requirement for a long-range bomber-escort was drawn up on April 12, 1940, and Lockheed undertook to design a plane fulfilling this need. Unfortunately, the entire program was plagued with changes of one type or another. First, the proposed Continental IV-1440 engines were cancelled and experimental Pratt & Whitney XH-2600-3/5 engines were substituted. At this time, it was decided to add a second crewman to operate a power turret in the fuselage rear. Nose armament was now to include two 20 mm cannons and four .50 cal. machine

guns. This was an addition of one cannon to the original proposal. Upon cancellation of the XH-2600 engines, supercharged Pratt & Whitney R-2800's of 2,350 hp were considered. The initial estimated maximum speed of 450 mph was altered with each engine change proposal, and, with the R-2800's, only 418 mph was anticipated. The Army felt this would not be adequate by the time the XP-58 became operational and requested the design be modified to accommodate two 2,300 hp Wright R-2160 Tornado forty-two cylinder radials. In addition, the decision was made to use two rearward-firing power turrets and a pressurized cabin. From an originally planned gross weight of 20,000 lbs., the XP-58 now was going to weigh 34,242 lbs. and the design was only in the mock-up stage! By October 10, 1941, the estimated gross weight was up to 35,350 pounds. It was then that Lockheed suggested a second prototype be built as a back-up, and in March 1942, the Army authorized the second airframe. At this point, the Tornado engine was running into problems and the delay allowed additional changes to be

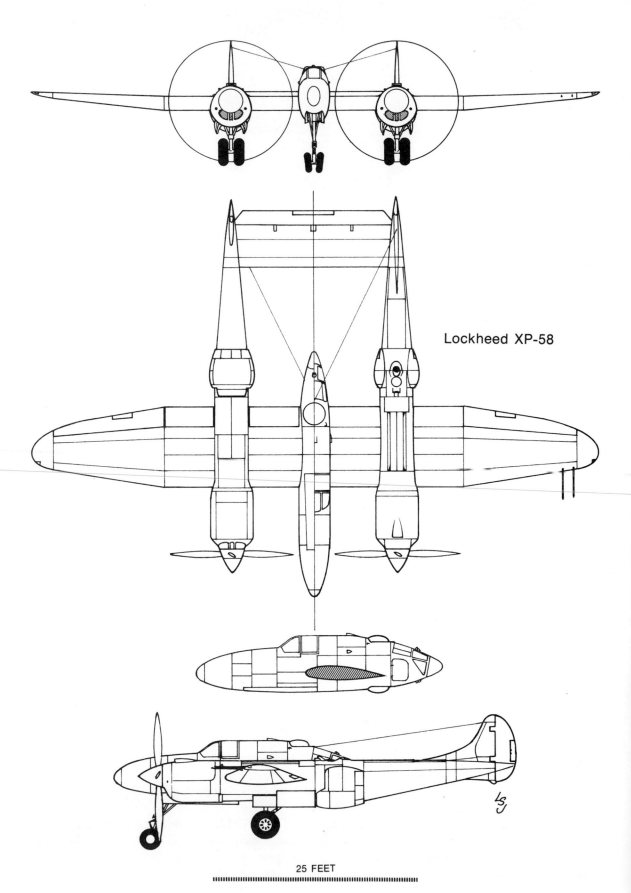

Lockheed XP-58

25 FEET

The V-3420 engines used in the XP-58 were made by coupling a pair of 12 cylinder Allisons to a common crank shaft, making it virtually a four engined fighter.   Lockheed

worked into the second XP-58.

Early in 1942, consideration was given to install an automatically-fed 75 mm cannon in the nose and use the XP-58 as a bomber destroyer. Before this decision was made, however, and when the airframe was some 25 percent complete, it was determined the XP-58 would become a low-altitude tank-destroyer. This change came about because the big plane could no longer compete with existing fighters. Now the power turrets were to be removed and cabin pressurization and supercharging were no longer required. This new design weighed 36,000 pounds and had a maximum speed of 355 mph. In October 1942, the second XP-58 was cancelled and the decision was made to modify the first plane for the ground-attack role. In its new role, the XP-58 was now a direct competitor of the Beechcraft XA-38 Grizzly, which had been designed from the outset as a tank destroyer. In view of this fact, the Army again reversed itself and the XP-58 once again was assigned the bomb-attacker duties with the second airframe reinstated.

Similar obstructions continued to hinder development of the Chain Lightning but the first, and only, prototype was eventually completed and made its maiden flight on June 6, 1944, over four years after its inception. The Tornado engine failed to materialize and the aircraft was fitted with two 2,600 hp Allison V-3420-11/13 twenty-four cylinder liquid-cooled engines with single-stage, single speed superchargers. The superchargers were a constant source of trouble, frequently torching and scorching the tail. The final weight of the XP-58 was 31,306 pounds empty, 38,874 pounds gross—nearly twice the original estimate.

The XP-58 had a 600 square foot wing with a span of 70 feet. Length was 49 feet 5 inches, and it stood 16 feet high. Despite its phenomenal growth, the XP-58 achieved a top speed of 436 mph at 25,000 feet and cruised at 274 mph. Internal fuel capacity was 650 gallons, but with external tanks this could be increased to 1,700 gallons. Range was 1,250 miles. Service ceiling was 38,400 feet.

Two alternate noses were designed for the XP-58. One carried the automatic 75 mm cannon with 20 rounds and two .50 cal. machine guns with 300 rpg. The other nose mounted four 37 mm cannons with 100 rounds. Neither nose was actually installed. The two power turrets were to carry two .50 cal. machine guns.

The second XP-58 was cancelled when sixty-five percent complete. The first machine was flown to Wright Field on October 22, 1944, where maintenance problems led to its abandonment and it was subsequently retired to ground instruction duties.

BELL
XP-59 & P-59 AIRACOMET

Continued development of the Bell XP-52 pusher fighter led to an enlarged design which was assigned the XP-59 classification. All development was put behind the larger fighter and the XP-52 program was cancelled in favor of the newer plane. Two prototypes were ordered and construction began on a mock-up of the twin-boomed fighter before the program was cancelled in favor of an even more advanced design.

Like the XP-52, the XP-59 was to have its engine mounted behind the cockpit with engine-cooling air taken from an opening in the nose and fed past the cockpit. The engine specified was a Pratt & Whitney R-2800-23 of 2,000 hp driving a six-bladed Hamilton Standard dual-rotation propeller located between the two tail booms. The leading-edge fairings of the booms each housed three .50 cal. machine guns with 300 rpg, and two 20 mm cannons were located in the nose of the power nacelle beside the cockpit. Each cannon was provided with 70 rounds of ammunition. Thus equipped, the XP-59 was expected to have a speed of 450 mph at 22,000 feet. Service ceiling was 38,-000 feet; the first 20,000 feet of this were to be reached within 6.3 minutes of take-off. Two hundred seventy gallons of fuel were to be carried, and range was estimated at 850 miles at a cruising speed of 380 mph.

The XP-59 design had a 40 foot wingspan, was 37 feet 3 inches long, and stood 12 feet high. Wing area was 286 square feet. Empty weight was 7,960 pounds with a design gross of 10,463 pounds.

To conceal the true power source of the secret jet Airacomet, a wooden propeller was attached to the nose for ground transportation at Muroc AFB. General Electric Co.

Aircraft design took a major step forward with the introduction of the jet propulsion engine. Although unknown to the Allies, the first pure turbojet-powered aircraft had already flown one month before World War II began in Europe, in the form of the German Heinkel He 178. By mid-1942, the Messerschmitt Me 262 was making itself known, and the British-designed Gloster E.28/39 had flown earlier in the same year.

As far back as September 4, 1941, the Army Air Force began a discussion that eventually led to the first American jet-powered aircraft, the Bell P-59 Airacomet. Though design of the airframe was American, the powerplant design was obtained from the British Whittle engine used in the Gloster jet. This engine was put into

150

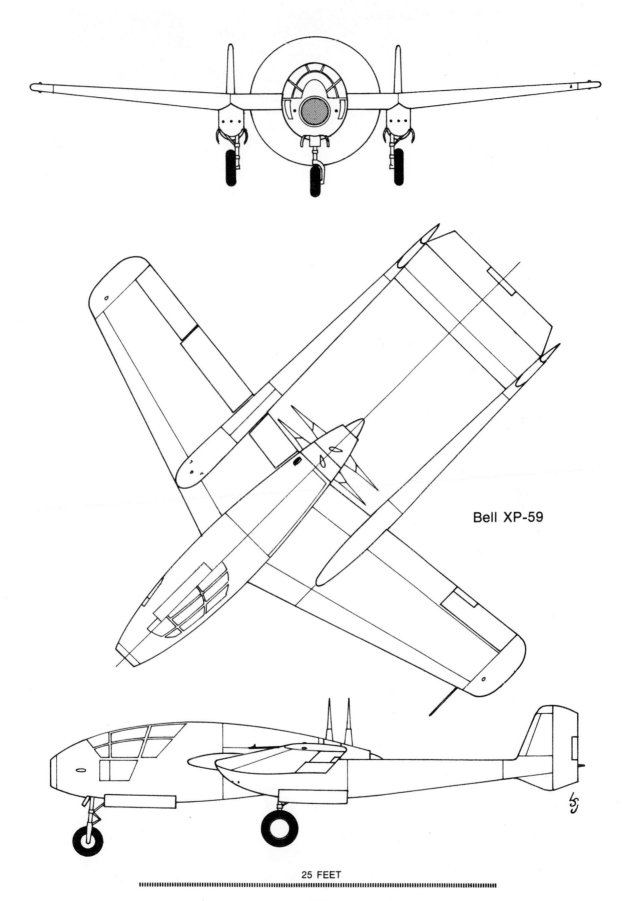

Bell XP-59

25 FEET

The first production P-59A (42-2609). The last two digits of the serial number have not yet been painted on the rudder.   *Bell*

America's first jet plane did not prove suitable as a fighter and was confined to the training role.
Gordon S. Williams

production by General Electric as their Model I-A, two of them being installed in the new Bell fighter.

The desire to keep the existence of the jet propulsion program absolutely secret led to the adoption of the designation already assigned to the defunct XP-59 pusher. On paper, it would appear that the jet was actually a continuing development of the propeller aircraft, thus camouflaging its true configuration. In fact, to keep this impression, the first XP-59A jet was fitted with a dummy wooden propeller whenever it was moved about on the ground, and the cavernous engine intakes were faired with canvas for concealment.

A contract for three XP-59A jet fighters was signed on October 3, 1941, and the first machine was completed at the Bell plant in Buffalo, New York, eleven months later. The fighter was dismantled and shipped to Muroc in the California desert for flight tests. The initial flight was made on October 2, 1942. The General Electric engines each developed 1,400 pounds of static thrust to push the fighter to a speed of 404 mph at 25,000 feet. The performance of the first American jet was not spectacular, but one of thirteen YP-59A's did establish a new unofficial altitude record of 47,600 feet. Following the order and delivery of the thirteen YP-59A Airacomets with 1,650 lb. thrust engines, the Army received 20 P-59A's and 30 P-59B's, all powered by J-31-GE-5 engines of 2,000 lbs. s. t.

Flight evaluation uncovered a tendency

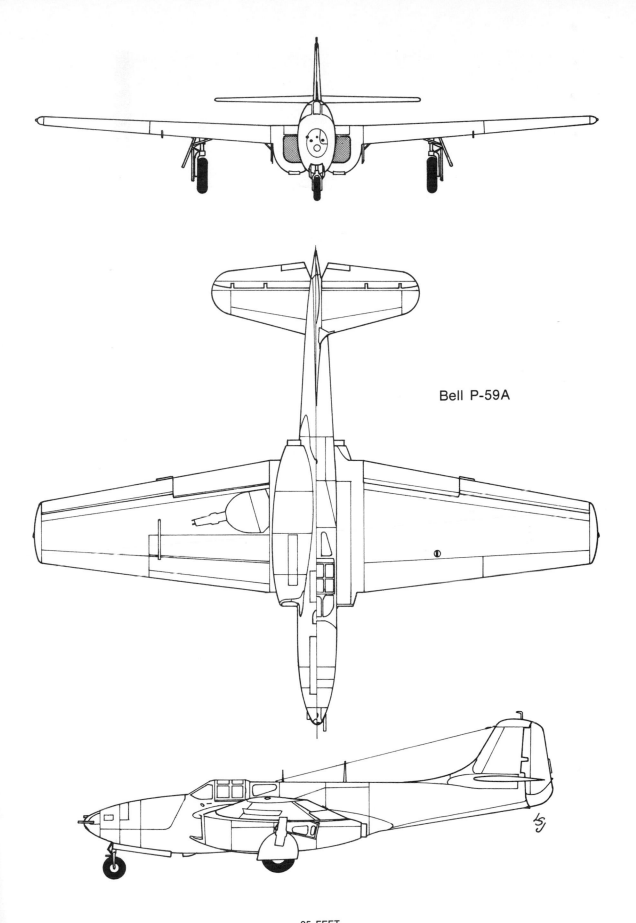

Bell P-59A

25 FEET

The first Airacomets had rounded wingtips and tail surfaces, as this YP-59A.   *Bell*

for the P-59 to yaw, or sway, from side to side making it unsuitable as a fighter. Instead, the planes were relegated to the training of jet pilots to prepare them for the new generation of fighters coming off the drawing boards. A proposal for a single-engine model of the Airacomet was labeled XP-59B with the engine being fed via intakes in the roots of the low-mounted wing and exhausting beneath the fuselage. The Bell Company was unable to devote the necessary time on the single-engine design, however, and this plan was passed on to Lockheed, eventually appearing as the Shooting Star.

The P-59B proportions were the same at the "A": wingspan was 45 feet 6 inches,

length was 38 feet 10 inches, and height was 12 feet. Wing area was 386 square feet, which, with a gross weight of 11,040 pounds, provided a fairly light wing-loading. In fact, the XP-59A made a very satisfactory glider, the test pilots often flying until the fuel ran out then gliding back to Muroc for a landing! Empty weight of the P-59B was 8,165 pounds.

Armament installed in the P-59 included three .50 cal. machine guns with 600 rounds and one 37 mm cannon with 45 rounds.

The P-59B had a maximum speed of 413 mph at 30,000 feet. Cruising speed was 375 miles per hour and service ceiling was 46,-200 feet. Fuel tanks held 290 gallons for a range of 400 miles at 375 mph.

Originally intended to be the XP-60B with a supercharged Allison V-1710-75 engine, this plane was fitted with an R-2800-10 and redesignated XP-60E.   *Dustin W. Carter*

Not since the Curtiss P-6 Hawk series of 1927-31 had one fighter designation been applied to so many different configurations as the various designs known as P-60's. In a concentrated effort to maintain its status as a primary supplier of American fighting machines, Curtiss continued its attempts to design a suitable replacement for its P-40. They hoped the P-60 would be the plane.

During the construction of the two XP-53 prototypes, the Army requested a Merlin-powered fighter with a laminar-flow wing. To expedite development of such an aircraft, Curtiss was asked to modify the second XP-53 to this configuration and reclassed it as the XP-60. Changes from the P-53 were to be kept minimal. The XP-53's Continental engine was, of course, replaced with a Rolls Royce V-1560-1 Merlin of 1,-300 hp and P-40-type rearward-folding landing gear was altered to retract inward. Otherwise, the XP-60 was quite similar to the original XP-53 concept.

The XP-60 first took to the air on September 18, 1941, and demonstrated a top speed of 380 mph at 20,000 feet. It soon became evident that demand for the Merlin

for P-51's and other types would delay deliveries of the British engine to Curtiss, and a turbo-supercharged Allison V-1710-75 was specified for production P-60's. A contract for 1,950 of these fighters was signed October 31, 1941. A few weeks later, the Army considered the Allison-powered plane unsuitable and recommended that Curtiss construct P-47's instead. At a meeting on January 2, 1942, Curtiss accepted the Army's suggestion to build 2,400 P-47's, 1,400 P-40's, 100 P-62's, and one each of three different versions of the XP-60.

The original trim lines of the XP-60 gave way to more portly proportions as bulky radial engines were introduced to the program. These models were designated XP-60C and XP-60E, each with a Pratt & Whitney R-2800 of 2,000 hp, and YP-60E with a 2,100 hp R-2800. In the meantime, the Allison-powered XP-60A was readied for flight testing. The exhaust manifold caused several minor fires during engine run-ups and this required removal of the turbo-supercharger and a redesign of the exhaust outlets. It was finally flown on November 1, 1942. This P-60 version had a

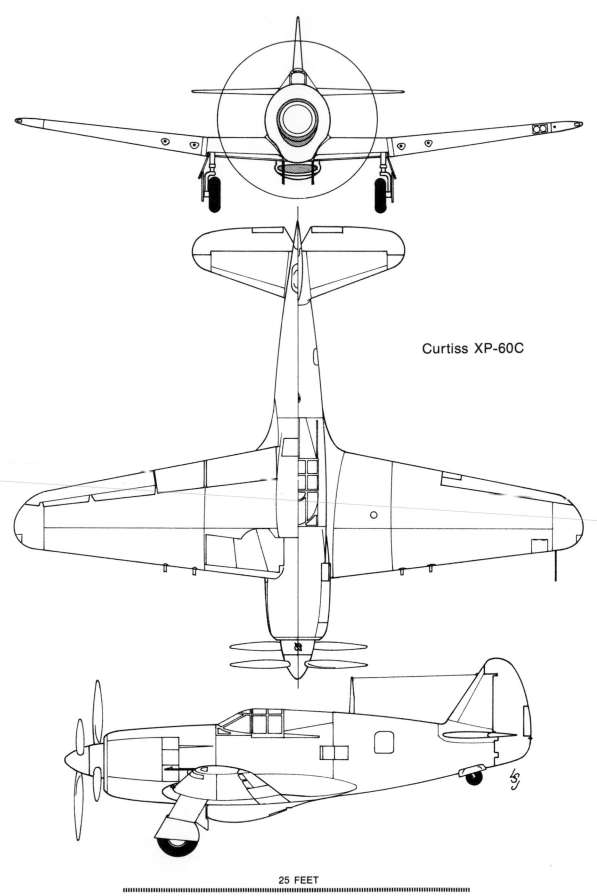

Curtiss XP-60C

25 FEET

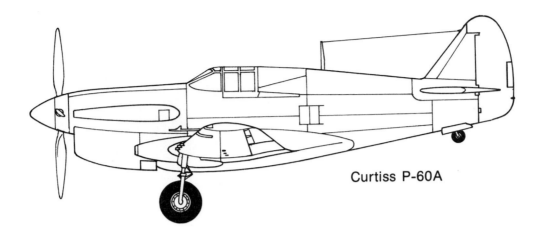

Curtiss P-60A

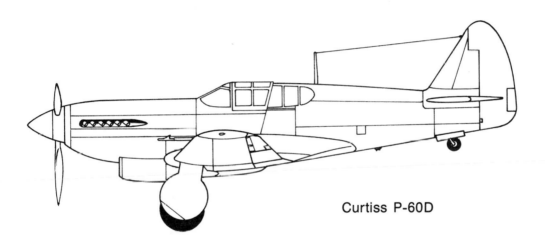

Curtiss P-60D

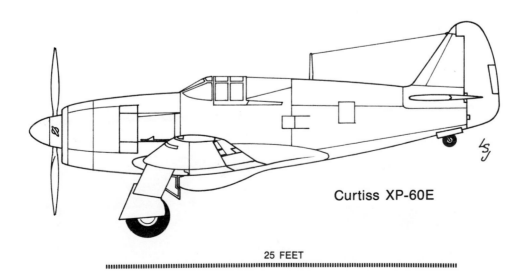

Curtiss XP-60E

25 FEET

This is the XP-60C with Curtiss Electric contra-props.   Gordon S. Williams

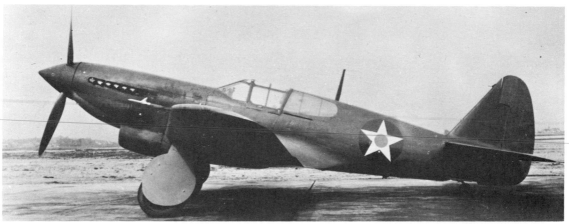

Installation of a more powerful Merlin engine and enlarging the tail surfaces of the XP-60 created the XP-60D.   Gordon S. Williams

Last of the series, the sole YP-60E was only flown twice.   Gordon S. Williams

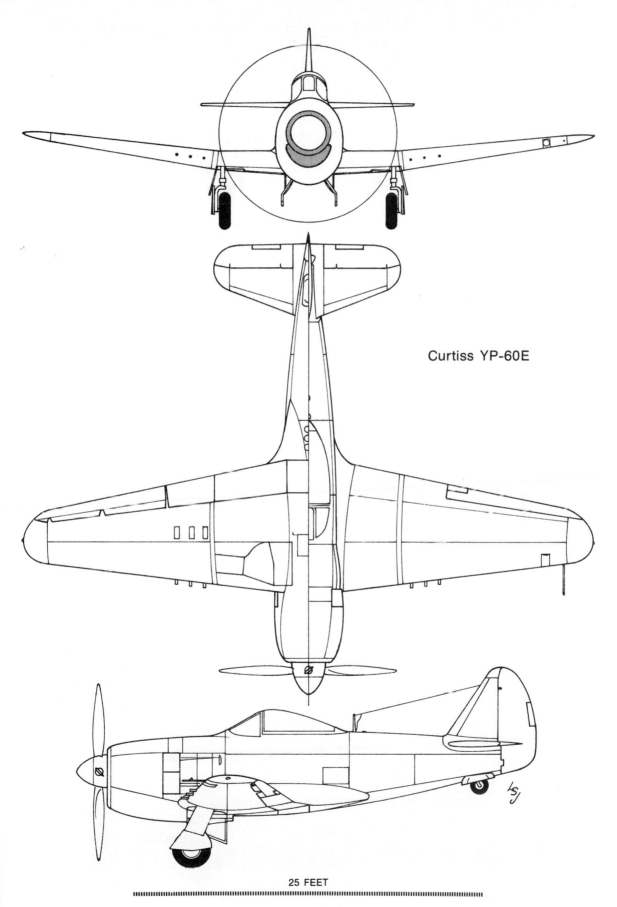

Curtiss YP-60E

25 FEET

top speed of 420 mph.

The first radial-powered example was the XP-60C with 12 foot 2 inch Curtiss Electric contra-rotating propellers. Original plans had called for this plane to use an experimental Chrysler XIV-2220 sixteen-cylinder inline engine, but problems with the airframe design dictated a change to the Pratt & Whitney. This one, first flown on January 27, 1943, had a top speed of 414 mph at 20,350 feet.. On May 26, 1943, the XP-60E took to the air and reached 410 mph in tests. Unfortunately, this model was damaged before testing could be finished. In order to complete testing of the XP-60E, the engine was removed from the damaged airframe and mounted to that of the XP-60C, which then became an XP-60E!

Testing of the Pratt & Whitney-powered P-60's was encouraging enough that the Army had ordered 500 of the planes in November 1942. As problems began to manifest themselves during the tests, and the performance of the series was not substantially improved over the Mustang and Thunderbolt, the contract for the P-60A was cancelled on June 3, 1943. Two YP-60E's were ordered instead, one of these eventually being dropped from the requirement. Thus on July 15, 1944, the last of the series was flown in the form of the YP-60E. This version reached 405 mph during tests and

was delivered to Wright Field in September. Various problems were suffered by each of the planes in the group and the entire program was finally cancelled, the last model being released for disposal on December 22, 1944.

Dimensions and weights of the P-60's were as follows:

XP-60 (Merlin) - 41 feet 5 inch wingspan, 33 feet 4 inch length, 14 feet 4 inches high, 7,010 pounds empty, 9,350 pounds gross.

XP-60A (Allison) - 41 feet 4 inch wingspan, 33 feet 8 inch length, 12 feet 4 inches high, 7,806 pounds empty, 9,616 pounds gross.

XP-60C (Pratt & Whitney) - 41 feet 4 inch wingspan, 34 feet 1 inch length, 15 feet high, 8,698 pounds empty, 10,525 pounds gross.

XP-60E (Pratt & Whitney) - 41 feet 4 inch wingspan, 33 feet 11 inch length, 15 feet high, 8,574 pounds empty, 10,320 pounds gross.

YP-60E (Pratt & Whitney) - 41 feet 4 inch wingspan, 33 feet 7 inch length, 13 feet 11 inches high, 8,285 pounds net, 10,270 pounds gross. Wing area for the entire series was 275 square feet.

It was proposed to arm the XP-60 with eight .50 cal. machine guns, the XP-60A with six .50's, the XP-60E and YP-60E with four .50's.

This XP-60 began as the second XP-53. The change was made during construction.   Gordon S. Williams

NORTHROP
P-61 BLACK WIDOW

A P-61A which was delivered without the dorsal turret due to buffeting problems.   *Northrop*

Northrop's large twin-engined Black Widow was the first American fighter designed specifically for the night-interception role. It was actually the precursor for today's all-weather fighters. Two XP-61 prototypes were contracted for on January 11, 1941; and the following March, thirteen YP-61's and one static test airframe were added to the order.

The need for fighters capable of nighttime operation became apparent to the British shortly after they were drawn into the Second World War. Douglas Havoc attack bombers had been hastily adapted to the night fighter role with a great degree of success. By the beginning of 1941, the U. S. Army Air Force realized the importance of having a similar weapon in its inventory. Before the first XP-61 was ready to fly, the original contract was again expanded to include 560 production P-61A's.

The bomber-sized XP-61 made its initial flight on May 21, 1942. It was powered by two Pratt & Whitney R-2800-10 engines of 2,000 hp, seated three crewmen and carried four 20 mm cannons under the cockpit canopy. A power turret on top of the fuselage carried four .50 cal. machine guns and was operated by a gunner located in the aft part of the fuselage. Normally, the turret was locked in the forward-firing position to supplement the cannons. The third crewman operated the radar set.

The YP-61's and thirty-seven P-61A's were delivered with the power turret, but a tail-buffeting problem was traced to the turret and the following 163 P-61A's were delivered without the turret. This also eliminated the need for the gunner. The first 200 P-61B's were delivered without the dorsal turret, too, but the buffeting was eventually corrected and turrets were installed on the 201st P-61B and the remainder of the Black Widows produced.

The first P-61's reached the Pacific combat zone by mid-1944, and their first kill came on July 7. Most of the P-61's were painted a glossy black to blend into the dark skies, hence the name "Black Widow."

Throughout its operational life, the P-61 retained most of its original appearance. A one foot extension was made to the nose of the P-61B-10, and supercharger intakes were installed on the P-61D. The greatest

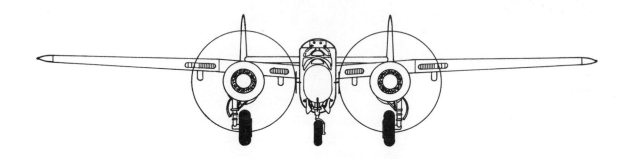

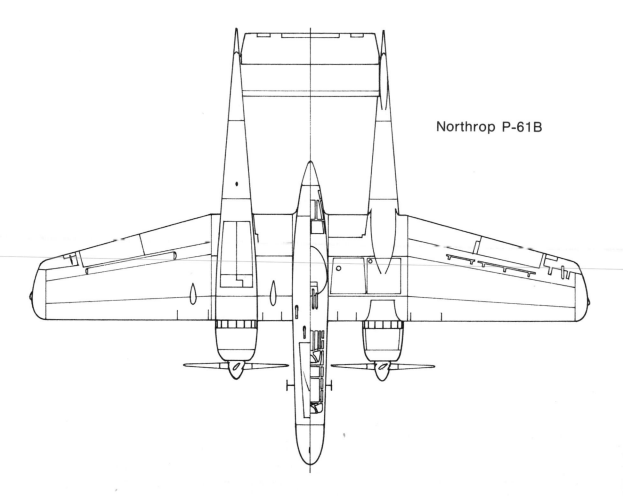

Northrop P-61B

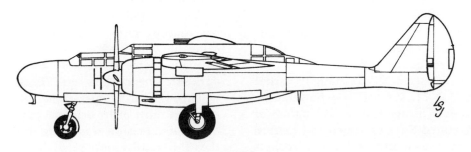

25 FEET

configuration change was made on the two XP-61E prototypes of a two-man day fighter. The crew was placed under a long bubble canopy on the altered central pod. Both the dorsal turret and gunner's greenhouse were eliminated on the "E's." Four .50 cal. machine guns were mounted in the nose, replacing the night-fighter's radar gear. The four 20 mm cannons were retained on this model, but no production orders were placed. Instead, 36 examples of an unarmed reconnaissance model were ordered as F-15A Reporters. Over 700 P-61's were delivered before production ceased after the war.

The aileron surfaces on the P-61 were extremely small and mounted at the wingtip to produce the necessary roll for a turn. Inboard of these, just forward of the almost full-span flaps, were a set of retractable spoilers which performed most of the action usually done by the ailerons. As a result, the Black Widow could reverse direction with great rapidity. The huge size of the landing flaps permitted the twelve-ton P-61B to touch-down as slowly as 93 mph.

The Black Widow's gull wing had a span of 66 feet with an area of 664 sq. feet. The P-61B was 49 feet 7 inches long and was 14 feet 8 inches high. Each of the two Pratt & Whitney R-2800-65 engines delivered 2,000 hp to the four-bladed propellers. Maximum speed was 369 mph at 20,000 feet. Service ceiling was 33,100 feet. Up to 640 gallons were carried in the fuel tanks which provided a range of 400 miles at 318 mph.

In addition to the cannons and machine guns, provisions were made to carry up to four 1,600 pound bombs on underwing pylons.

The P-61C introduced turbosupercharged engines which became standard for the Black Widow. Northrop

The P-61E was to be a two-man day fighter and was similar in appearance to this F-15A Reporter. Thirty-six of these reconnaissance versions of the Black Widow were built. *Northrop*

163

The XP-62 was too much airplane for the power available. As a high altitude fighter, its performance was disappointing.
Gordon S. Williams

The last of Curtiss' wartime fighter designs to fly was also the largest single-seat, single-engine fighter to be built in the United States during the war. It was the materialization of a request by the Army in 1941 to create a fighter for the new Wright R-3350 eighteen cylinder radial engine. The requirements included a pressurized cabin, an armament of either four or eight 20 mm cannons and a speed of 468 mph at 27,000 feet. A delivery date fifteen months from the contract date for the first article was also specified.

A contract for one XP-62 and one XP-62A was received on June 27, 1941. Within days, it was learned that the special supercharged engine and dual-rotation propellers could not be ready in time for the contracted delivery date. As an alternative, Curtiss-Wright recommended completion of the plane with a standard engine and propeller. This suggestion was taken and Curtiss also requested approval for an increase in gross weight and a reduction to 448 mph for the guaranteed speed. By January 1, 1942, it was apparent that the XP-62 was going to be too heavy for the an-

ticipated high-altitude performance called out in the requirements. Curtiss was advised to remove more than 500 pounds from the airframe.

On January 13, 1942, the Army received a proposal from Curtiss to build 100 P-62's, the first to be delivered in May 1943. A contract to this effect was signed on May 25, 1942. When it was learned that the production of P-62's would require a cutback in deliveries of the Curtiss-built P-47's, which were deemed superior to the new fighter, the production contract was withdrawn on July 27, 1942.

With the termination of the contract, the fate of the XP-62 was sealed. By now, the prototype was more than three-fourths complete and flight testing was scheduled to begin in nine months. The cabin pressurization gear was delayed, however, and the XP-62 was not ready to fly until ten months later than the scheduled date, and even then the pressurization system was not installed.

By the time the XP-62 made its long-delayed take-off, it was of little value to anyone. The pressure cabin could provide some useful data and work began on its in-

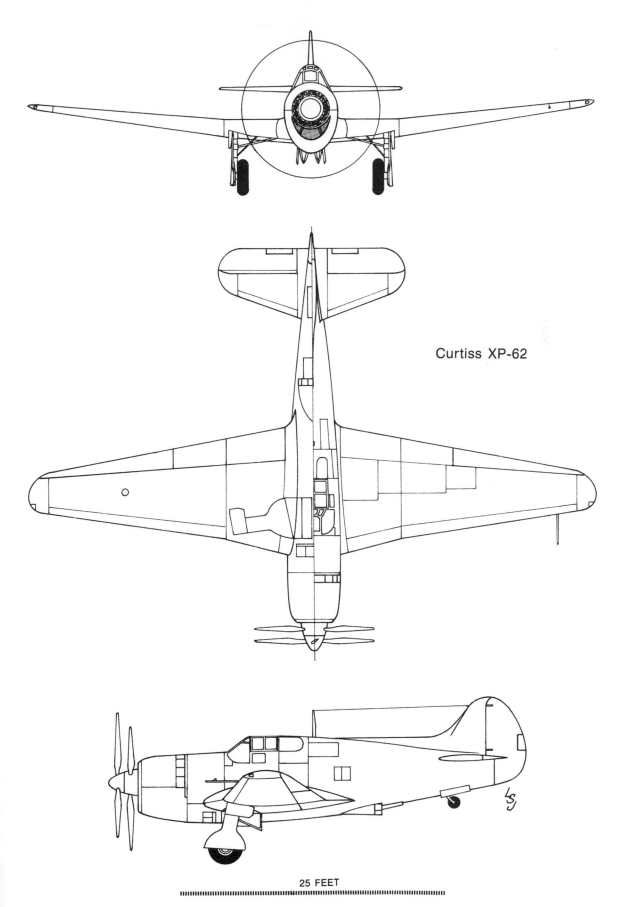

Curtiss XP-62

25 FEET

stallation. Since the plane was of no worth in the war effort, it received a low priority and finally all interest was lost and the plane was scrapped without flying again.

The XP-62 was only flown for a few hours and the full range of its abilities can only be estimated. It had a wingspan of 53 feet 8 inches, was 39 feet 6 inches long and 16 feet 3 inches high. Wing area was 420 square feet. The empty airframe weighed 11,773 pounds and grossed 14,660 pounds. Maximum speed was 448 mph at 27,000 feet. Service ceiling was 35,700 feet. Fuel capacity was 384 gallons. Powerplant was one Wright R-3350-17 Cyclone eighteen-cylinder twin-row engine of 2,300 horse power.

By the time the XP-62 was ready to fly, it was of little value except for cabin pressurization tests.

Dustin W. Carter

BELL
P-63 KINGCOBRA

A production P-63A, most of which were delivered to Russia under Lend-Lease.   Bell

Developments which led to the design of the Bell P-63 Kingcobra began on April 10, 1941, when the Army ordered three P-39D Airacobras with laminar-flow wings as XP-39E's. The tests were promising, and on June 27, 1941, two XP-63 prototypes were ordered.

The Kingcobra bore a strong resemblance to the earlier Airacobra, but was in fact a totally new design. It featured the laminar-flow wing and the Allison V-1710-47 engine tested on the P-39E. The first XP-63, S.N. 41-19511, was flown on December 7, 1942, but was written off the following month. On February 5, 1943, the second XP-63 was flown; and it too was lost in a crash three months later. The third Kingcobra, the XP-63A, flew on April 26, 1943, and deliveries of production models ordered in September 1942, began in October 1943.

Like the Airacobra, the P-63 found itself cast in the role of an attack aircraft and was ideally suited to the requirements of the Russians. A total of 2,456 P-63's were sent to Russia under the Lend-Lease program.

With the abandonment of a proposed Merlin-powered P-63B, the next version of the Kingcobra was the P-63C. This followed 1,725 "A" models and displayed a recontoured empennage with a ventral fin for improved stability. Of the 1,227 P-63C's built, most were shipped to Russia; while 300 were supplied to France and the Royal Air Force evaluated two of them.

None of the USAAF Kingcobras were used operationally. Several variations were made to the basic design for evaluation; among them was a Vee tail and bubble canopy. In one of its more unusual roles, the P-63 became a rather unique flying pinball machine with a red light in the wing that lit up when the plane was hit by special frangible bullets during gunnery training. Three hundred thirty-two of these planes were built as RP-63's.

The P-63C Kingcobra was only slightly larger than the Airacobra, with a wingspan of 38 feet 4 inches, a length of 32 feet 8 inches, and a height of 12 feet 7 inches. Wing area was 248 sq. feet. Maximum speed was 410 mph at 25,000 feet. Fuel capacity was 128 gallons for a range of 320 miles at 275 mph.

167

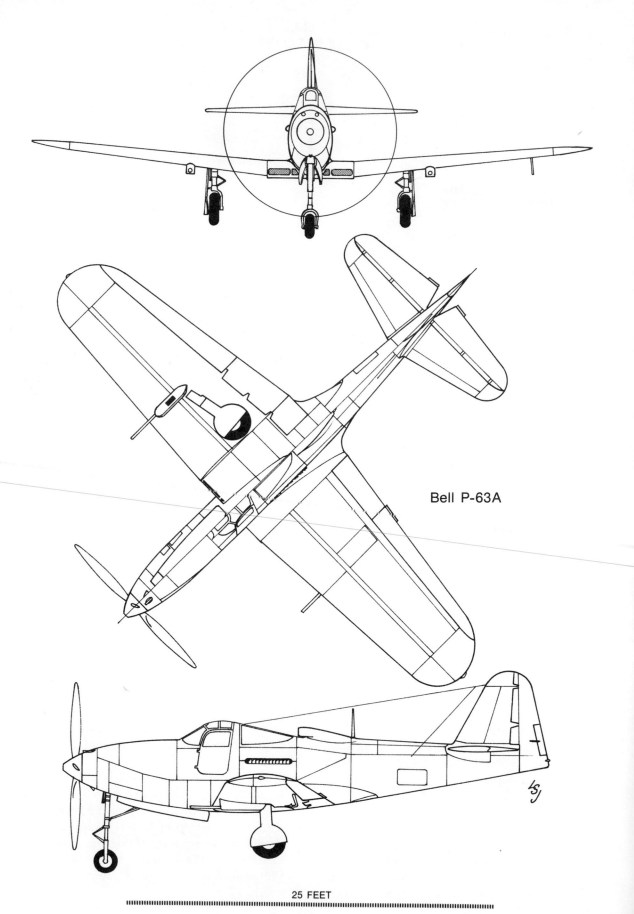

Bell P-63A

25 FEET

As on the Airacobra, the P-63's 1,510 hp Allison engine was located behind the pilot and drove a four-bladed Aero Products propeller through an extensive shaft. A 37 mm cannon fired through the spinner with with two .50 cal. machine guns situated in the nose, firing through the propeller. A second pair of .50's were mounted under the wings in external pods.

The Kingcobra had an empty weight of 6,800 pounds and grossed out at 7,500 pounds maximum.

One of several P-63A's used to evaluate different canopy configurations.   *Bell*

This is the XP-63A, the third prototype of the Kingcobra series, and one of the fastest with a speed of 421 mph.   *Bell*

Six NA-50A's were built for Siam. Before they could be delivered, Siam fell to the Japanese and the fighters were absorbed into the Army as P-64's.
Rockwell International

On August 1, 1938, the Peruvian Government initiated a contract with North American Aviation to supply them with seven fighters developed from the North American NA-16 trainer. As single-seat fighters, these planes received the designation NA-50. Their appearance left no question as to their origin, as they were essentially a single-place version of the popular trainer. The seven fighters were delivered to Peru by May 1939.

On December 30, 1939, a similar order for the trainer-cum-fighter was received from the Siamese Government. This contract was for six modified NA-50A fighters. The modifications to these planes were mainly in the shape of the rudder and differences in armament. The six NA-50A's were shipped from North American in June 1941, and were awaiting transhipment from Pearl Harbor to Siam on December 7, 1941. Following the attack on Pearl Harbor, and with the fall of Siam to the Japanese immi-

nent, the U. S. Army confiscated the planes and absorbed them into their inventory as P-64's.

The Armament was removed from the six fighters, and they were used as advanced trainers at Luke Field, Arizona. Four of the P-64's were later assigned to the training command headquarters for liaison.

As originally built, the P-64 had a wingspan of 37 feet 3 inches, length of 27 feet, and was 9 feet high. Wing area was 228 square feet. Empty weight was 4,660 lbs., loaded the P-64 weighed 5,990 lbs. Armament consisted of two .30 cal. machine guns and two 20 mm cannons. Provisions were made to carry two 100 lb. bombs plus one 550 lb. bomb. The 870 hp Wright R-1820-77 engine gave a top speed of 270 mph at 8,700 feet. With 170 gallons of fuel, the P-64 had a range of 900 miles at 235 mph.

One example of the P-64 is still in use in the U. S. and is often displayed at air shows.

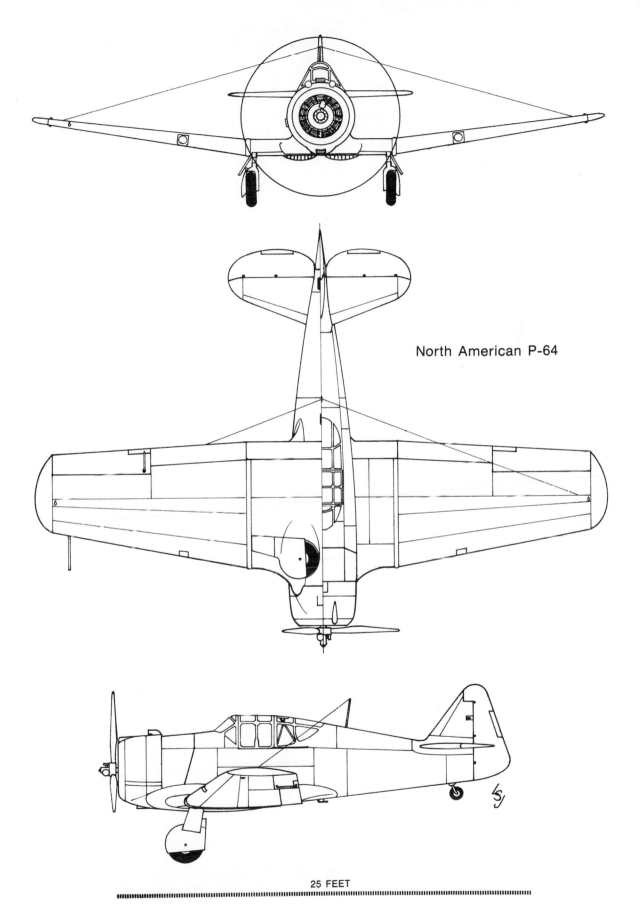

North American P-64

25 FEET

The only remaining P-64 is this privately-owned example, often seen at air shows. Rockwell International

The XP-65 was to have been a replacement for Grumman's XP-50. The Army tested this XF7F-1 at Wright Field and found it unsuited to its use.
Grumman

With the crash of the Grumman XP-50 in May 1941, the designers turned their attention to the refinement of an enlarged, twin-engine fighter for the Air Corps. Bearing the company designation G-51, two examples were ordered by the Air Corps as XP-65's on May 19, 1941. Funding for the XP-50 program was transferred to the XP-65 project.

The XP-65 was to be developed in parallel with a carrier-based version for the Navy, the XF7F-1. The major difference between the two types was the use of superchargers on the Air Corps version. The XP-65 was to be powered by two 1,700 hp Wright R-2800-22W engines for an anticipated speed of 427 mph at 19,200 feet. Four 20 mm cannons and four .50 cal. machine guns were to be carried by the XP-65. The normal fuel capacity of 426 gallons would give a range of 825 miles at 180 mph.

Dimensions of the proposed fighter show a wingspan of 52 feet 6 inches, a length of 46 feet 5 inches, and a height of 15 feet 2 inches. Empty weight was 15,943 pounds, gross weight being 21,425 pounds.

As the Army and Navy designs progressed, it became apparent that the requirements for each of the services were so different that no one design would be satisfactory for both roles. (This was the same problem they would again face some twenty years later with the F-111 program.) Since Grumman had been a major supplier of Navy equipment for many years, it was decided that the XP-65 would be discarded in favor of the XF7F-1 which was eventually produced as the Tigercat.

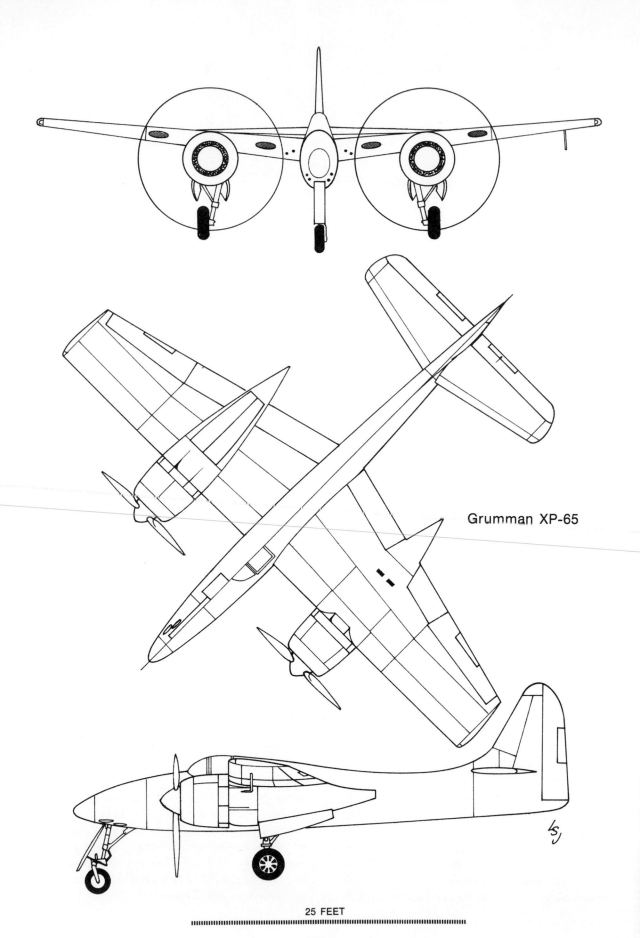

Grumman XP-65

25 FEET

Although the XP-65 was not built, it was virtually identical to the Navy's XF7F-1 Tigercat, as shown here.

Grumman

VULTEE
P-66 VANGUARD

Vultee's Model 48 was a company-funded attempt to earn a military contract. The long cowling was intended to reduce the drag of the radial engine.
Dustin W. Carter

As in the case of the North American P-64, the Vultee P-66 Vanguard became a part of the American fighter inventory through an indirect route.

Bearing Vultee's model number 48, the Vanguard first appeared in September 1939. The radial R-1830-S4C4-G engine was enclosed in a low-drag cowling reminiscent of the XP-42 by Curtiss. The same cooling problems experienced by the XP-42 led to the removal of the long cowling and a conventional cowl was adopted.

No orders for the Vanguard were forthcoming from the Army Air Corps, but a contract for 144 of the planes was received from Sweden on February 6, 1940. The first of the Swedish Vanguards was ready for delivery by September 1941; but by this time, the U. S. Government had placed an embargo on the export of the planes to Sweden and Vultee was not permitted to ship them. The British Government, recognizing their value as trainers, took over the Swedish contract. But before any Vanguards were delivered to them, the

planes were diverted to China who eventually received 129 of them. In the meantime, the Vanguard had been given the American fighter designation P-66. The remaining 15 planes were absorbed by the Air Corps, although official documents show all 144 planes received American serial numbers (42-6832 to 42-6975). The first two production Vanguards also received the British serial numbers BW 208 and BW 209. The American P-66's were assigned to West Coast training groups.

Specifications of the P-66 were: wingspan 36 feet, length 28 feet 5 inches, height 13 feet 1 inch, wing area 197 sq. feet. Empty weight was 5,235 pounds, gross weight was 7,100 pounds. The P-66 was armed with four .30 cal. machine guns in the wings and two .50 cal. guns in the nose. The engine used was a Pratt & Whitney R-1830-33 fourteen cylinder air-cooled radial of 1,200 hp. This provided a maximum speed of 340 mph at 15,100 feet. Range was 850 miles with 290 gallons of fuel.

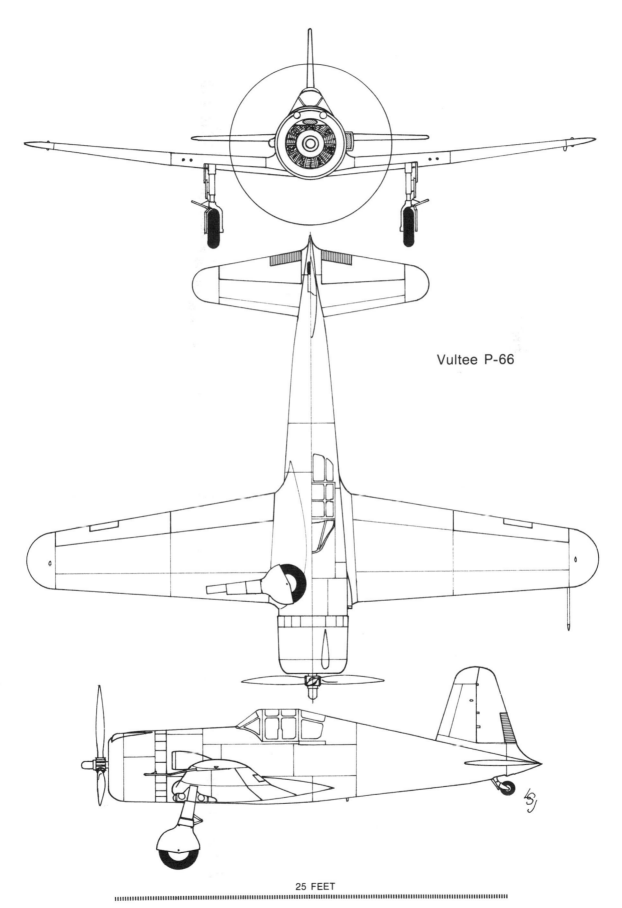

Vultee P-66

25 FEET

The Vultee Vanguard was designated P-66 after export models of the plane were taken over by the U. S. Army.   *Dustin W. Carter*

The first production prototype of the Vultee Vanguard.   *Convair*

The radical XP-67 represented a bold step for a new company.   *McDonnell Douglas*

The first design to emerge from the McDonnell Aircraft Company, formed in July 1939, was the distinctive-appearing XP-67, known variously as "Bat," "Moonbat," or "Bomber Destroyer." When it was ready for its first flight on January 6, 1944, the XP-67 represented the culmination of a design that was begun late in 1939.

Starting with a proposal to the Air Corps for an Allison V-3420- or Pratt & Whitney H-3130-powered long-range fighter, McDonnell inquired about a contract to construct the plane. The Air Corps wasn't too excited about the plan to bury the engine behind the pilot and drive a pair of pusher propellers through right angle extension shafts, but did permit the company to submit the design for Proposal R-40C. The unconventional design, competing with what became the XP-54, -55, and -56, did not fair well but did warrant an order for more engineering details. A revised proposal for a more conventional fighter was submitted to the Air Corps in June 1940, but again rejected. McDonnell returned on May 22, 1941, with a re-engineered design and received a contract for construction of two XP-67's.

The first, and in the event only, XP-67 was completed by December 1, 1943. Its graceful lines were a study of aerodynamic simplicity. The twin-Continental XI-1430-17/19 engines and their superchargers were housed in torpedo-shaped nacelles which blended smoothly into the wings. Similarly, the fuselage flared outward to receive the wings with a flowing fillet.

Flight tests were accompanied by a series of fires and engine problems. Regarding the latter, the main concern was the fact that the engines did not provide the rated 1,350 hp, falling nearly 300 hp short. Without the extra power, the guaranteed speed of 448 mph could not be met. Actual speed obtained was 405 mph at 25,000 feet, even with the assist of jet-augmented exhaust. The reduced power also compelled an excessive take-off run. Although the handling characteristics of the XP-67 were considered acceptable, pilots reported it felt underpowered. On September 6, 1944, just as the fighter was being prepared for its official USAAF performance tests, the starboard engine caught fire, and though a safe

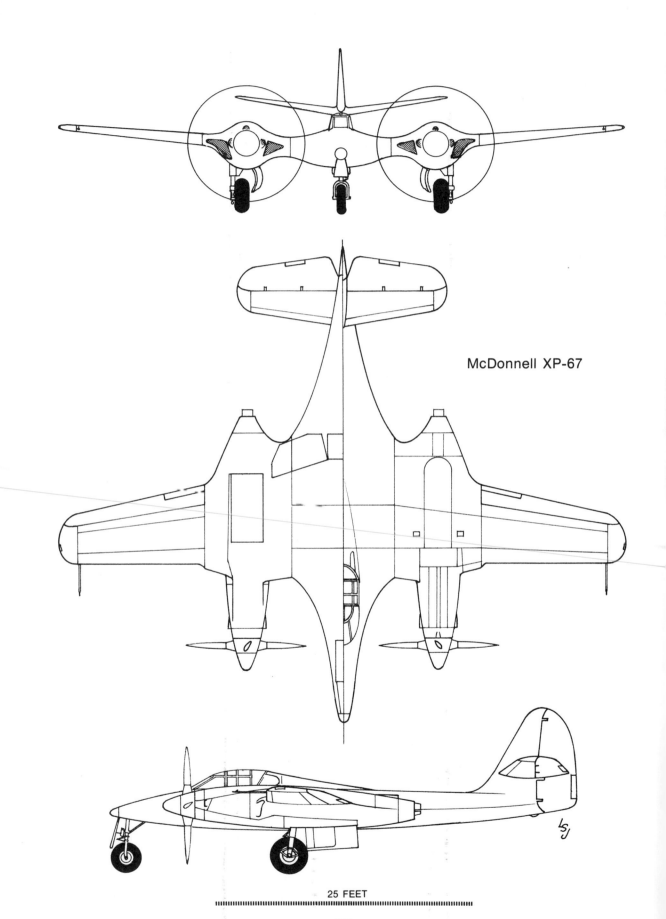

McDonnell XP-67

25 FEET

landing was made, the flames were blown over the fuselage and the plane was destroyed.

The second prototype XP-67 was cancelled following the accident, despite the improved performance that would be obtained through the use of two Merlin and two 2,300 lb. s.t. jet engines.

Dimensions of the XP-67 included a wingspan of 55 feet, length of 42 feet and height of 14 feet 9 inches. Wing area was 414 square feet. Service ceiling was 37,000 feet. With an internal fuel capacity of 735 gallons, the XP-67 had a range of 2,000 miles at 210 mph. Weights were 17,745 pounds empty and 22,114 pounds loaded. The formidable armament of six 37 mm cannons with 270 rounds was intended for the XP-67, but no weapons were installed.

Although not entirely successful, the XP-67 was the first of a line of significant McDonnell fighters.

Air Force Museum

The augmentor exhaust stacks are visible in this view of the sleek XP-67.   *Air Force Museum*

This wooden mock-up of the XP-69 was three-quarters the size of the proposed fighter.   *Republic*

One of the more interesting aircraft power plants under development in the United States during World War II was the Wright R-2160 engine with 2,500 hp. Its 42 cylinders were in six rows and had a displacement of 2,160 cubic inches. A large-diameter contra-prop was planned to deliver the power. It was this engine that was intended to propel Republic's huge AP-18 fighter, designated XP-69 in July 1941, when two examples were ordered.

A three-quarter scale mock-up of the XP-69 was inspected in June 1942, but by May 11, 1943, the Air Force felt the Republic XP-72 would fulfill their requirements and the XP-69 was discontinued.

The final configuration of the XP-69 differed slightly from that shown in the photos of the mock-up. Provisions had been made for a long bubble canopy, no doubt for improved rearward vision. The mid-mounted engine was to receive cooling air through a large intake below the wing. Power was to be transmitted to a pair of 13 foot 8 inch contra-rotating propellers by means of an extension shaft passing beneath the cockpit. An armament of two 37 mm cannons and four .50 cal. machine guns was to be installed in the wings, with 1,280 total rounds.

Wingspan of the proposed XP-69 was 51 feet 8 inches with 505 sq. feet of area. Overall length was 51 feet 6 inches and the height was 17 feet 3 inches. Empty and maximum gross weights were 15,595 lbs. and 26,164 lbs. respectively. It was estimated that a speed of 450 mph could be reached at 35,000 feet and that altitude could be attained twenty minutes after take-off. Service ceiling was to be 48,900 feet. Fuel capacity was to be 700 gallons and range was to be 1,800 miles.

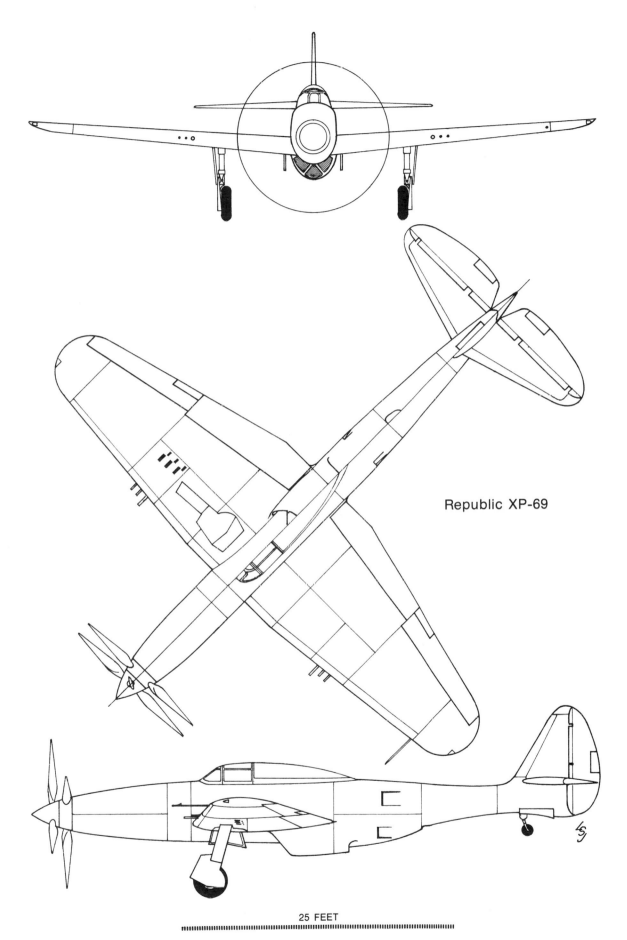

Republic XP-69

25 FEET

183

DOUGLAS
P-70

America's first night fighter was originally an attack bomber. The glass nose was retained but painted black with the rest of the plane.

Douglas

It is not unusual for a fighter to be adapted to the bombing role, but the reverse is somewhat unique. In the case of the Douglas P-70, the need for a night-fighter was urgent, but the large proportions of early radar equipment required the use of a plane the size of a medium bomber in this role.

The first use of the Douglas A-20 type bomber as a night-interceptor was made by the British Royal Air Force after England took over a French contract for 100 DB-7A's. About eighty of these planes had solid noses replacing the bomb aimers glazed position. Twelve machine guns were mounted in the new nose along with radar gear, and the Havoc II's, as they were called, were used with some degree of success.

The USAAF had already ordered the P-61 Black Widow at the beginning of 1941, but these could not be available for a year or so. The need for a radar-guided night-fighter was clear, and with the success of the RAF in their Havocs, the U. S. also turned to the Douglas bomber. A new radar set of the type developed for the P-61 was installed in an A-20, which was redesignated XP-70, and the first American night-fighter was

born. The armament consisted of four 20 mm cannons in a tray mounted below the bomb bay, and the glass nose was painted black with the rest of the plane.

When the Japanese attacked Pearl Harbor, the P-61 was still nearly a year from delivery. Although the P-70 was not fitted with high-altitude engines, it was the only night-fighter available. Therefore, as soon as additional radar sets could be obtained, more P-70's were built. Fifty-nine P-70's were delivered by September 1942, followed by 104 P-70A's with four .50 cal. machine guns added to the nose. One hundred five P-70B-2 trainers were delivered to units awaiting delivery of the P-61's.

The P-70 had a crew of two, the second man operating the radar set and guiding the pilot to the intercept point. Wingspan was 61 feet 4 inches, length was 47 feet 7 inches, height was 18 feet 1 inch, and wing area was 465 square feet. Two 1,600 hp Pratt & Whitney R-2600-11's were used for power and provided a top speed of 338 mph at 14,-000 feet. Service ceiling was 28,250 feet. The fuel tanks could hold 270 gallons. The P-70 weighed 15,730 pounds empty, 19,750 pounds loaded.

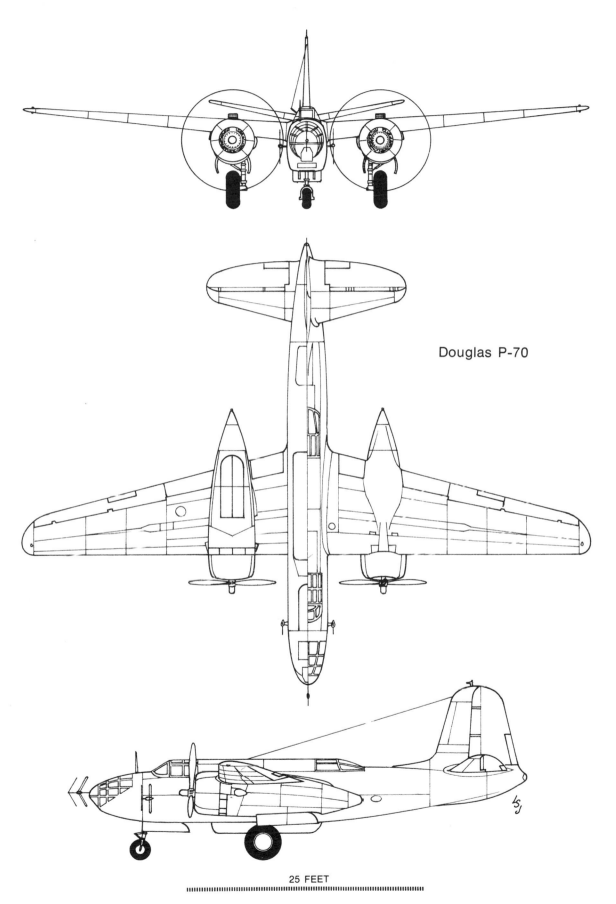

Douglas P-70

25 FEET

Some of these P-70's saw action in the Pacific, others were used as trainers until the P-61 was available.

Harry Gann

The advisability of designing an escort fighter that was as large, and weighed as much as the bombers it was to guard, seems questionable at least. However, in November 1941, Curtiss proposed just such a machine to the Army Air Force. The mammoth fighter was to be powered by two turbo-supercharged 3,450 hp Pratt & Whitney R-4360-13 Wasp Major engines driving a pair of 13½ foot contra-props behind the wings. Two prototypes were ordered as Curtiss XP-71-C's, but the project was cancelled before construction had begun.

The proposed long-range fighter had a wingspan of 82 feet 3 inches. Overall length was 61 feet 10 inches and the rudder tip stood 19 feet above the ground. Wing area was 902 square feet, 50 percent more than a B-25 bomber. With an estimated gross weight of 39,950 pounds, the XP-71 would have weighed five tons more than the bomber. Empty weight was to be 31,060 pounds. Equally as formidable as its proportions was the armament planned for the XP-71. Two 37 mm cannons with 60 rpg and one 75 mm cannon with 20 rounds were to be installed in the nose. A two-man crew was to be seated in tandem in a pressurized cabin.

Despite the proportions and weight of the XP-71, it was estimated that the huge fighter would reach a velocity of 428 mph at 25,000 feet yet land as slowly as 97 mph. It was to take 12.5 minutes for the XP-71 to reach 25,000 feet. Service ceiling was 40,000 feet. Since long-range was a prerequisite for an escort fighter, the XP-71 design was provided with a fuel capacity of 1,940 gallons which, it was anticipated, would provide a range of 3,000 miles.

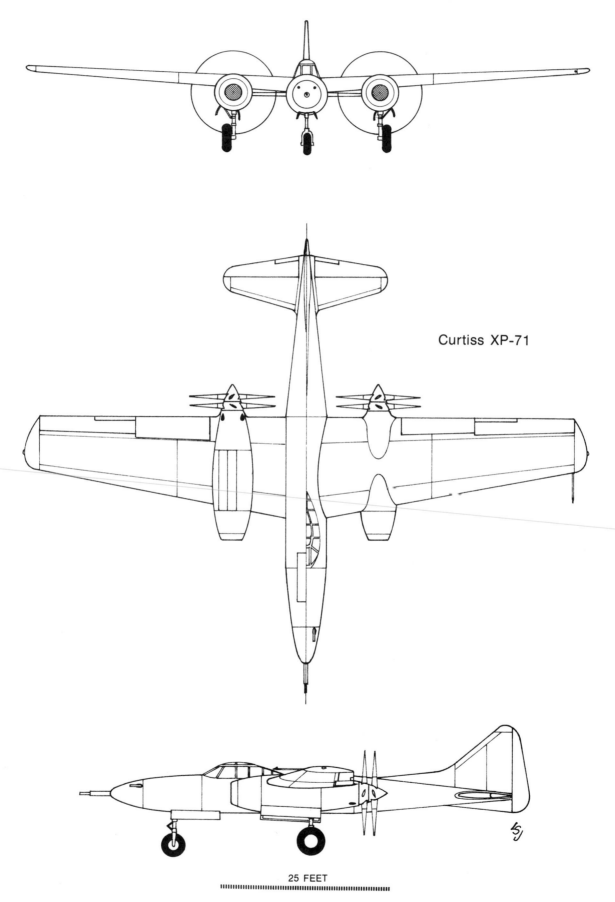

Curtiss XP-71

25 FEET

The second XP-72 used a contra-rotating propeller, but the performance of the two planes was virtually the same.
                                                                                                    Republic

The most powerful piston engine to reach production in any country during World War II was Pratt & Whitney's 3,500 hp Wasp Major. When Republic engineers were considering a means of upgrading their P-47 Thunderbolt, they turned to this engine for their powerplant. Design studies began in July 1941, scarcely two months after the XP-47B first flew. By June 18, 1943, the USAAF felt the prospects of the new design were worthy of a development contract and ordered two prototypes as XP-72's.

When the first XP-72 was flown on February 2, 1944, it had much of the appearance of the P-47, differing primarily in the slimmer nose created when the supercharger intake was moved back to the wing. The big 28 cylinder R-4360-13 engine was contained within a close-fitting cowling and cooled by a fan behind the spinner. The supercharger was located in the fuselage rear, as on the P-47, but the belly was deeper due to the intake fairing. Features which proved advantageous on the Thunderbolt were retained on the XP-72. These included the teardrop-shaped cockpit canopy and compressability-recovery flaps for slowing the fighter rapidly as it ap-

proached the speed of sound.

The first XP-72, S.N. 43-36598, was fitted with a conventional four-bladed propeller, but the second prototype was delivered with an Aero Products 13½ foot contra-prop. During flight testing, the two XP-72's showed outstanding performance characteristics, and a contract for 100 P-72's was approved. It was intended to use the planes as Buzz-bomb interceptors because of their rapid acceleration to 490 mph at 25,000 feet. Before production commenced, the Air Force revised its requirements in favor of long-ranging bomber escorts and the production order was rescinded.

The XP-72 had a wingspan of 40 feet 11 inches, a length of 36 feet 7 inches, height of 16 feet, and wing area of 300 sq. feet. Service ceiling was 42,000 feet. The prototype XP-72's carried six .50 cal. machine guns with 1,600 rounds, but production models were to carry four 37 mm cannons. Provision was also made to mount two 1,000 pound bombs under the wings. Fuel capacity was 370 gallons which was to give a range of 1,200 miles at 300 mph. The XP-72 weighed 11,475 pounds empty and 14,444 pounds loaded.

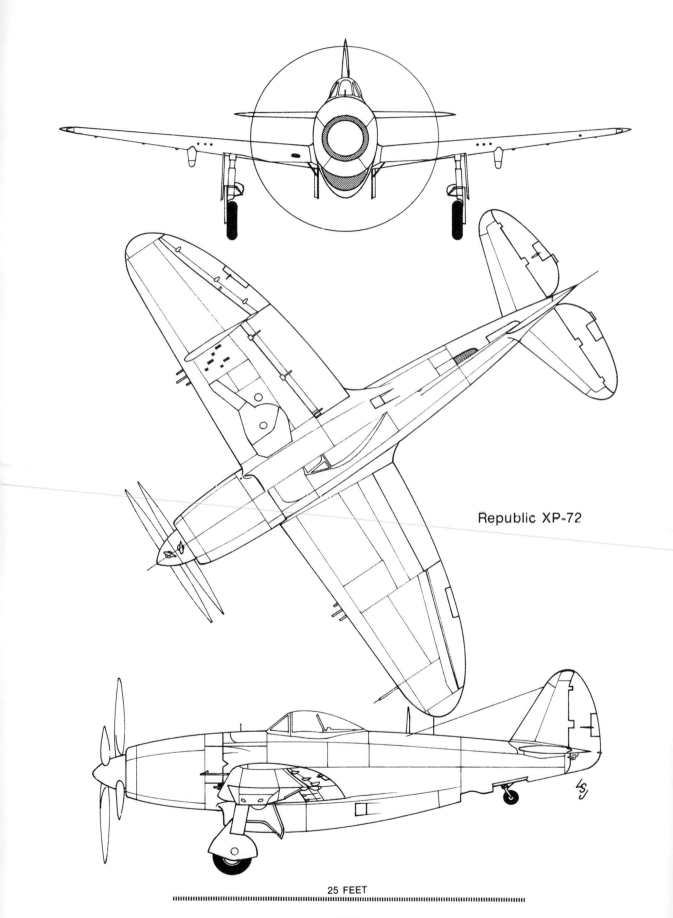

Republic XP-72

25 FEET

The XP-72 was basically a Thunderbolt with a 3,500 hp engine.　　　　　*Republic*

According to Republic, the second XP-72 reached 504 mph at full rated power during testing.　Republic

Following failure of the composite XP-75, the entire plane was redesigned to make the P-75A.

Gordon S. Williams

The numbers -73 and -74 were not assigned to any fighter projects. Some historical sources indicate this was done in order to designate the Fisher Eagle as the P-75, comparing it to the famous French 75 cannon of World War I. Whatever the case, the fighter designed and built by the Fisher Body Division of General Motors bore that symbolic number.

As radical in concept as it was strange in appearance, the XP-75 was a conglomeration of parts from existing production aircraft. Oddly enough, the idea for such composite design came from the man who designed the Curtiss P-40. In itself, the idea was realistic—to use proven componants from aircraft in production, thus reducing development and unit costs. The only problem was that each of these parts was designed to function as an integral unit to a specific airframe. Mixing them with parts from other aircraft could, and did, produce some unusual results.

The original requirement that spawned the XP-75 urged the development of an interceptor with an initial climb rate of 5,600 feet per minute, a top speed of 440 mph at

20,000 feet, and a service ceiling of 38,000 feet. With Fisher's promise to deliver the first Eagle seven months after receiving the contract, two XP-75's were ordered on October 10, 1942. First appearing on paper with inverted-gull wings using P-51 Mustang outer panels, F4U Corsair landing gear, and A-24 Dauntless empennage, the XP-75 soon was subject to design changes. The inverted-wing design was replaced by a straight surface using P-40 outer panels before the configuration was frozen. By mid-1943, the interceptor role was changed to that of a long-range escort, and on July 6, 1944, six additional planes were ordered in this capacity. At the same time, production of no less than 2,500 P-75A-GC's was authorized, but with the stipulation that the entire contract could be cancelled if the as-yet-unflown XP-75 should fail to meet the requirements.

On November 17, 1943, the first XP-75 took to the air. Power was obtained from an Allison V-3420-19 liquid-cooled engine buried in the fuselage and driving contra-props via an extension shaft. Handling characteristics were not as anticipated. The

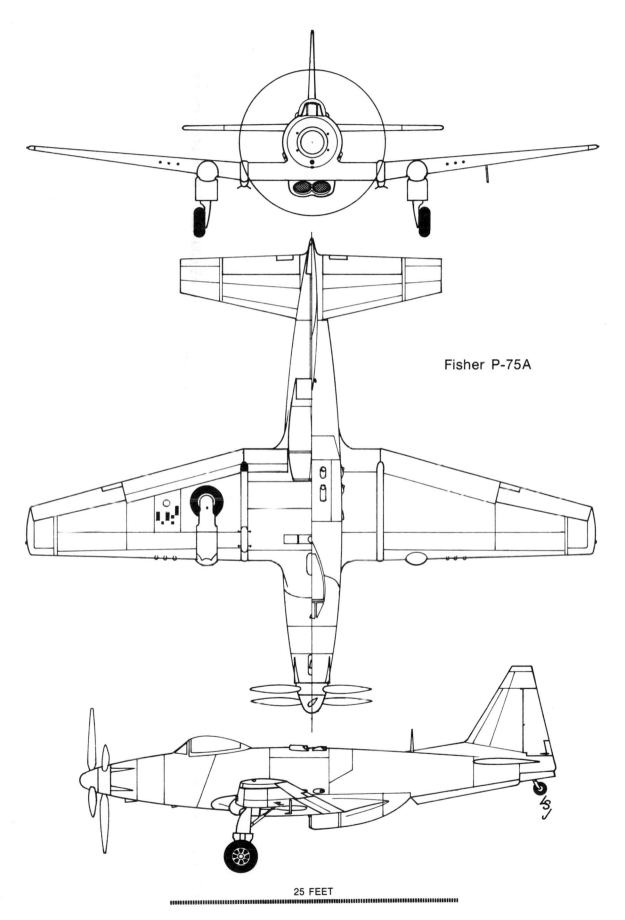

Fisher P-75A

25 FEET

big plane taxied and took off well but was too stable to be a satisfactory fighter. The aileron forces were heavy and the engine did not provide the rated power. Added to this was the embarrassing fact that the engineers had miscalculated the aircraft's center of gravity. The long-range XP-75's had already been subjected to some redesign, but even this was not enough. When the first P-75A appeared, it was virtually a new airplane. Performance was somewhat improved, but even the pre-production Eagles were unable to attain the required results. Three of the planes had been lost in crashes, two of them fatal, and the entire program was staggering under development problems when the Air Force cancelled the production contract on October 27, 1944. By this time, six production Eagles had been delivered—five of them fly-ing and the sixth was retained for spare parts.

The P-75A had a wingspan of 49 feet 4 inches, a length of 41 feet 4 inches, and a height of 15 feet 6 inches. Wing area was 347 square feet. Empty weight was 11,255 lbs., gross 13,600 lbs., maximum 19,420 lbs. With the 2,885 hp Allison engine, the maximum speed attained was 404 mph at 22,000 feet, although one of the XP-75's did reach 418 mph at 21,600 feet during the program. Service ceiling was 36,400 feet.

The P-75A had a normal fuel capacity of 638 gallons with a range of 3,150 miles at 250 mph. Armament was to consist of four .50 cal. guns with 300 rpg or, alternatively, ten .50 cal. machine guns with 261 rpg. Provisions were made to carry two 1,000 pound bombs.

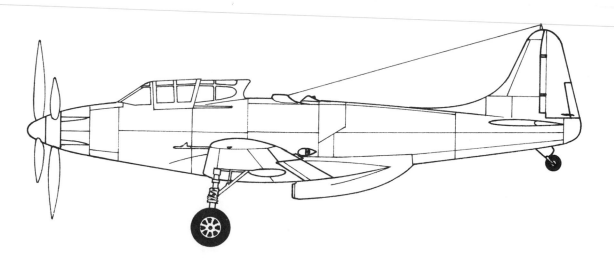

Fisher XP-75

Notice the multiple exhaust ejectors for the 24 cylinder Allison V-3420 coupled engine.   Gordon S. Williams

The XP-75 was a strange-looking aggregation of parts from several different planes.   Gordon S. Williams

BELL
XP-77

The second example of Bell's XP-77 wooden interceptor.   *Bell*

The tiny Bell XP-77 was an attempt to solve two problems facing the American aircraft industry following the outbreak of World War II. The first was the possibility of shortages of light metal alloys used in airframe construction. The war had caused a rapid increase in the use of these metals, and it was feared that their production could not keep pace with the demands of the industry. The second problem was that presented by the appearance of the highly maneuverable Japanese Zero-Sen, a fighter far more agile than its American opponents. Therefore, the XP-77 was intended to out-maneuver the Zero-Sen and be constructed mainly of wood.

The lightweight fighter concept had intrigued designers for many years. In Europe, nimble wooden fighters had already been built and used with some degree of success. In contrast, American fighters had increased in weight and speed but maneuverability had suffered. Bell proposed building their Tri-4, a wooden fighter with an estimated top speed of 410 mph at 27,000 feet, carrying two 20 mm cannons and two .50 cal. machine guns, yet

weighing only 3,700 pounds! Procurement of twenty-five of the little Tri-4 fighters as P-77's was authorized on May 16, 1942, but unavailability of a supercharger for the selected engine led to a reduction to six aircraft. The first of these was ready for flight testing on April 1, 1944, by which time the contract had already been cancelled because the need for such a fighter no longer existed. Nevertheless, Bell was requested to complete the second XP-77 for flight trials.

The 520 hp unsupercharged Ranger XV-770-7 did not deliver the estimated performance, and the XP-77 had a top speed of only 330 mph at 4,000 feet. Further evaluation showed that the little wooden fighter did not offer any advancement over existing production fighters.

The engine, mounted rigidly to the airframe, caused excessive vibration at some speeds. On October 22, 1944, the second XP-77 was destroyed when the pilot attempted an Immelmann turn which resulted in an inverted spin.

Although the speed of the XP-77 was disappointing, the designers did manage to keep the actual weight within the estimated

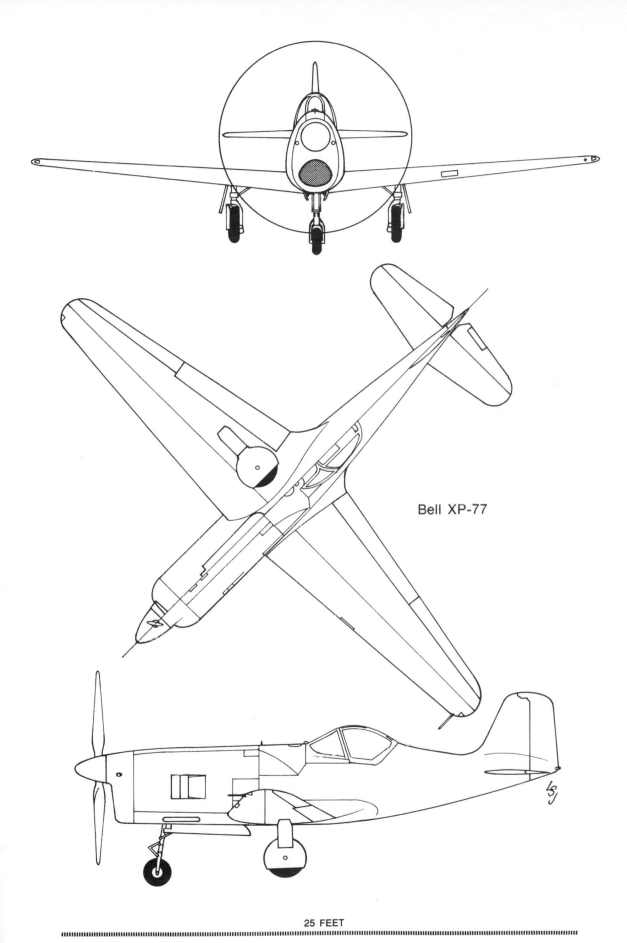

Bell XP-77

25 FEET

figure; empty weight was 2,760 pounds, gross was 3,583 pounds, and overload weight was 4,028 pounds. The XP-77's wing spanned 27 feet 6 inches, it was 22 feet 10½ inches long and stood 10 feet 11 inches high. Wing area was 100 square feet. With a fuel capacity of 56 gallons, the XP-77 had a range of 550 miles at 270 mph. Service ceiling was 30,100 feet.

Although the XP-77 was basically of wooden construction, many metal panels are apparent in this view.
Gordon S. Williams

The lightweight XP-77 looked more like a racer than a fighter. It is shown here during its flight test program in 1944.
Air Force Museum

For years the all-wing airplane was a Northrop trade mark.   U.S. Air Force

The first reaction-powered flight of a piloted aircraft took place on June 30, 1939, when the German Heinkel He 176 rocket flew for 50 seconds. Continuing development of the powerplant led to the introduction of the rocket-propelled Messerschmitt Me 163 Komet, first flown in April 1941. The Japanese also tested a rocket-intercepter patterned after the Komet design.

In the United States, the first serious thought given to the development of a rocket-powered fighter came in late 1942 when Northrop devised a flying wing aircraft driven by a liquid-fuel rocket motor. In January 1943, three of these fighters, designated XP-79, were ordered from Northrop. Since Northrop did not have the space to assemble their new fighter, the program was subcontracted to Avion, Inc. for actual construction. The project was handled with the greatest of secrecy; and new techniques in metal fabrication were devised, such as welding magnesium.

Two months after the rocket-powered XP-79A's were ordered, it was decided to alter the third airframe to use two

Westinghouse turbojets in place of the rocket motor. The jet version was designated XP-79B. Difficulties with the Aerojet rocket motor led to the priority being placed on completion of the jet-powered XP-79B. Eventually the rocket versions were cancelled; however, a development of the program, the MX-324, was flown by rocket power on July 5, 1944.

The XP-79B was transferred to Northrop on December 1, 1944, for completion. The magnesium structure created an extremely sturdy machine, and some thought was given to using the fighter as an aerial battering ram to slice wings and tails from attacking bombers. How practical this would be remains to be seen. Other design features of interest were the prone cockpit position, enabling the pilot to withstand up to 21 g's, wingtip bellows instead of conventional rudders, and a four-point landing gear system.

In June 1945, the XP-79B was delivered to the test facilities at Muroc for flight evaluation. Taxi testing seemed to be causing the most problems, the tires constantly blowing out during high-speed dashes.

Northrop XP-79B

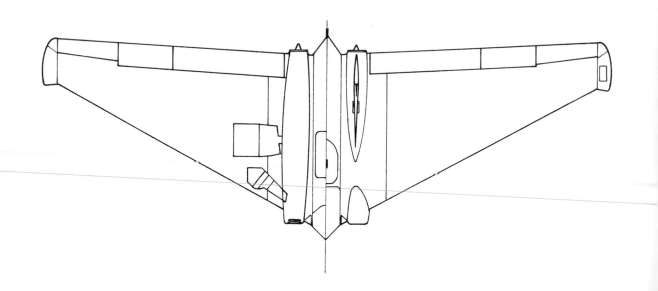

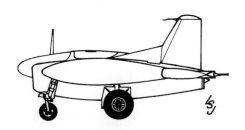

25 FEET

Finally, on September 12, 1945, the XP-79B was taken into the air. For about 15 minutes, the fighter seemed to perform normally; then, at an altitude of some 7,000 feet, the XP-79 started into a slow roll from which it failed to recover. The pilot bailed out at 2,000 feet, but was struck by the revolving aircraft and was unable to open his parachute. The magnesium XP-79B was totally consumed by fire following its impact with the desert.

No armament had been installed, but the XP-79B was expected to carry four .50 cal. machine guns with 250 rpg. Span of this flying wing fighter was 38 feet, length was 14 feet and height was 7 feet 6 inches. The two Westinghouse J30 turbojets provided a total of 2,300 lbs. of thrust for the 9,600 pound gross fighter. Empty weight was 6,250 pounds. Since the plane was destroyed before actual performance figures could be determined, the maximum speed of 547 mph at sea level is only an estimate. Three hundred gallons of fuel could be carried.

The Northrop MX-324, a test vehicle for the rocket-powered XP-79A.   Northrop

A close-up view showing one of the XP-79B's wingtip rudder bellows. The jet XP-79B was constructed primarily of magnesium.
U.S. Air Force

LOCKHEED
F-80 SHOOTING STAR

The Shooting Star was America's first true combat jet.   *Lockheed*

Too late to see action in World War II, the Lockheed Shooting Star nevertheless became one of the outstanding combat planes to emerge from the war. Development of America's first jet fighter began as a single-engine modification of the Bell Airacomet as the XP-59B. Bell, unable to fulfill the additional commitment required for the new design, relinquished the project to Lockheed. Within 143 days of receiving the contract, Lockheed was ready to fly their XP-80 with a British-built de Havilland Goblin engine. Even though the 3,000 lb. thrust engine delivered only 2,460 lbs. of power, the XP-80 reached a speed of 502 mph following its first flight on January 9, 1944. This was the first time an American fighter had ever exceeded 500 mph. On June 11, 1944, the second Shooting Star was flown with an American-built GE J33 engine. The performance of the P-80 was so outstanding, the Air Force ordered 5,000 Shooting Stars. With the surrender of Japan and the end of World War II, this order was cut back to 917 planes. The potential of

the Shooting Star was such that one airframe was modified for an attempt at breaking the world's speed record. Known as "Racey," the XP-80R, used a 4,600 lb. engine with the added boost of water-alcohol injection to set a record of 623.8 mph on June 19, 1947. This plane now forms a part of the Air Force Museum near Dayton, Ohio.

Growth of the Shooting Star, known as F-80 after June 1948, continued; when the Korean War erupted on June 25, 1950, the F-80 was a fully developed combat weapon. On November 8, 1950, an F-80C and a Russian-built Mig 15 tangled in the world's first jet-to-jet dogfight. The Shooting Star was the victor.

Ejection seats were first installed on F-80B's, but the earlier -A's were retrofitted to bring them up to the -B standards. The bubble canopy had become the accepted cockpit cover on the new generation of fighters, and it added a touch of grace to the clean lines of the F-80.

A two-seat trainer model of the Shooting

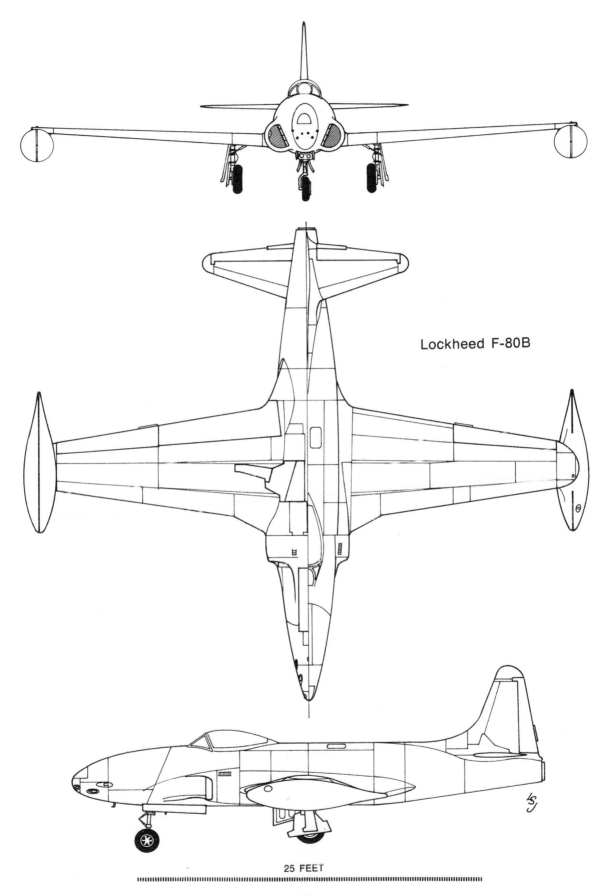

Lockheed F-80B

25 FEET

Star was constructed in August 1947, and designated TF-80C. A production contract was awarded for the trainer as the T-33, which ironically, led to the creation of more trainers than fighter versions of the Shooting Star. Fighter production reached 1,714 of all types while there were a total of 5,691 T-33's assembled.

The F-80 Shooting Star was the Air Force's first true jet-powered fighter and led America straight into the jet age. It had a wingspan of 39 feet, wing area of 238 square feet, a length of 34 feet 6 inches, and was 11 feet 4 inches high. The F-80C, the final production model of which 798 were built, reached a maximum speed of 580 mph at 7,000 feet. Empty weight was 8,240 pounds, gross weight was 15,336 pounds. Fuel capacity with external tanks was 755 gallons. Range was 1,380 miles and service ceiling was 42,750 feet.

F-80R "Racey", world speed record setter. This plane was specially modified for the attempt and bears a highly-polished coat of gray paint.   *Lockheed*

The F-80 made an ideal mount for aerobatic teams. These are the Acrojets.   *Lockheed*

CONVAIR
XF-81

The turboprop exhaust can be seen in front of the main gear door in this view.   *Convair*

The distinction of being the first American turboprop-powered aircraft to fly goes to the XF-81 long-range fighter built by Consolidated-Vultee. The high fuel consumption of the early jet fighters was a serious problem in the development of the new generation of high-performance jets. Convair's solution was to combine a relatively fuel-efficient turboprop with a pure turbojet for the best in both performance ranges. Two prototypes of the composite-powered fighter were ordered on February 11, 1944.

The first XF-81, with its 3,750 lb. thrust Allison J33-GE-5 jet engine installed, was completed before the General Electric TG-100 (XT-31) turboprop was available. Rather than wait until the problems with the TG-100 engine were solved, it was decided to proceed with flight testing using a Packard V-1650-7 Merlin in the interim. The nose section of a P-51D Mustang was adapted to the XF-81 fuselage and flight testing began on February 11, 1945. Flying characteristics were considered very good. After some ten hours of flying, the XF-81

was returned to the manufacturer for installation of the turboprop engine. Flying was resumed on December 21, 1945, with the XT-31 engine.

Flight testing with the turboprop engine was disappointing. Of an anticipated 2,300 ehp, plus a residual 600 lbs. of exhaust augmentation, the XT-31 only provided 1,-650 shaft hp—just 200 hp more than the Merlin had produced. There was virtually no difference in the performance of the aircraft with either the turboprop or Merlin engine.

An order for thirteen YF-81 pre-production machines was cancelled as a result of the poor performance of the turboprop engine, but a second XF-81 was completed. With the failure of the turboprop engine to deliver full power, the total range of performance of the XF-81 was not explored. It was anticipated that with both the turboprop and jet engines operating at rated power, the maximum speed would be 507 mph at 20,000 feet. On the turboprop alone, the XF-81 was to cruise at 275 mph at 25,000 feet. Since the

205

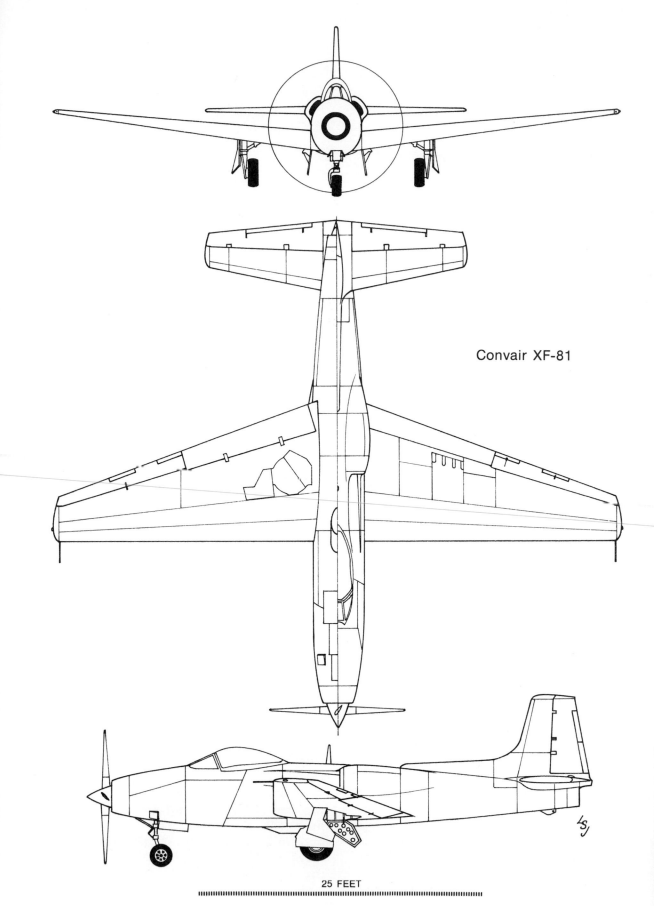

Convair XF-81

25 FEET

jet engine was to be used for take-off and combat boost, it would not normally be flying on the jet alone.

The XF-81 was a fairly large aircraft having a wingspan of 50 feet 6 inches; length was 44 feet 10 inches and height was 14 feet. Wing area was 425 sq. feet. Service ceiling was 35,500 feet. The fuel tanks held 811 gallons for a range of 2,500 miles. Weapons bays in the wings could hold six .50 cal. machine guns or six 20 mm cannons. Two 1,600 lb. bombs could be carried on underwing pylons.

The Convair XF-81 was powered by a turbo-prop and jet combination.   *Convair*

Despite its name, the Twin Mustang was not made from two mustang fighters, but was an entirely new Mustang development.
North American (Rockwell)

The piston-powered F-82 seems an anachronism in the midst of the jet age; but in fact, it was planned in 1943 as a super-long-range escort fighter. The war in the Pacific was often fought by pilots who were spending as many as eight hours in the cockpit. The long over-water flights required a great deal of attention for proper navigation. The need for a second man in the cockpit to assist with the navigational chores and relieve the pilot was quite evident.

As can be seen by its appearance, the F-82 concept was essentially to join two P-51 Mustang fuselages together by a common wing and stabilizer. In fact, though the fuselages are similar to the P-51, they are totally new structures. The pilot, located in the left fuselage, was provided with a complete set of instruments and controls. The co-pilot/navigator had adequate instrumentation and controls to safely guide the plane.

Construction of the first of two XF-82's (44-83887) began in January 1944, and the plane was ready to fly on April 15, 1945; but even before this event took place, 500 F-

82B Twin Mustangs had been ordered. The XF-82 was powered by two Merlin V-1560-23/35 engines turning opposite-rotating propellers. The third, and only XF-82A, used two Allisons turning their props in the same direction. The production F-82B's were powered by the Merlins as on the XF-82's. With the end of the war, all but twenty of the F-82B's were cancelled. Two of the F-82B's were used as test-beds to develop a new night-fighter prototype. Carrying the designations F-82C and F-82D, they differed primarily in the type of radar carried in a large pod mounted to the central wing segment. Results of the night-fighter project led to an order for 250 more of the planes, 100 as F-82E day escort fighters and 100 as F-82F and G night-fighters. By the end of 1949, the F-82 had replaced the Air Force's fleet of P-61 Black Widows. F-82's were deployed to Korea when that war began; and on June 27, 1950, Lt. William Hudson, flying an F-82G, became the first pilot of the new U. S. Air Force to score a kill. This was also the first American aerial victory in the war. After the war, fourteen F-82F and G's were modified

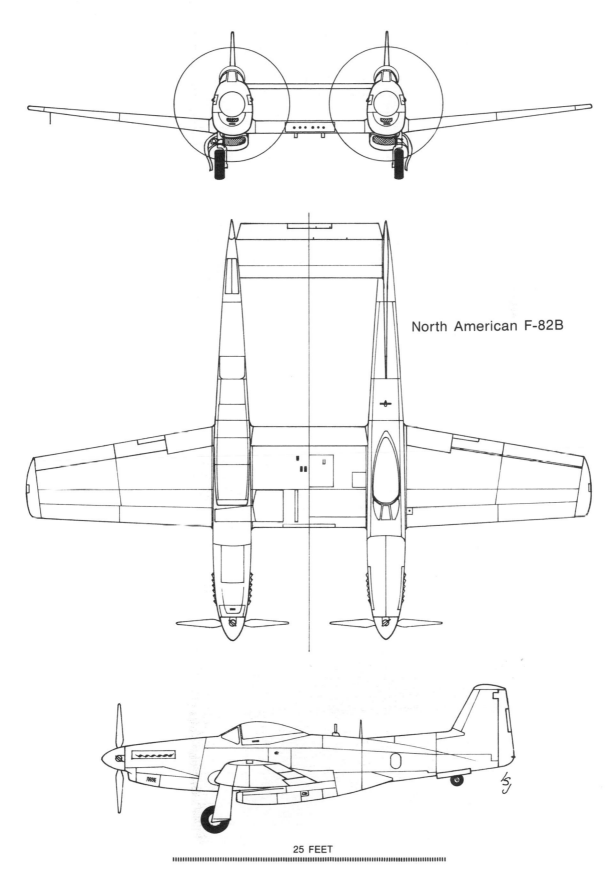

North American F-82B

25 FEET

for the cold weather of Alaska and redesignated F-82H.

The F-82B had a wingspan of 51 feet 3 inches with an area of 408 square feet. Length was 38 feet 1 inch, but the addition of the radar pod on the night-fighters increased their length to 42 feet 5 inches. Height was 13 feet 10 inches. The F-82B weighed 13,405 pounds empty and grossed 19,100 pounds. It was powered by two Packard-built Merlin V-1350 engines of 1,-860 hp each. Top speed was 482 mph at 25,-100 feet. Service ceiling was 41,600 feet. Ar-

mament was six .50 cal. machine guns and either 4,000 pounds of bombs or twenty-five 5 inch rockets.

The night-fighting F-82G weighed 15,-997 pounds empty, 25,891 pounds gross. It was powered by two Allison V-1710-143/145 engines of 1,600 hp each. This version had a top speed of 461 mph at 21,000 feet. Fuel capacity was 576 internal gallons which could be supplimented by external drop tanks to provide a range of 2,240 miles.

The F-82D night fighter prototype.   *North American (Rockwell)*

The F-82C with a radome on the center wing segment. Note the two canopies are different because of the radio gear.   *North American*

The XF-83 with a pair of auxiliary jets under its wings.

The Bell XF-83 was another attempt to overcome the problem of limited range caused by the high fuel consumption of the early jet engines. Huge internal tanks could hold 1,150 gallons of jet fuel which gave a range of 1,580 miles to the big fighter. External tanks with an additional 600 gallons could increase the distance to 2,200 miles. However, there is more to a fighter than long range; and the weight of all that fuel took its toll on the performance of the XF-83, and only the two prototypes were completed.

Engineering work began on the XF-83 in March 1944, the contract for two prototypes being received on July 31, 1944. Relying heavily on their Airacomet experience, the XF-83 appeared to be an enlargement of the basic P-59 concept. Mounting the twin General Electric J33-GE-5 engines on the fuselage sides offered two advantages. First, it left the fuselage free for the installation of fuel cells; and second, the failure of one engine would not cause appreciable control

difficulties since their thrust lines were so close to the aircraft centerline.

The first XF-83 made its initial flight on February 25, 1945, but as subsequent testing showed, the XF-83 did not offer any increase in performance over existing fighters. The pilot of the XF-83 rode in a pressurized cockpit, a feature which was becoming standardized in American fighters due to the extreme altitudes at which they performed best.

Proportions of the big Bell fighter were: wingspan 53 feet, length 45 feet, height 14 feet, wing area 431 square feet. Empty weight was 14,105 pounds; but with the addition of the fuel, flight gear and ammunition, the XF-83 weighed 24,090 pounds, while maximum take-off weight was 27,500 pounds. At normal loaded weight, the XF-83 could reach 522 mph at an altitude of 15,660 feet. Service ceiling was 45,000 feet. Six .50 cal. machine guns were fitted into the nose, each gun being provided with 300 rounds of ammunition.

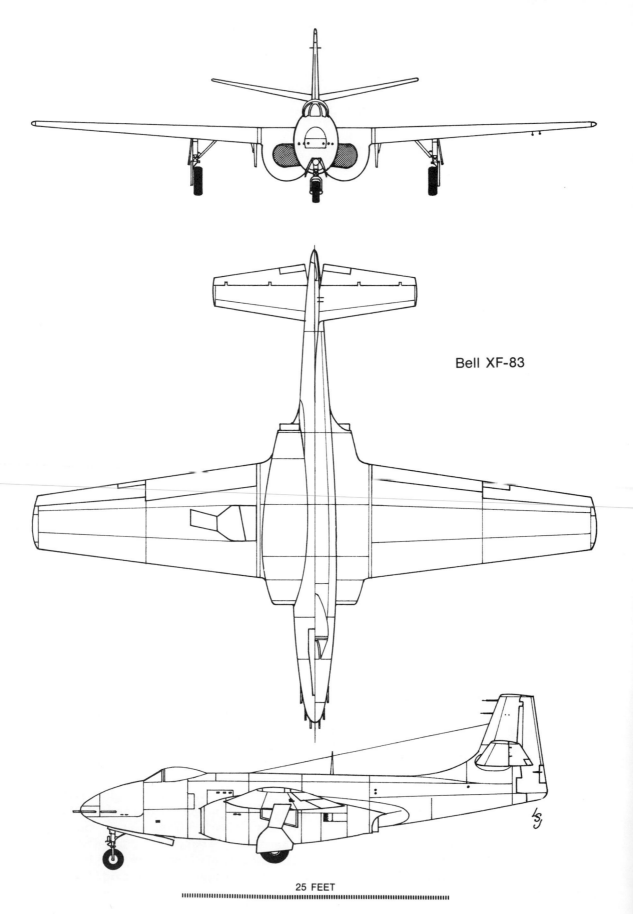

Bell XF-83

25 FEET

Bell's XF-83 was an outgrowth of the original Airacomet design.   *Bell*

The bulk of the XF-83 was caused by the need to carry the large quantity of fuel for its duties as an escort fighter.
                                                                        U.S. Air Force

REPUBLIC
F-84 THUNDERJET

The F-84G was distinguished by a reinforced canopy. This one is operated by the Royal Netherlands Air Force.   *Jurrie van der Woude*

America's first new fighter to fly following the ending of World War II was the jet successor to Republic's P-47 Thunderbolt, the F-84 Thunderjet. The uncomplicated design of the Thunderjet produced a graceful airplane of utmost simplicity. The air intake in the nose fed past the cockpit and directly into the 3,750 pound thrust General Electric J-35-GE engine in the aft fuselage, the now-standard location for fuselage-mounted jets.

The first Republic jet fighter was originally conceived in mid-1944 as a jet-propelled adaptation of the P-47, with a jet power unit installed in the lower fuselage of the Thunderbolt replacing the piston engine. By the end of the year, it was decided to build a totally new machine for the General Electric engine. Three of the Republic fighters were ordered early in 1945, and the first of them was completed by December of the same year. The first flight took place at Muroc Air Force Base, California, on February 28, 1946. The second XF-84 was finished by August, and on September 6, was flown to a speed of 611 mph to establish a world's record. The third

XF-84 was not produced; instead, sixteen YF-84's were built for service tests. The latter had six .50 cal. machine guns and could carry tip tanks for extended range.

Production models, bearing the designation F-84B, began to reach the Air Force in June 1947. These were equipped with ejection seats which were now considered a necessity due to the high operating speeds of the jet fighters. From the 85th production Thunderjet on, the planes were fitted with retractable under-wing rocket launchers. Two hundred twenty-four "B" models were built before the "C" version supplanted it. The 191 "C's" differed mainly in their electrical systems. Additional internal improvements distinguished the 154 F-84D's and 843 F-84E's which followed. From the original 3,750 lb. s.t. engine in the XF-84's, the power grew to 5,000 lbs. s.t. with an Allison J35-A-17D engine. Last of the straight-winged F-84's was the "G" version which had been developed to deliver nuclear weapons. It was powered by a 5,-600 lb. s.t. J35-A-29 engine and could be refueled in flight by a flying-boom system. Now, with its range extended by air-to-air

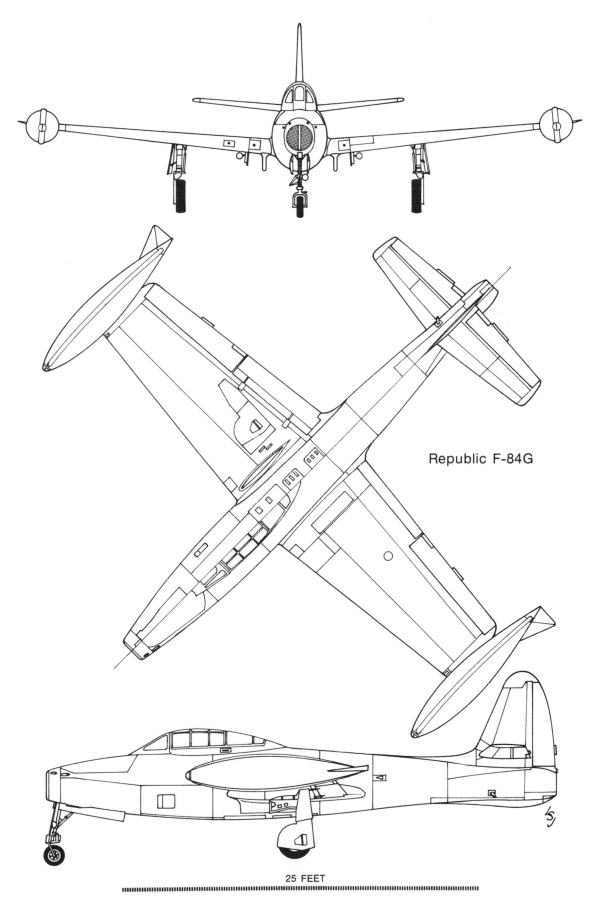

Republic F-84G

25 FEET

refueling, the F-84G was fitted with an autopilot, the new answer to pilot fatigue on long-distance flights. Of the 3,025 F-84G's built, 1,936 were supplied to NATO Air Forces, along with 100 F-84E's.

The Thunderjet, like the Shooting Star, found itself involved in the Korean War. Beginning service as B-29 escorts, they often engaged Mig 15's. Later, they became effective ground-support fighter-bombers.

The F-84G, final version of the Thunderjet, had a wingspan of 36 feet 5 inches, a length of 38 feet 1 inch and stood 12 feet 7 inches high. Wing area was 260 square feet. Empty weight was 11,095 pounds and gross was 23,250 pounds. Maximum speed was 622 mph at sea level. Service ceiling was 40,500 feet.

The first F-84E-1.   *Republic*

The simple lines of the Thunderjet are apparent in this photo.   *Republic*

REPUBLIC
F-84F THUNDERSTREAK, YF-96A

The original Thunderstreak. In this form, it was designated YF-96. Note the differences between this and the production models.
Republic

As successful as it was, the F-84G Thunderjet, with its 5,600 lb. s.t. engine had reached the upper limits of its development. The straight-wing imposed strict limitations on speed. Taking the fuselage of an F-84E, Republic attached new swept wings and tail surfaces to create the XF-84F. A long, more streamlined, cockpit topped off the changes, and the new fighter flew on June 3, 1950. At this point, about 60 percent of the airframe came from the F-84E. For a short time, the prototype was designated YF-96A; but on August 6, 1950, it was officially declared to be F-84F.

Now at the low end of its development scale, the F-84F, called Thunderstreak, was able to absorb the thrust of a more powerful engine, in this case, the Wright J65 Sapphire of 7,220 lbs. s.t. Because of the greater volume of air consumed by the J65, it was necessary to enlarge the Thunderstreak's fuselage. This was done by splicing a 7 inch section into the center of the fuselage, creating an oval cross-section. In addition, a new upward-rising canopy was devised. Thus modified, the second XF-84F flew on February 14, 1951, and set the pace for the following production Thunderstreaks, eventually to total 2,711 planes.

After production was established, the second XF-84F was further modified to test various air inlet positions. A streamlined nose replaced the gaping air intake and flush inlets were built into the fuselage sides. Later, the intakes were moved to the leading edges of the swept wings. This arrangement was not adapted for the fighter, but the spacious nose was able to accommodate a battery of cameras. A total of 718 models of the reconnaissance RF-84F Thunderflash were subsequently built.

The F-84F Thunderstreak's swept-wings have a span of 33 feet 7 inches. Overall length is 43 feet 5 inches and height is 15 feet. Wing area is 325 square feet. Maximum speed is 695 mph at sea level (Mach 0.91). Empty weight is 13,645 pounds, gross weight is 25,226 pounds. The F-84F has a normal fuel capacity of 1,479 gallons. With in-flight refueling, the F-84F's normal range of 860 miles can be extended to the limits of the pilot's endurance. The Thunderstreak is armed with six .50 cal.

These Thunderstreaks had a top speed of nearly 700 mph.　　　*Republic*

Sweeping the wings back on the F-84 increased the operational life of the series.　　　*Republic*

Republic's turboprop fighter was based on the Thunderflash reconnaissance plane.　　　*Republic*

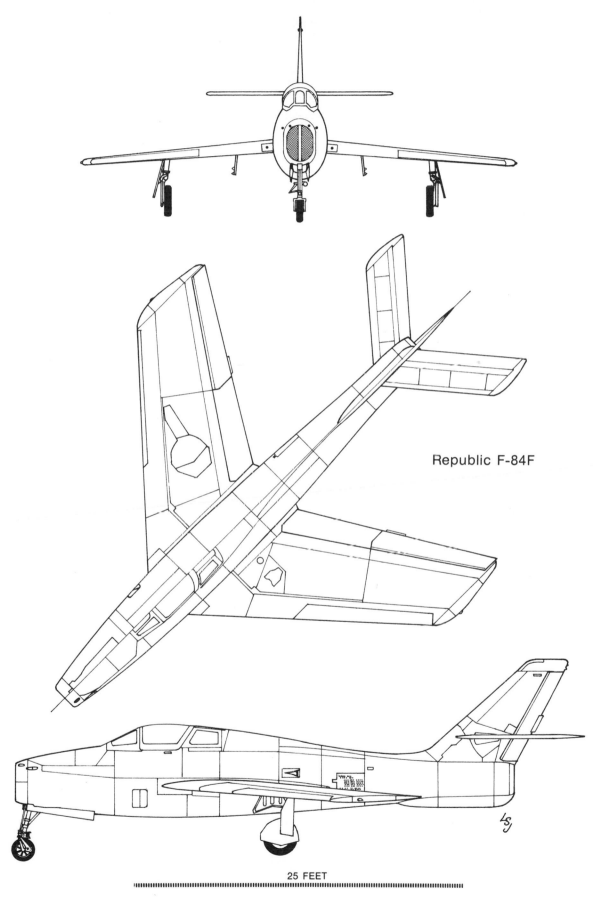

Republic F-84F

25 FEET

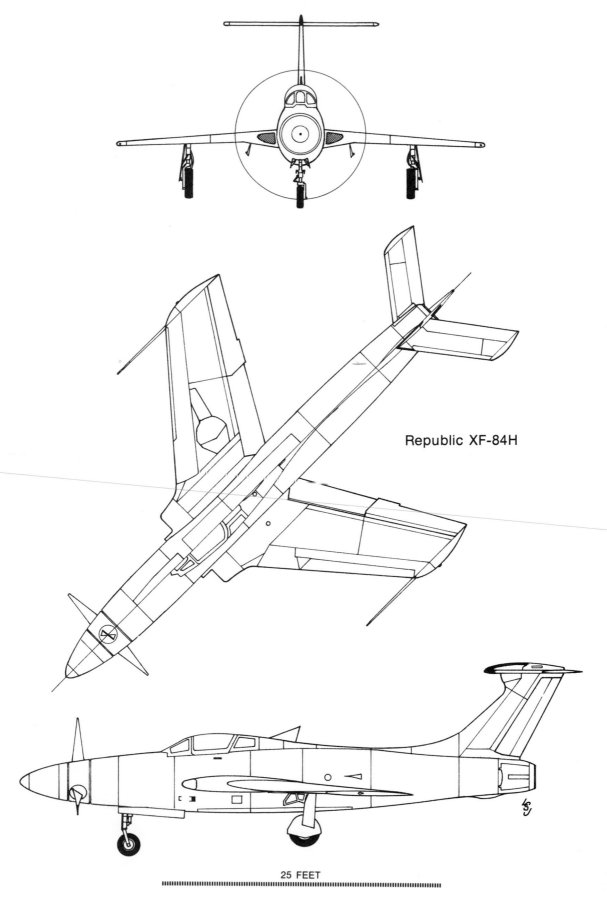

Republic XF-84H

25 FEET

machine guns and can carry up to three tons of external ordnance, including rockets and bombs.

In 1951, the Air Force and Navy were seeking a turboprop-driven strike fighter with performance enabling it to operate from the Navy's carriers. In response, Republic proposed their Model AP-46, a modified RF-84F airframe adapted to take a 5,850 eshp Allison XT-40-A-1 turboprop. A development contract for three planes was signed, providing two of the fighters for the Air Force with the third to test an afterburning XT-40 for the Navy. The planes were briefly designated XF-106, but were reclassed as XF-84H's before completion.

Arriving at Edwards Air Force Base (formerly Muroc AFB) in March of 1955, the first XF-84H was readied for testing. The most obvious differences between it and its pure-jet brother were the "T" tail, a shark-like anti-torque fin behind the cockpit, and of course, the large spinner with its supersonic propeller. It was the latter which created the most unique problems in the development program. An automatic governor controlled engine RPM to maintain a constant speed. The throttle operated the propeller pitch to provide the

necessary thrust for forward motion. On the ground, the propeller could be reversed for braking. During a ground run-up, the 12 foot diameter Aero Products propeller produced hypersonic sound waves which, though inaudible, created acute nausea in anyone within several hundred feet of the plane. Problems with the brakes, gearbox and hydraulic leakage delayed the first flight until July 22, 1955, when it reached an altitude of 20,000 feet.

Although flight testing was limited, the handling characteristics of the XF-84H were reported as very good. Troubles with the engine and propeller finally led to the abandonment of the program. The second XF-84H was completed but not flown, and the third, with the afterburning engine, was never built; the Navy had lost interest in the project. The performance characteristics of the XF-84H have never been declassified, but it is reported to have been the fastest propeller-driven plane in the world, though it is not fair to compare a jet-augmented powerplant with a piston-driven unit.

The XF-84H had the same 33½ foot wingspan as the Thunderstreak, with 325 square feet of area. Length was 51 feet 6 inches and height was 15 feet 4 inches.

The turboprop Thunderstreak was used as an engine and propeller test bed. The wafer-thin blades could revolve at supersonic speed.
Republic

221

McDONNELL
XF-85 GOBLIN

The diminutive Goblin was literally wrapped around a jet engine.   McDonnell Douglas

One of the boldest departures from the usual Air Force fighter concept is represented by the diminutive McDonnell XF-85 parasite fighter. Parasite fighters were not new, the most famous of these being the Navy's squadron of Curtiss F9C Sparrowhawks carried in the Macon and Akron dirigibles. During the 1930's, the Russians had devised a method of carrying up to five parasite fighters on a TB-3 four-engine bomber, and actually used the system in combat on August 25, 1941. At this same time, preliminary planning which was to lead to the XF-85 was underway in the United States.

When the Air Force ordered the giant B-36 bomber in December 1941, it was faced with the necessity of providing a fighter escort for its 10,000 mile range. Rather than work on a heavy, multi-seat fighter, the development of a tiny single-seater was undertaken. Design responsibilities were assigned on October 9, 1945, to McDonnell. The company model number 27 was given the project before the official XF-85 designation was applied.

The original intent was to design the XF-85 for use with the B-29 Superfortress and B-35 Flying Wing as well as the B-36, but this idea was abandoned and only its ultimate use with the B-36 was considered. In June 1946, the mock-up was suspended from a dummy trapeze in a plywood B-36 fuselage and shown to Air Force officials. Nine months later, two XF-85's were ordered. The first of these was completed and sent to Moffett Field, California, for wind tunnel testing on January 8, 1948. While being hoisted into the tunnel, the prototype was damaged when the hook-latch slipped and the XF-85 dropped some 40 feet to the floor and suffered the first of several indignities to befall it during its relatively short life. While the first plane was being repaired, the second XF-85 successfully completed the wind tunnel tests. These tests indicated the need for increased vertical area, and both planes were modified before flight testing was undertaken.

The two XF-85's were only flown by one person, McDonnell test pilot Edwin F.

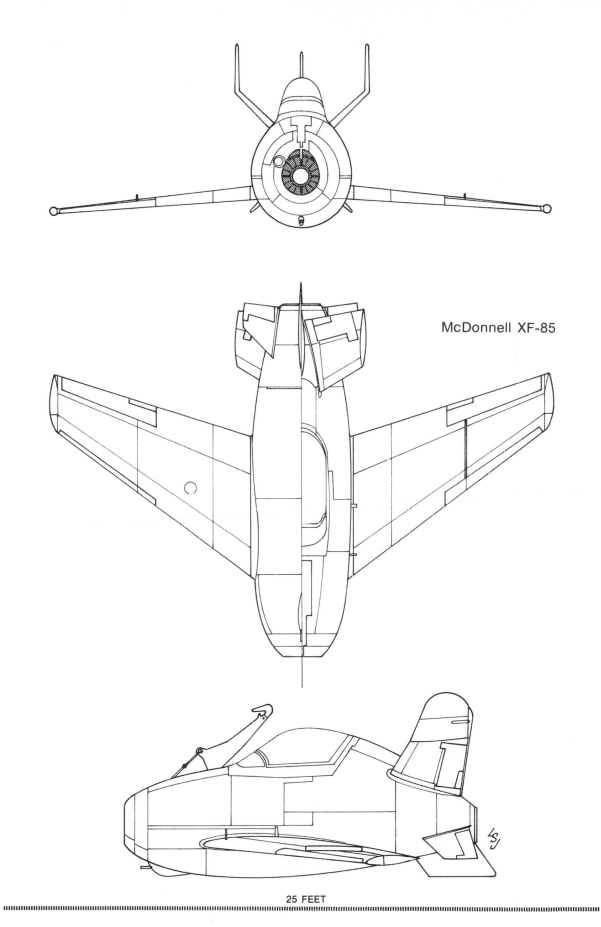

McDonnell XF-85

25 FEET

Schoch. The first "flight" of the XF-85 was made on July 22, 1948, while the tiny plane remained attached to the trapeze below an EB-29B mother ship, aptly named "Monstro." Flying at 20,000 feet over Muroc AFB, the XF-85 was lowered into the slip stream, the engine started and controls tested. Three more captive flights were made before the first actual, or free, flight was made on August 23, 1948. After being released at 20,000 feet, the XF-85 was put through a series of performance and handling tests which lasted for ten minutes. Returning to the mother ship, three attempts were made to engage the trapeze behind the churning propellers. On the third attempt, the trapeze bar smashed through the canopy and knocked the pilot's helmet off. A quick evaluation indicated the damage was minor and the pilot elected to make a belly landing on the desert below, a procedure that was to be common during the test program.

The second, third and fourth free flights concluded with successful airborne recoveries, but the following flights were all concluded in the dust of the California desert. After a total of 2 hours and 19 minutes of flight testing, the entire XF-85 program was terminated. By then, it had been determined that a great deal of pilot skill would be required for aerial recovery even under ideal conditions—circumstances seldom found in combat. The endurance of only thirty minutes severely limited the fighter's effectiveness, and the cost of refining the design to eliminate the numerous problems encountered made it impractical to proceed.

Aside from the parasite factor, the XF 85's performance was quite acceptable as a fighter. Chase pilots reported difficulty in staying with the XF-85 in turns. The test pilot himself was quite enthusiastic about the little fighter, indicating it was very maneuverable. No maximum speed runs were attempted since the recovery procedures had taken up most of the testing program, but the highest speed reached was 362 mph. Estimated maximum speed was 648 mph at sea level, 573 mph at 40,000 feet. Service ceiling was to be 48,200 feet.

The XF-85 Goblin had a wingspan of 21 feet 1½ inches, length 16 feet 3 inches, height 8 feet 3¼ inches. Wing area was 90 square feet. The wings could be folded to enable the XF-85 to fit into the B-36 bomb bay. Empty weight was 3,740 pounds, gross was 4,550 pounds. Fuel capacity was 201 gallons in two fuselage and two wing tanks. All this was literally wrapped around a Westinghouse J34-WE-22 engine of 3,000 lbs. thrust. An armament of four .50 cal. machine guns was proposed.

Information gained during testing of the XF-85 was applied to a similar project in which modified Republic RF-84's were carried in the bomb bay area of reconnaissance B-36's, the combination being called FICON for FIghter-CONveyor.

"It followed me home, can I keep it." The Goblin, taken aloft by mother ship "Monstro." McDonnell Douglas

NORTH AMERICAN
F-86A, E, F, H SABRE

The fuselage of the F-86H was widened to accommodate a larger engine. The dihedral was eliminated from the horizontal stabilizer on this model.   *North American (Rockwell)*

On November 27, 1946, North American flew its first jet fighter for the Navy. The pudgy, straight-winged carrier plane, called FJ-1 Fury, was ordered into production on May 18, 1945. At the same time, the Air Force ordered a similar plane for its use as the XP-86. Although the straight-winged mock-up was approved in June, the manufacturer suggested that the performance could be vastly improved by sweeping all flying surfaces back at an angle of 35 degrees. Documents obtained from the Germans following World War II indicated swept wings would delay compressibility and permit higher speeds without a tremendous increase in engine power. Swept wings had already been flown successfully by the Germans, and their research data was now in the hands of the American aircraft industry. On November 1, 1945, the revision was approved.

The first American swept-wing combat plane was flown from Muroc on October 1, 1947. On April 26, 1948, the new fighter went into a shallow dive and became the first American fighter to pass Mach 1. By this time, 33 production F-86A's were already under construction; and 188 F-86B's, redesigned with a wider fuselage and larger tires, had been ordered. The latter order was transferred to F-86A's when the development of high pressure tires eliminated the need to enlarge the fuselage.

A proposed F-86C was such a radical change that it was redesignated F-93.

Events which were to have a significant effect on the history of the F-86 were soon to take place in Korea as the production of the swift fighter was gaining momentum. The first fighter squadrons to receive the plane, now called Sabre, were becoming familiar with the F-86; and by June 1949, eighty-three planes had been delivered. By mid-1950, license-built Sabres were leaving production lines in Canada and the F-86E was under construction at North American when the North Korean invasion began. The importance of air supremacy was still fresh in American minds following World War II; and the first generation jets, so far advanced beyond the last wartime fighters, were quite capable of maintaining the advantage over the Russian types which had been encountered over Korea. But in November, the introduction of the Mig 15 radically changed the picture. Swooping down on the slower P-51's, F-80's and F-84's, the swept-winged Mig 15's quickly gained the tactical edge. On November 8, 1950, the Sabres were ordered into combat. Soon after their arrival, the balance of air power swung back in favor of the United Nations forces and remained to the end of the fighting. The F-86 achieved a kill-loss ratio of 14-to-1 and was the mount of all 39 Allied jet aces during the war.

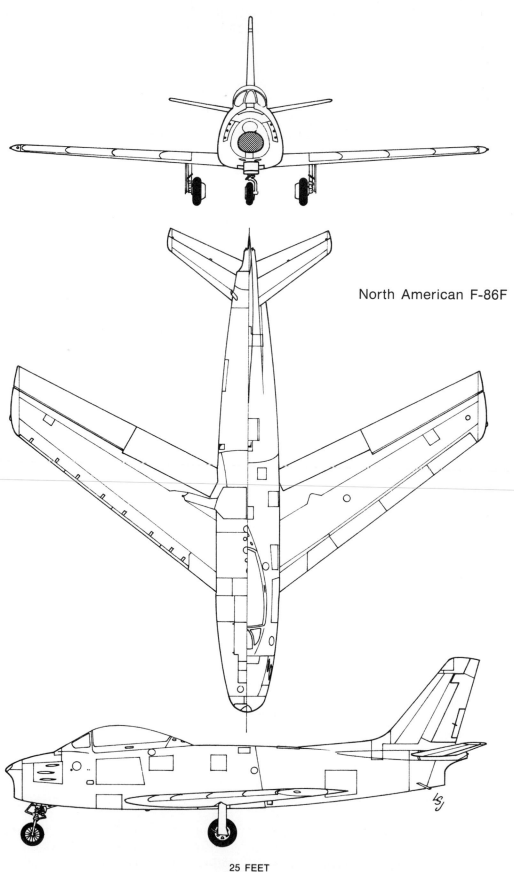

North American F-86F

25 FEET

Late model F-86H's, as shown by this example, carried four 20 mm cannons instead of six .50 cal. machine guns.
North American (Rockwell)

This F-86F was flown in Korea by astronaut John Glenn. Three Mig kill markings appear under the windshield.
North American (Rockwell)

F-86A's of the California Air National Guard.   *Calif. Air National Guard*

The first two F-86's were powered by a Chevrolet-built J35-C-3 engine of 3,750 lbs. thrust. Production F-86A's were propelled by General Electric J47-GE-1 engines with 4,850 lbs. of thrust. With the F-86E, a new all-flying tail was installed, in which the entire stabilizer moves with the elevator. Three hundred ninety-six of the "E's" were built. The next production version, the F-86F, used a new high altitude wing with a leading edge slat that extended forward 6 inches at the root and only 3 inches at the tip. Called the "6-3" wing, it eliminated the need for the vertical fences on the wing; and like the all-flying tail, was to be found on all later production Sabres. The "F" production amounted to 2,540 planes.

The next 473 Sabres displayed a noticeable configuration change to accept a 9,300 lb. thrust General Electric J73-GE-3 engine. Designated F-86H, its fuselage was deepened 14 inches to increase the volume of air for the engine, the wingspan was increased two feet, and dihedral was eliminated from the horizontal stabilizers. From the 117th F-86H on, the six .50 cal. nose guns used by the F-86 up to now were replaced by four 20 mm cannons. With the larger engine, the F-86H had a maximum speed of 692 mph—17 mph faster than the F-86A.

The F-86F is representative of the series. It has a wingspan of 37 feet 1 inch, length of 37 feet 6 inches and stands 14 feet 8 inches high. Wing area is 288 square feet. It has an empty weight of 10,950 pounds with a maximum gross of 17,000 pounds. Fuel capacity is 476 gallons plus 400 gallons in drop tanks. Range without tanks is 785 miles, tanks extending this distance to over 1,200 miles.

The 5,970 lb. thrust J47-GE-27 provides the F-86F with a speed of 690 mph at sea level and 610 mph at 35,000 feet. Service ceiling is 50,000 feet. Armament consists of six .50 cal. machine guns beside the pilot, plus two 1,000 lb. bombs or sixteen 5 inch rockets under the wings.

The F-86K was similar to the "D" with the exception of the rocket armament which was replaced with four cannons.   *North American (Rockwell)*

Progressive development of the F-86 led to the introduction of the radar-guided, rocket armed F-86D or "Dog Sabre." This model differed in so many respects from the original F-86 that it was given the designation YF-95A, but was ultimately reclassified as F-86D.

For its role as an all-weather fighter, the F-86D carries an APS-6 radar set in a prominent nose above the air intake. The fuselage was widened and the General Electric J47-GE-17 engine is provided with an afterburner which delivers 7,650 lbs. of thrust and a top speed of 707 mph at sea level. During its test phase, the F-86D set two world's speed records over a three kilometer course flying 698.505 mph on November 19, 1952 and 715.697 mph on July 16, 1953, making it the first American plane to break its own speed record.

The all-missile armament carried by the F-86D is mounted in a retractable tray in the fuselage just behind the nose wheel well. When the rockets are fired, the tray drops below the fuselage and up to twenty-four 2.75 inch Folding Fin Aircraft Rockets (FFAR) can be fired. These rockets are 48 inches long, weigh 18 pounds, and one hit is sufficient to knock down a plane. The ac-

tion of the launching tray is instantaneous; the tray is extended only long enough to allow the missiles to clear.

The first of 2,504 F-86D's was delivered to the Air Force in March 1951. The designation F-86G was temporarily assigned to a J47-GE-33-powered version, but the 406 "G's" were redesignated F-86D-20. In 1956, nine hundred eighty-one Dog Sabres were given F-86H wings and new electronic gear to create F-86L's.

The F-86D has a span of 37 feet 1 inch ("L's" have a 39 foot 1 inch span). Length is 40 feet 4 inches and height is 15 feet. Wing area is 228 sq. feet (313 sq. feet on the "L"). Empty weight is 12,470 pounds, gross is 17,-100 pounds. The F-86D cruises at 525 mph and has a service ceiling of 54,600 feet. Initial rate of climb is 17,800 fpm. Internal fuel capacity is 608 gallons.

A further alteration to the line produced the F-86K, armed with four 20 mm cannons instead of the rockets. The F-86K is two feet longer than the other two versions of the series. Power for the F-86K comes from an afterburning J47-GE-33. This model was assembled by both North American and Fiat, in Italy, for NATO forces in Europe.

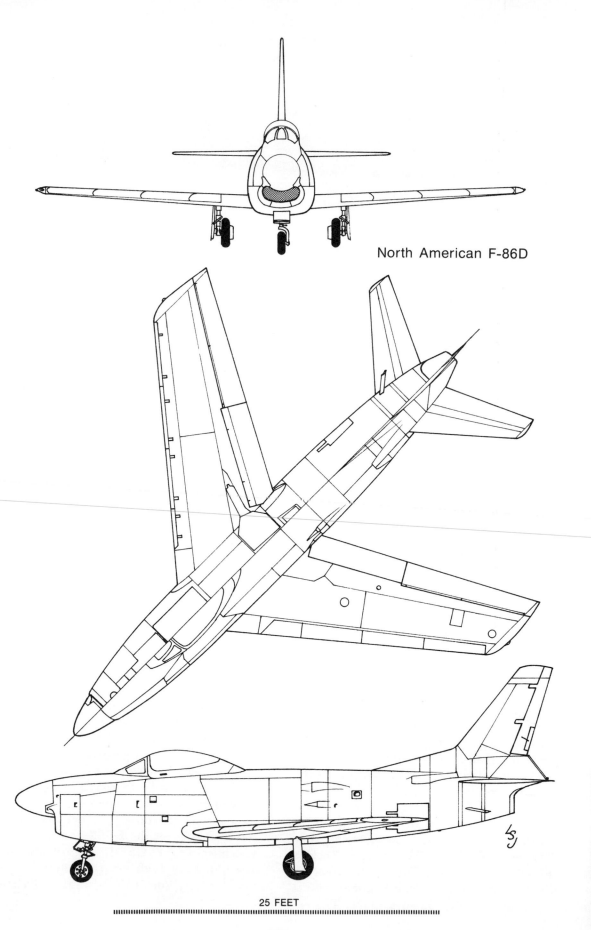

North American F-86D

25 FEET

This F-86D was used to test underwing rocket pods.   North American (Rockwell)

A "Dog Sabre" launches a salvo of Mighty Mouse rockets. This was a test plane and camera windows are visible on the fuselage and wing.
North American (Rockwell)

CURTISS
XF-87 BLACKHAWK

Despite its size, the Blackhawk still looked like a fighter.   *Air Force Museum*

The last airplane to bear the name Curtiss was conceived in 1945 as an answer to an Air Force specification for a jet fighter able to operate under all weather conditions. In its original form, the proposed Curtiss fighter was a single-place, twin jet design with an estimated weight of 32,000 pounds. This layout was rejected by the Air Force in March 1945, because the engines of the day could not deliver the required performance. Here Curtiss' failure to keep pace with fighter development in the jet age was to present a severe drawback in their all-weather fighter project. While other airframe manufacturers were well into high performance jet types, Curtiss was stepping into an area in which it had no experience and was fettered by an ailing management. Despite the rejection of the fighter, Curtiss was authorized to proceed with a similar design for an attack plane, the XA-43.

On November 21, 1945, Curtiss received notice to transfer the XA-43 funds and efforts into the construction of a pair of two-place, four engine all-weather fighters. In keeping with the tradition of naming their aircraft "Hawk," it was natural that the name "Blackhawk" be chosen, although the name "Bat" had been considered. Officially designated XF-87, the big plane was beset with difficulties from the beginning. The major problem was, obviously, weight. The automatic fire control system alone accounted for more than ten percent of the entire aircraft weight. The four Westinghouse J34-WE-7 engines were intended to run on gasoline which, though lighter than regular jet-grade kerosene, required a much greater storage area. There wasn't enough room in the aircraft to house the fuel needed for the specified range. This problem was finally resolved, but the 3,000 lb. thrust Westinghouse engines proved to be a poor choice of powerplant.

The mock-up was inspected on May 14, 1946; several of its features were noteworthy. Most unusual was the revolving nose with swivelling guns allowing the four 20 mm cannons to fire in a 60 degree arc around the nose. The guns could be angled from zero to 90 degrees from the centerline. Development of the turret was assigned to the Glenn L. Martin Co. Another feature was the side-by-side seating arrangement for the two crewmen. This increased the fuselage width adding to frontal area, but it also allowed installation of a huge fuselage fuel tank without further drag concessions.

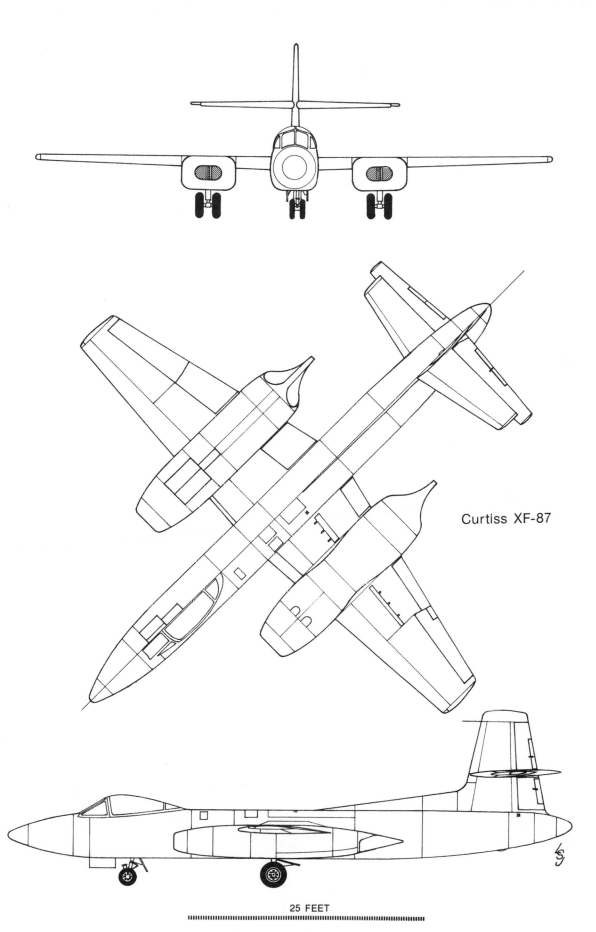

Curtiss XF-87

25 FEET

The XF-87, #46-522, began preliminary taxi tests at the Curtiss plant in Columbus, Ohio, in October 1947, before it was disassembled and trucked to Muroc for flight testing. Damage during the trip and early taxi tests delayed the first flight until March 1, 1948. The first flight was generally satisfactory, although the main gear doors did not close, and at speeds above 220 mph the plane began to buffet. General flight characteristics were good in spite of the buffeting.

On June 10, 1948, Curtiss received a contract for 88 production F-87A's to be powered by two General Electric J47 engines of 6,000 lbs. thrust, and for awhile it appeared that the Curtiss name would once again grace a combat plane. At one point, thirty reconnaissance models of the F-87 were placed on contract. These were designated FP-87A, RP-87A or RF-87C, depending on the date of the document concerned.

Any enthusiasm generated by the new contracts was soon dispelled as continuing troubles plagued the test program. The most serious of these, the buffeting, was never fully solved. Finally, on October 18, 1948, the ax fell on the last Curtiss aircraft program to permit use of the funds for other, more successful, types entering production.

The Martin nose turret was not installed on the prototype XF-87, and even that facet of the program was scrapped as missile armament was proving its effectiveness. The second XF-87 was never completed, although it was to use two General Electric J47's.

The Blackhawk's wing spanned 60 feet, overall fuselage length was 62 feet, height was 20 feet 4 inches. Wing area was 600 square feet, but production models were to use a 740 square foot surface. Empty weight was 25,930 pounds with a gross of 37,350 pounds. Fuel capacity was 2,600 gallons which would have given the XF-87 a 1,000 mile range at 450 mph. Top speed was 600 mph at sea level and service ceiling was 41,000 feet.

The size of the Blackhawk is apparent by the two figures in the foreground.   Gordon S. Williams

McDONNELL
XF-88 VOODOO

After the Voodoo test program was revised, the first airframe was fitted out as a turbo-prop test bed.

McDonnell Douglas

In mid-1946, the Air Force, still seeking a long-ranging escort for its bomber fleet, ordered two versions of a new class of combat planes called "penetration fighters." Contracts were issued to McDonnell for two XF-88's and to Lockheed for two XF-90's. Both were generally similar in appearance.

The XF-88 was designed around two 3,-000 lb. thrust Westinghouse J34-WE-13 engines housed amidship in the fuselage—a configuration which was to become a McDonnell trade mark. The penetration fighter concept represented no great technical advance in the state of the art. It was simply the necessity of providing the Air Force with fighter protection for its new superbombers deep in enemy territory. As a result, the XF-88 was an uncomplicated design, its most notable feature being its great size for a single-seat fighter. The size, of course, was due to the need for great quantities of fuel for its escort duties over distances of 1,500 to 1,700 miles.

The original XF-88 was rolled-out on October 20, 1948, and flown nine days later. Soon after, the second Voodoo joined the program; but with the limited amount of power to be obtained from the Westinghouse engines, the maximum speed attained was 641 mph. In order to explore the Voodoo's potential more thoroughly, the second plane was returned to the manufacturer for installation of afterburning J34-WE-15 engines of 3,600 lbs. of thrust. With afterburners, it became the XF-88A. Performance was improved to the point that 700 mph was exceeded with the new engines, but this was not enough to merit further investment in the design; and by the middle of 1950, with 210 total hours, the program was concluded. Both planes were placed in storage.

Now again, the Korean War enters the picture. Republic F-84 Thunderjets, used for escorting B-29's in raids on North Korean targets, were being pushed to their limits. They did not have the range or speed for such duties. In February 1952, the XF-88A was restored to flight status and a new development program was undertaken. The results of the new evaluation culminated in the creation of an entirely new long-range fighter based on the XF-88 design, the F-101 Voodoo.

While the XF-88A was undergoing further testing, the original XF-88

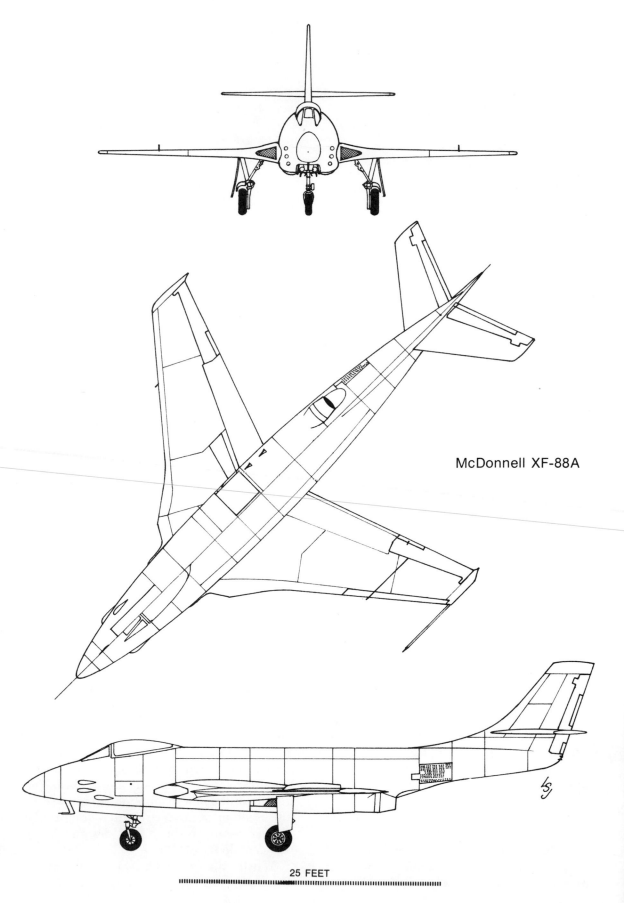

McDonnell XF-88A

25 FEET

prototype was also getting some attention. A visit to the McDonnell factory led to the installation of afterburning engines, added an Allison XT-38A turbo-prop engine to the nose, and changed the designation to XF-88B. On April 14, 1953, the tri-motored Voodoo was first flown. While the information obtained from the composite powerplant was of some value, it also proved again that the turbo-prop/jet combination was not practical for such aircraft. Both XF-88's were permanently retired and eventually scrapped.

The XF-88's had a wingspan of 39 feet 8 inches, a length of 54 feet 2 inches and a height of 17 feet 3 inches. The wing was swept-back 35 degrees and had an area of 350 square feet. Empty, the airframes weighed 12,140 pounds; loaded, 18,500 pounds. A fuel capacity of 734 internal gallons could be supplemented by two 350 gallon tip tanks to give a range of 1,737 miles. Service ceiling was 36,000 feet. Armament was to consist of six 20 mm cannons mounted in the nose.

McDonnell's XF-88, the first of a new class of penetration fighters.   McDonnell Douglas

NORTHROP
F-89 SCORPION

The XF-89, first of the Scorpions. Tip tanks were removable on this plane but were permanent on production models.   *Northrop*

The first successful all-weather fighter to be designed specifically for the role was Northrop's F-89. Outlined in a proposal made to the Air Force in December 1945, a development contract was approved in May 1946. The mock-up passed inspection in September, and the first of two prototypes flew on August 16, 1948. The XF-89 carried jettisonable wingtip tanks, but production models had permanent tanks mounted to the tips. The bulbous nose of the prototype was also subject to change on the production planes. The original intent had been to install a Martin nose turret of the type to be used in the Curtiss XF-87, but this was abandoned and conventional nose armament was mounted. Although large, the fuselage was relatively slim, this due to the tandem placement of the crew members. An upswept tail led to the name "Scorpion."

During flight testing, the ailerons on the XF-89 were replaced by a combination aileron/speed brake of the type used on the Flying Wings. Working conventionally as ailerons, the new controls divided top and bottom when used as speed brakes. Called "decelerons" by Northrop, they became standard equipment on all production Scorpions.

Production of the F-89A was approved on July 14, 1949, and 18 of this model were completed before an improved F-89B replaced them on the line. This model differed mainly in internal gear. Both the "A" and "B" models originally carried external balances on the elevators to dampen a high-frequency vibration. They were eliminated by development of an internal balance system. Thirty F-89B's were delivered before the first of 164 "C" types entered production. The first three production models carried six 20 mm cannons in the nose with the radar gear.

In 1951, an F-89B was redesignated YF-89D and flown with two wingtip pods, each carrying 52 Mighty Mouse rockets plus fuel. Production F-89D's carried these rocket/fuel pods instead of the cannon armament. Six hundred eighty-two of these were built. Additional underwing tanks on the "D" increased its fuel capacity and range.

With each model change, there was an accompanying uprating of the engines. The first Scorpion flew with two 4,000 lb. thrust Allison J35-A-15 engines. The F-89D was propelled by a pair of afterburning J35-A-33A's or -41's with 7,200 lbs. maximum thrust. The single YF-89E was an engine test bed.

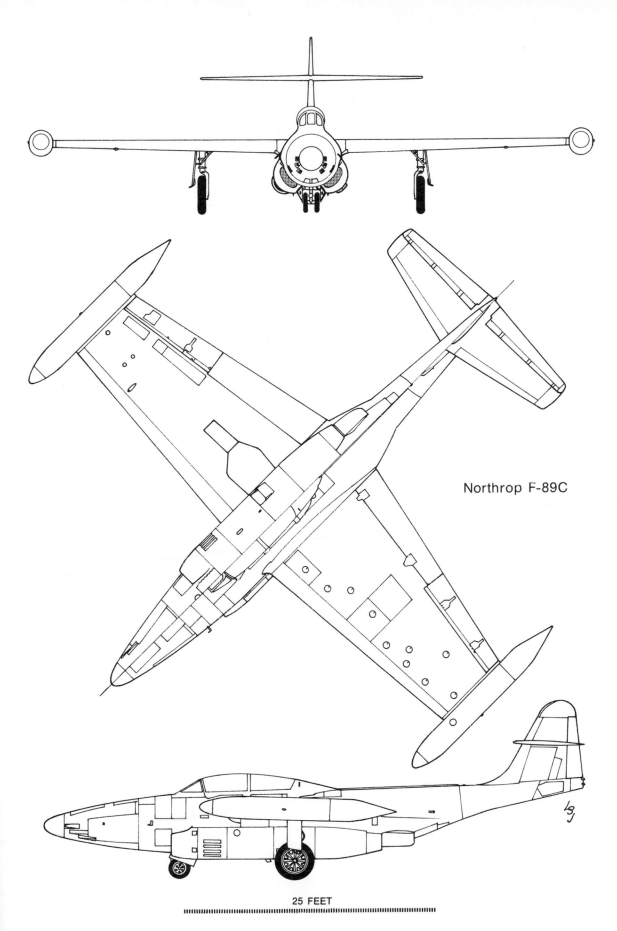

Northrop F-89C

25 FEET

The final production Scorpion was the F-89H with tip pods constructed to carry three Hughes Falcon missiles and 21 Mighty Mouse FFAR rockets. An additional six FFAR's could be mounted beneath the wings. Two J35-A-35's provided the driving force for this model. Modifications to permit launching of Douglas MB-1 Genie missiles changed the designation of 350 "D's" to F-89J's.

The design of the F-89F was a major departure from the Scorpion configuration. Although it reached the mock-up stage, technical problems involving the use of nuclear weapons led to its cancellation.

Huge tanks were mounted at the midspan of the wing, these housing the main units of the landing gear, fuel and missiles. The fuselage was faired straight back from the front cockpit and a one-piece stabilizer was attached to the fuselage.

The F-89H has a span of 59 feet 8 inches and a wing area of 650 square feet with tip pods. Overall length is 53 feet 10 inches, height is 17 feet 7 inches. Empty weight is 25,194 pounds and gross weight is 42,241 pounds. The F-89H has a maximum speed of 636 mph at 10,600 feet. Range is 1,300 miles. Service ceiling of the F-89H is 49,200 feet.

The F-89J was armed with two Genie MB-1 nuclear tipped AAM's.   *Northrop*

The proposed F-89F Scorpion. This plane reached the mock-up stage but was cancelled before development was completed.

The Lockheed F-90 penetration fighter. *Lockheed*

Developed in parallel with McDonnell's XF-88, the Lockheed XF-90 was slightly larger and mounted its two Westinghouse J34-WE-11 engines in the tail. Otherwise, the concepts of the two planes were quite similar.

The first XF-90, with Lockheed test pilot Tony LeVier at the controls, made its maiden flight on June 6, 1949. The two Westinghouse engines provided a total of 6,200 lbs. of thrust for the 27,200 pound fighter. Obviously underpowered, the second XF-90 had short afterburners fitted to its J34-WE-15 engines. (One of these small afterburners had been installed on an F-80 Shooting Star for evaluation, creating an unusual one-of-a-kind model.)

The afterburners of the second XF-90 increased the total power to 8,000 lbs. of thrust; but the highest speed achieved was 665 mph, though Mach 1 could be attained in a dive.

For its planned role of long-range bomber escort, the XF-90 was designed to carry 1,665 gallons internally and in jettisonable wingtip tanks. Ports for six 20 mm cannons peered from beneath the engine air intakes, but the armament was not installed on either plane. Again, the requirement for great quantities of fuel dic-

tated massive proportions of the Lockheed fighter, but despite its relatively large size, the XF-90 presented a trim, almost futuristic, appearance. The horizontal stabilizer, mounted on the vertical fin, was adjustable to vary the incidence. To achieve this, the entire vertical surface could be tilted fore and aft. This unusual feature was later to find its way onto Lockheed's JetStar executive transport.

The comparative tests between the XF-90 and XF-88 were concluded in June 1950, with a production order for one of the designs anticipated. The eruption of the Korean War turned the Air Force's attention to planes already in production and neither plane was ordered, although the Air Force was later to return to the long-range fighter program as a direct result of the war.

Dimensions of the XF-90 were: wingspan—40 feet; length—56 feet 2 inches; height—15 feet 9 inches; wing area—345 square feet. Empty and gross weights were 18,520 pounds and 27,200 pounds. With the 4,000 lb. thrust afterburning engines, the XF-90 reached 665 mph in level flight at 1,000 feet and cruised at 473 mph. Range was over 2,300 miles and its service ceiling was 39,000 feet.

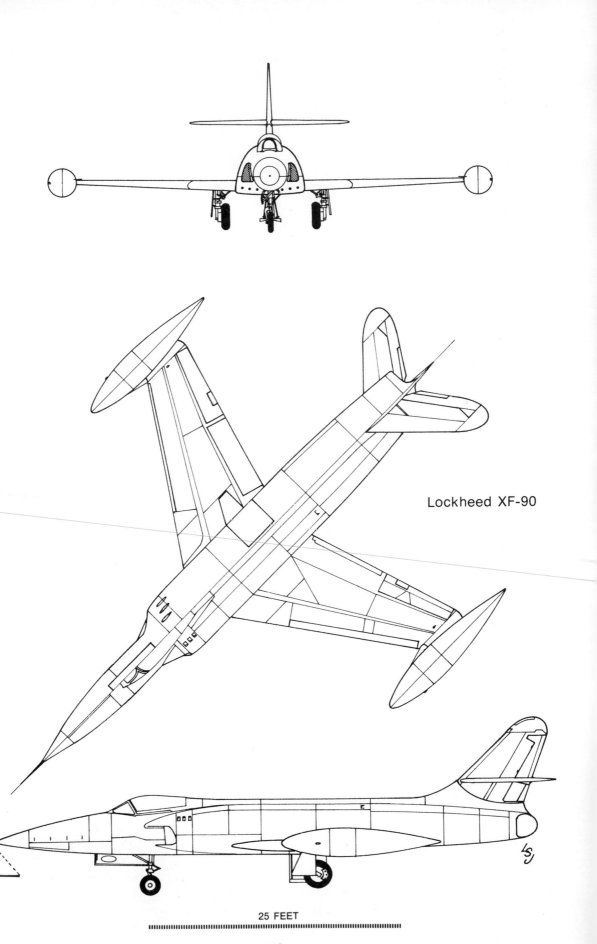

Lockheed XF-90

25 FEET

REPUBLIC
XF-91 THUNDERCEPTOR

The Thunderceptor's four rocket motors were housed in the fairings in the empennage. *Republic*

Rocket engines as an aircraft power source had long intrigued aircraft engineers. The German Me 163 Komet had come close to success, but its 10 minute duration severely restricted its use for anything more than a limited-area defender, as the Komet had been. Nevertheless, the thought of a tremendous spurt of power to drive a fighter beyond Mach 1 still drew the attention of aircraft designers. Jet engines were gradually reaching the point where supersonic speeds could be sustained. In 1946, however, when the Republic XF-91 was being developed, the most powerful jets were in the 7,000 lb. thrust class, this with afterburning.

The prescribed role for the XF-91 was daytime interceptor. This necessitated a rapid acceleration and climb capability which could readily be provided by a rocket motor. Therefore, the two XF-91 Thunderceptors were fitted with four Reaction Motors XLR11-RM-9 rocket motors of 1,500 lbs. of thrust each to supplement the primary General Electric J47-GE-3 of 5,200 lbs. thrust with an afterburner. The rockets were mounted in pairs above and below the jet.

The rocket boosters were not the most unusual feature of the XF-91. The 35 degree swept-wing could be adjusted to vary the incidence to the most effective angle for take-off, landing or cruise. But most novel was the inverse-taper configuration in which the thickest and widest portion of the wing was at the tip instead of next to the fuselage. This provided greater lift outboard and, with leading-edge slats, reduced the tendency of the wingtip to stall at low speeds. Since the wing was too thin inboard to receive the main landing gear, these units were retracted outward to fit into the thickened tips.

On May 9, 1949, XF-91 number one, S.N. 46-680, was flown on the power of the jet alone. After five months of testing, the afterburner and four rocket motors were installed for evaluation of the fighter's high-speed characteristics. In December 1952, the big interceptor was pushed beyond Mach 1 by the 11,200 lbs. of combined thrust from its jet/rocket engines. Although the XF-91's were intended to serve as prototypes for production fighters, no order was placed and the two airframes were subject to continuing testing. The original plane, which

243

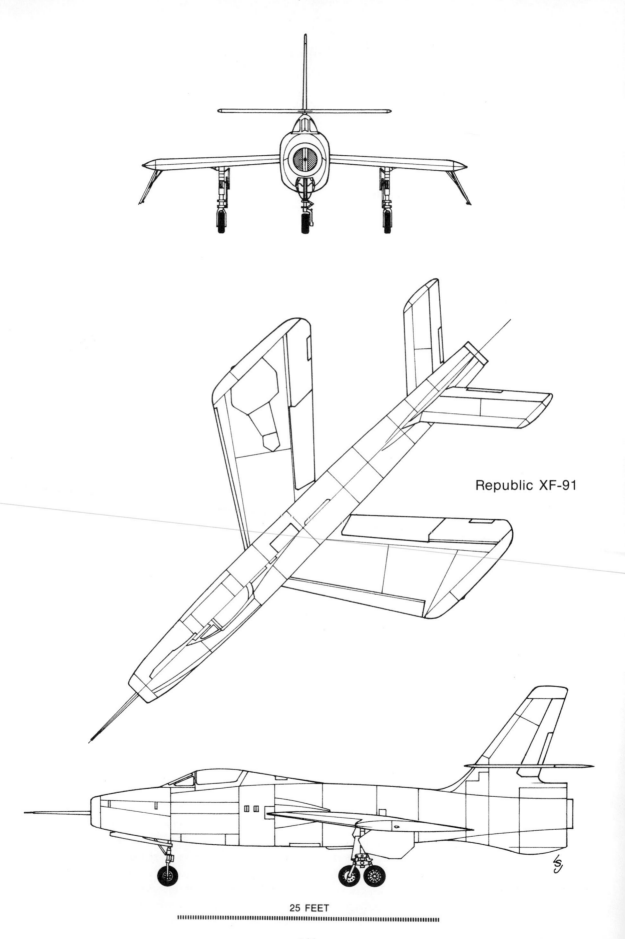

Republic XF-91

25 FEET

Variable incidence wing and outward retracting landing gear were features of the Thunderceptor.   Republic

Using its rocket boosters, the XF-91 was capable of exceeding Mach 1 in level flight.   Republic

245

now forms a part of the Air Force Museum collection, was fitted with a radar nose cone giving the plane an appearance similar to the F-86D "Dog Sabre." The second XF-91 ended its career with a "butterfly" Vee-type empennage before its destruction as a "victim" in a simulated crash-rescue operation.

The two XF-91 Thunderceptors had wingspans of 31 feet 3 inches, lengths of 43 feet 3 inches and stood 18 feet 8 inches high. Wing area was 320 square feet. Empty weight was 15,853 pounds, gross was 23,807 pounds; maximum take-off weight was 27,329 pounds. Fuel capacity was 1,440 gallons with two huge underwing tanks. With afterburner and rocket power, the XF-91 reached 1,126 mph at 50,000 feet. This altitude could be reached in 5½ minutes. Cruising speed was 539 mph for a range of 1,171 miles. No armament was installed in either plane.

This view shows the XF-91's inverse tapered wing in which the tip is thicker than the root.   Republic

The XF-92A design was based on German delta-winged research material.   Convair

During World War II, German aviation technology surpassed that of nearly every other nation. One of their most noted designers was Dr. Alexander Lippisch, who had done considerable research into radical wing shapes for supersonic aircraft. Among these was the triangular, or delta, wing. Several German designs utilizing the delta wing had been proposed, but no aircraft had actually been flown with the wing.

Dr. Lippisch's data had been obtained by the U. S. Air Force, and in cooperation with the doctor himself, Convair undertook the design of the first delta-winged aircraft. Again hindered by relatively low-thrust engines, it was decided to use a Westinghouse J30 of 1,560 lbs. thrust plus six 2,000 lb. thrust nitro-methane rockets for a total push exceeding 13,000 lbs.! Enough fuel was to be provided to allow five minutes of combat and ten minutes of cruise. This operational time-table represented only a slight advancement beyond that of the Me 163 Komet of World War II; but the delta fighter was to reach a speed of 825 mph at 50,000 feet—275 mph faster than the German rocket. Given the

Air Force designation XF-92, the Convair fighter was to be armed with four cannons, have a semi-delta wing and a butterfly tail.

To test the radical new wing design, Convair built a flying mock-up using parts from five other aircraft to reduce construction time. Officially labeled Convair Model 7002, the craft was powered by a 4,600 lb. thrust Allison J33-A-23 engine. By injecting water and methanol into the fuel, the thrust level could be increased to 5,400 lbs. No provision was made for any armament or military equipment.

The first flight of a delta-winged aircraft took place on June 8, 1948, when the Convair test pilot gingerly nudged the Model 7002 into the air. The plane immediately proved stable and a full scale testing program was begun. On June 9, 1949, development of the XF-92 rocket was terminated and the Air Force purchased the test vehicle, giving it the designation XF-92A.

The delta wing had a leading-edge sweep of 60 degrees. Only three control surfaces were required, a conventional rudder and combination elevator/ailerons, or elevons.

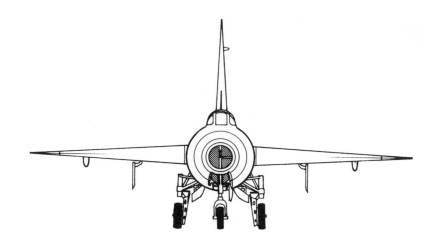

Convair XF-92A

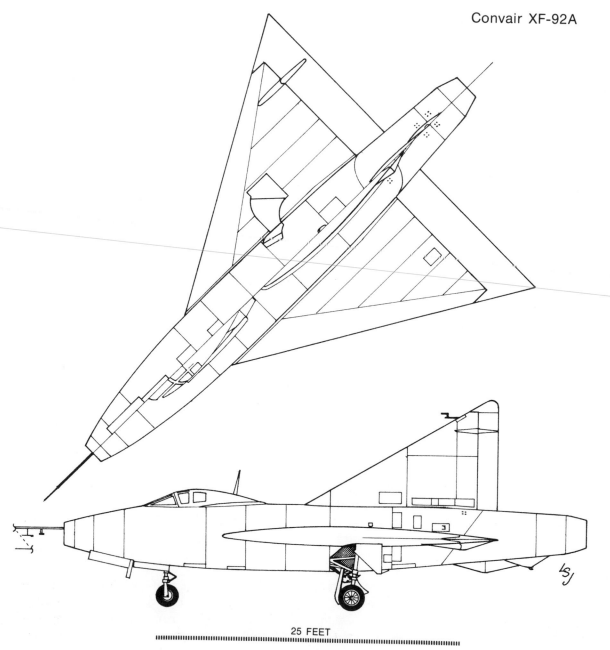

25 FEET

Before the tests were completed, the little delta received an afterburning Allison J33-A-29 providing a maximum of 7,500 lbs. thrust. With this, the XF-92A could reach Mach .95 or 630 mph, above 45,000 feet. The plane was not capable of supersonic flight.

The XF-92A's 230 square foot delta wing spanned 31 feet 3 inches. Length, with the afterburner extension, was 42 feet 5 inches and height was 17 feet 8 inches. Empty weight was 8,500 pounds and gross, with 295 gallons of fuel, was over 15,000 pounds.

To speed the construction of the radical delta-winged fighter, the XF-92A was built using parts from five existing airplanes.   *Convair*

During flight tests, cotton tufts were taped to the wing and photographed to show air flow patterns. Convair

The air intakes of the first prototype YF-93 were modified, as shown here. The second plane was built with these more conventional inlets.   North American (Rockwell)

With production of the F-86 Sabre well under way, North American began studies to expand the potential of their swept-wing fighter. Work was begun on the F-86C as an offering for the competition that was to lead to the XF-88 and XF-90. In the intended penetration role, the F-86C would require an increased fuel capacity and room for electronic gear. The nose intake duct was replaced by two flush, side-mounted NACA-type scoops, thus providing a spacious nose for the necessary black boxes. The general proportions of the fuselage were increased to accommodate a 6,250 lb. thrust Pratt & Whitney J48-P-1 with after-burner and a large amount of fuel. Since the weight, too, had increased, dual wheels were attached to the main landing gear struts. Although still basically a Sabre, the plane had been changed so extensively that the Air Force redesignated the design YF-93A; and on June 9, 1948, placed an order for 118 of the new planes.

Two YF-93A prototypes were constructed, and on January 25, 1950, the first of these was flown. However, as developments in the field of fighter re-

quirements had changed while the planes were being assembled, the production contract had already been withdrawn. The novel flush intakes proved of interest to designers, and the YF-93A found itself used as a research tool in the evaluation of inlet ducting.

The second YF-93A was completed with more conventional lateral intakes and joined its sister in the test program. Both planes were acquired by the National Advisory Committee on Aeronautics (NACA) where they served as test vehicles until their retirement and eventual scrapping.

The YF-93's used the basic Sabre wing with the span increased 1 foot 8 inches to total 38 feet 9 inches. Wing area was 306 square feet. The fuselage of the flush-scoop YF-93 was carefully contoured to reduce frontal area and, therefore, drag. The fuselage sides above the wing were slightly concave, giving it a slim-waisted appearance—a shape which was eventually to become a standard form on high-performance aircraft. Overall fuselage length, plus the swept-back vertical tail, was 44 feet 1 inch. The tip of the fin was 15 feet

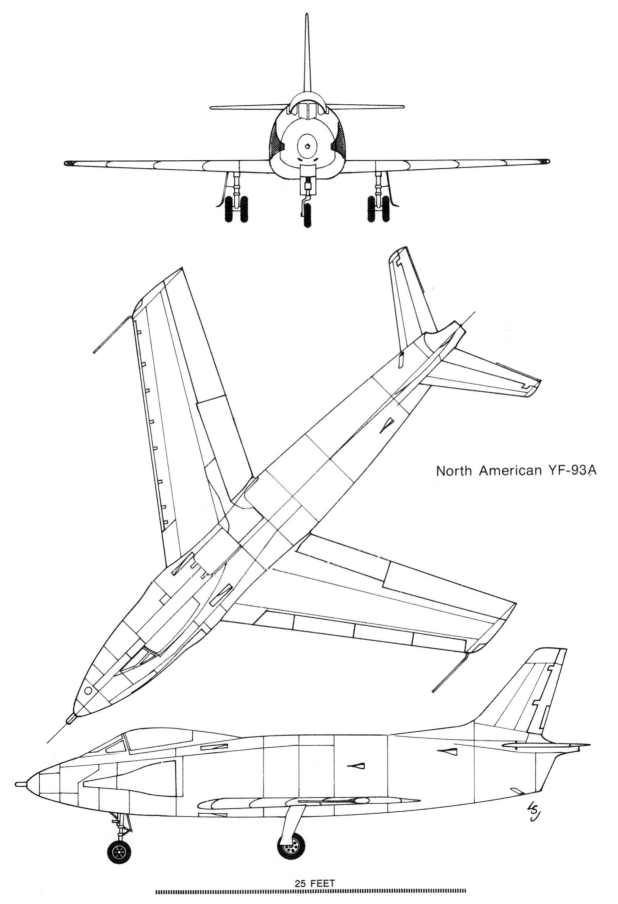

North American YF-93A

25 FEET

8 inches above the ground when the plane was static. The afterburner increased the thrust from 6,250 lbs. to 8,750 lbs.; and with this power, the YF-93's could reach 708 mph at sea level and 622 mph at 35,000 feet. The empty weight was 14,035 pounds, and with a full load of 1,581 gallons of fuel, the maximum gross weight climbed to 26,-516 pounds. Normal gross was 21,610 pounds. With this fuel, range was 1,967 miles. Service ceiling was 46,800 feet. Initial climb rate, with afterburning, was 11,960 fpm.

Flush air inlets were a distinctive feature of the YF-93.   North American (Rockwell)

Begun as the F-86C, this plane developed into an entirely new design and became the YF-93.
North American (Rockwell)

LOCKHEED
F-94A & B STARFIRE

The F-94A Starfire was adapted from the T-33 by the addition of radar and an afterburner.   *Lockheed*

When deliveries of the F-94A began in June 1950, the Lockheed Starfire became the first jet-powered all-weather fighter to enter service with the U. S. Air Force. The Starfire was virtually an off-the-shelf fighter, sharing wing, landing gear and tail surfaces with the F-80 Shooting Star. In fact, the prototype for the Starfire series had actually been built as an F-80 which had become the TF-80C, first of the famous T-33 trainers. Lockheed engineers revised the contours of the trainer's nose to accept radar. In this form, the YF-94 (#48-356) was first flown on April 16, 1949.

Incorporation of an afterburner on production F-94A's gave the interceptor another first; no other operational Air Force plane had used the speed-boosting device. The Allison J33-A-33 engine normally produced 4,600 lbs. of thrust; but by dumping raw fuel into the afterburning chamber, the thrust was increased to 6,000 lbs. With this power, the F-94A was capable of short bursts of speed to 606 mph or a rapid climb of 11,274 feet in a minute. The first purchase of F-94A's amounted to 110 machines.

In the first months of 1951, an improved Starfire began arriving at Air Force bases. The F-94B had large 350 gallon fuel tanks mounted on the ends of the wings, differing from the underslung tip tanks used by the F-94A. New hydraulics and electronics were less apparent to the observer, but were among the improvements in the plane. A total of 357 F-94B's were delivered to operational units.

The radar operator sat in the rear cockpit of the F-94, guiding the pilot to the target. Once located, it became the pilot's duty to deal with the intruder by means of four .50 cal. M-3 machine guns firing from beneath the radome.

The F-94B Starfire had a wingspan of 38 feet 11 inches, not including the tanks. Wing area was 238 square feet. Length was 40 feet 1 inch, height was 12 feet 8 inches. Empty and gross weights of the Starfire were 9,557 pounds and 12,919 pounds. With a fuel capacity of 648 gallons, the F-94B had a range of 1,079 miles.

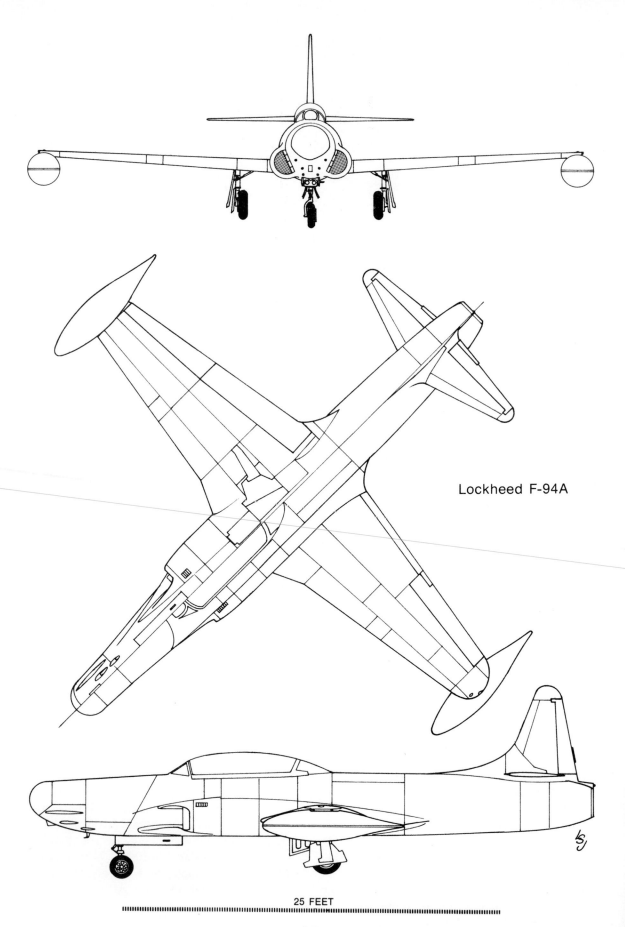

Lockheed F-94A

25 FEET

The F-94B was credited with several night interceptions during the Korean War.   *Lockheed*

Lockheed's F-94B differed from the "A" by using large tip-mounted drop tanks and improved electronic and hydraulic systems.
Lockheed

LOCKHEED
F-94C, YF-97A STARFIRE

Tony LeVier (left) and technician inspect the YF-97A prior to flight testing. Lockheed

While the conversion of the Shooting Star into a two-place night fighter was generally successful, the designers proceeded to refine the fighter to achieve more efficiency. Internal fuel capacity was restricted by the addition of the radar operator. This trade-off exacted an even greater range penalty when the fuel-gulping afterburner was required for increased speed. The F-94A's high wing loading, due to its greater weight on the unmodified F-80 wing, was responsible for poor high-altitude performance. If the Starfire was to keep abreast of its competitors, an extensive redesign was in order.

To improve the performance of the Starfire, a more powerful Pratt & Whitney J48-P-5 engine offering 6,250 lbs. of thrust was selected. Coupled with an afterburner, up to 8,300 lbs. could be obtained. A thinner wing of greater area was designed and the new model was designated F-94B. Further changes, including a swept horizontal stabilizer to raise the limiting Mach number to 0.85 and a parachute drag brake, compelled the Air Force to reclass the design as the YF-97A. The F-94B designation was assigned to the less-modified second production batch. Initially, the YF-97A retained the radar and cannon nose con-

figuration of the earlier F-94's; but after flight testing had begun, it was subjected to further alterations. While the radome remained in the extreme nose, the cannons were removed and a ring of twenty-four rocket tubes was installed. A production order for 108 F-97A's was placed; and two months later, the new Starfire was again redesignated, becoming the F-94C. Further orders brought the total number of F-94C's to 387 planes.

The first F-94C's mounted a hemispherical radome, but this was replaced by a more streamlined conical dome as production increased. The all-missile armament was another first for the Starfire. The tubes were grouped behind four retracting doors which snapped open to permit firing of the Mighty Mouse FFAR's. Twenty-four more FFAR's could be carried in pods attached to the leading edge of the wing. A frangible plastic dome streamlined the pods until they were fired. The DF-94C was adapted to fire Hughes GAR-1 homing missiles.

The F-94C proportions were larger than the other two Starfire types. Wingspan over the Fletcher-built tip tanks was 42 feet 5 inches, the enlarged fuselage was 44 feet 6 in-

256

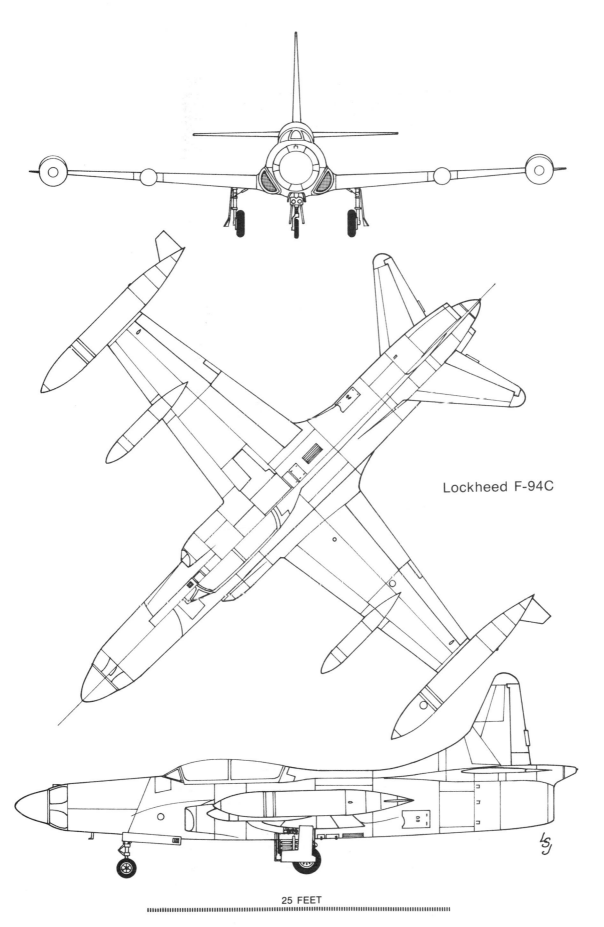

Lockheed F-94C

25 FEET

ches long, and the plane stood 14 feet 11 inches high. Wing area was 338 square feet. The F-94C weighed up to 27,000 pounds fully loaded. The Pratt & Whitney engine provided enough push to reach a maximum speed of 646 mph at sea level and 585 mph at 35,000 feet. Normal range was 1,200 miles, service ceiling was 55,000 feet.

A single-seat F-94D was built as a close-support fighter, and 112 copies were ordered on May 1, 1951; but the contract was withdrawn after the single example was evaluated.

The F-94C was the first American fighter to be armed entirely with missiles. Here, rockets belch from a Starfire's supplementary wing pods.   *Lockheed*

An early production F-94C with the round radome.   *Lockheed*

HUGHES
F-98 FALCON (GAR-1)

Hughes GAR-1 and -2 missiles being launched from an F-102.   *Hughes*

Two pilotless interceptors received fighter designations, the first of these being the Hughes Falcon, originally ordered as the F-98.

Development of the Falcon began in 1947 under the name Project Dragonfly, and the first example was ready for testing two years later. It weighed 120 pounds, was six-and-a-half feet long, and was powered by a solid propellant rocket motor. The explosive warhead was as powerful as an artillery shell. This first missile became the nucleus of an entire family of air-to-air weapons.

Designated GAR-1, quantity production of the Hughes missile began in 1954. The airframe is constructed of a light-alloy reinforced with plastic. Aerodynamic lift is obtained from small delta-shaped wings with guide vanes mounted near the exhaust nozzle. The GAR-1 is launched from an aircraft, and the rocket motor accelerates at a rate of 48g to hurl the weapon toward its objective at Mach 2 speeds.

The rocket-powered GAR-1D is guided toward the target by the reflection of a radar signal transmitted by the launching aircraft. A radar receiver in the nose of this Falcon tracks the target reflection from as far as five miles away. The similar GAR-2A is guided to its quarry by heat energy reflected from the target, such as jet exhaust.

GAR-1 and GAR-2 Falcons are used as offensive weapons on the F-101B, F-102A and F-106; and, during their operational lives, were fitted to the F-89J and "K." The GAR-1 became operational in March 1956, with the infrared seeking GAR-2 reaching service status the following year. Externally, the only difference between the two missiles is the nose cone. Both weapons are carried by the fighters to complement each other as circumstances require.

Approximately 4,000 GAR-1's were produced before the improved GAR-1D replaced it. About 12,000 of the latter completed production of the GAR-1 series. GAR-2A deliveries were concluded after 9,500 of the weapons had been constructed.

The span of the GAR-1D is 20 inches, the body is 78 inches long with a diameter of 6.4 inches. Weight is 121 pounds.

Later models of this missile include the

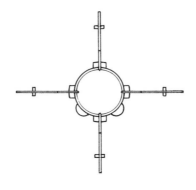

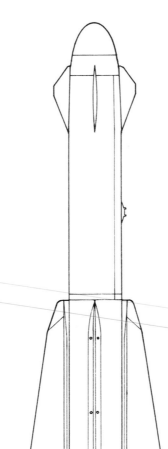

Hughes GAR-1D
(F-98)

24.53"=25 FEET

more powerful GAR-3 with greater range and destructive force, GAR-4 which is more sensitive and capable of picking up smaller, more distant targets, and the Nuclear Falcon, GAR-11. The latter is the first guided air-to-air missile to be armed with an atomic warhead.

The radar-guided GAR-1D. This missile was initially designated F-98.   *Hughes*

Left, the GAR-2A heat seeking Falcon; and the beam-riding GAR-1D on the right.   *Hughes*

BOEING
F-99 BOMARC (IM-99)

This Bomarc B rides the blast of its rocket engine on its way toward a simulated target. Boeing

The second "unmanned incerceptor", as the Air Force termed their first offensive missiles, was the Boeing-built IM-99. Designated XF-99 when first authorized in 1949, the more accurate Interceptor Missile classification was assigned to the production models.

Development of the Bomarc was undertaken by Boeing and the Michigan Aeronautical Research Center, hence the name Bo-MARC. The first F-99 was test fired in September 1952, and a more sophisticated model, with full instrumentation, was launched on February 24, 1955, to display its operational value. The purpose of the missile is area defense, and it was designed for a 200 mile intercept range. Following hundreds of test firings, the Bomarc evolved into a complete weapon system. The first production IM-99A was unveiled on December 30, 1957.

Each Bomarc is housed in its own concrete and steel shelter, 60 feet long, 20 feet wide and 12 feet high. Upon command from a direction center, located from 50 to 300 miles distant, the roof rolls back and the missile is elevated to a vertical position. When the electronic launch order is received by the missile, a fuselage-mounted Aerojet General LR59-AG-13 liquid-propellant motor is ignited to begin the first of three flight phases.

Immediately following its vertical launch, the IM-99 is under automatic, programmed guidance. Directional control and trim are achieved by a gimballed rocket exhaust nozzle. As the missile nears Mach 1, the aerodynamic controls become effective. By this time, two 10,000 lb. thrust Marquardt RJ43-MA-3 ramjets ignite to become the primary propulsive force. The liquid rocket is expended at about 30,000 feet.

The second phase of the flight begins as the Bomarc approaches its cruise altitude of 60,000 to 80,000 feet. A static pressure control directs the missile to its preselected altitude while ground control takes command of the cruise portion of the flight.

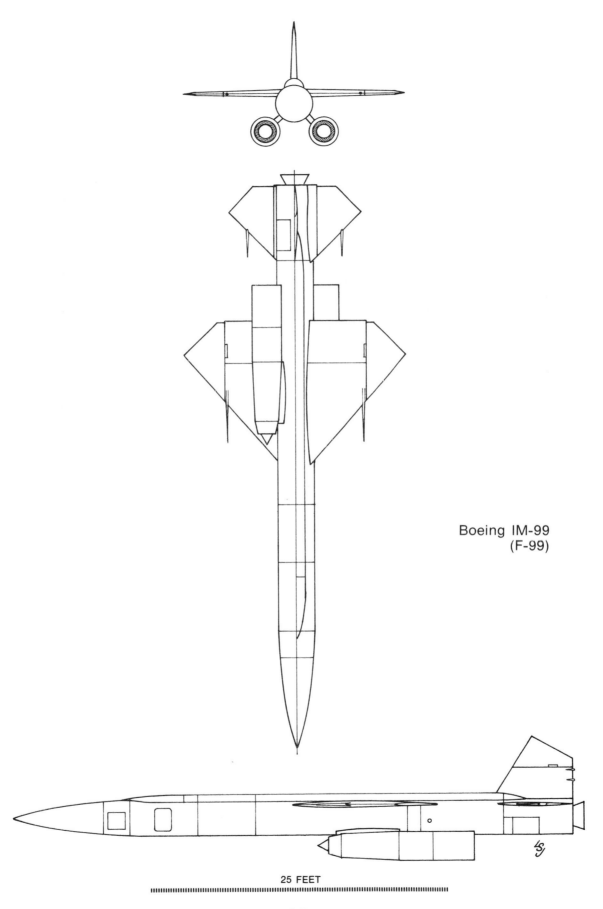

Boeing IM-99
(F-99)

25 FEET

Ground control computes an estimate of the intercept point and determines if the missile is to climb or dive to locate its goal. The Bomarc is then told when it should start its climb or dive. This command is known as TRUD (Time Remaining Until Dive) and is stored by the missile along with any changes dictated by ground control. When TRUD equals zero, the IM-99 responds to the climb or dive command. If the connection between the missile and its earth-bound directors is broken, the Bomarc will continue on the last command it received until zero TRUD, at which time the prescribed maneuver will be made. Among the signals sent to the interceptor are target-seeker sweep angles indicating where the missile should look for its objective. When the prey is found, the target seeker locks on and takes control for the third phase. A proximity fuse detonates the warhead to complete the mission. Either conventional or nuclear warheads can be mounted.

The IM-99B is a refined version of the Bomarc and is known as Advanced Bomarc or Superbomarc. The rocket motor is a more powerful Thiokol solid-fuel rocket. The cruise powerplant consists of two Marquardt RJ43-MA-7 ramjets which have carried the vehicle to Mach 3.95 at 100,000 feet. A highly sensitive terminal-homing target seeker in the IM-99B permits the weapon to home from 70,000 feet on a target flying at only 50 feet.

The Bomarc IM-99B has an 18 foot 2 inch wingspan. The wingtips are hinged to perform as ailerons. Fuselage length, excluding the rocket nozzle is 47 feet 4 inches, height is 10 feet 3 inches. Fuselage diameter is 34.6 inches. Launch weight is 15,500 pounds. The missile is constructed of welded stainless steel with a fibreglass radome.

The Bomarc A, shown here, was powered by a liquid-rocket engine for take-off. The ramjets will ignite before the missile reaches an altitude of 30,000 feet.
Air Force Museum

264

NORTH AMERICAN
F-100 SUPER SABRE

The Super Sabre was the world's first supersonic fighter.   *North American (Rockwell)*

Progenitor of the U. S. Air Force's Century Series of fighters, North American's F-100 Super Sabre was so far advanced beyond any existing fighting plane that it was truly a forerunner of a new generation of warplanes. It was the world's first production supersonic airplane and was designed from the outset to operate at speeds above Mach 1 for sustained periods. However, the technical advances which produced the F-100 also fringed on an unknown area of supersonic flight. Consequently, the Super Sabre became a victim of unexpected aerodynamic phenomena which were to have an effect on the design of all subsequent fighters.

The Super Sabre began as a company-funded project known as the Sabre 45, due to the 45 degree angle of the swept-back wing. Following two years of study, the project was approved by the Air Force which authorized construction of two YF-100's and 110 F-100A's on November 1, 1951. The prototype of the series, designated YF-100A, was flown on May 25,

1953, from the Air Force Flight Test Center at Edwards AFB.

On October 29, 1953, the initial production version of the Super Sabre was flown by North American while the Air Force was using the prototype to establish the world's first supersonic speed record. The official speed was 755.149 mph, achieved in the last low-level record attempt. Because of the potential danger and difficulty in tracking a supersonic aircraft, as well as the improved jet performance in the thinner air, all following absolute speed attempts have been on high altitude flights.

Deliveries to Air Force squadrons had begun in September 1954, when several of the new fighters crashed for unknown reasons. As a result, the F-100's were grounded on November 11, 1954, while an intensive study was made to determine the cause. It was found that when the Super Sabre was rolled, the long fuselage with its weight evenly distributed, caused the plane to pitch up and down and simultaneously sway from side to side. Normally, the ver-

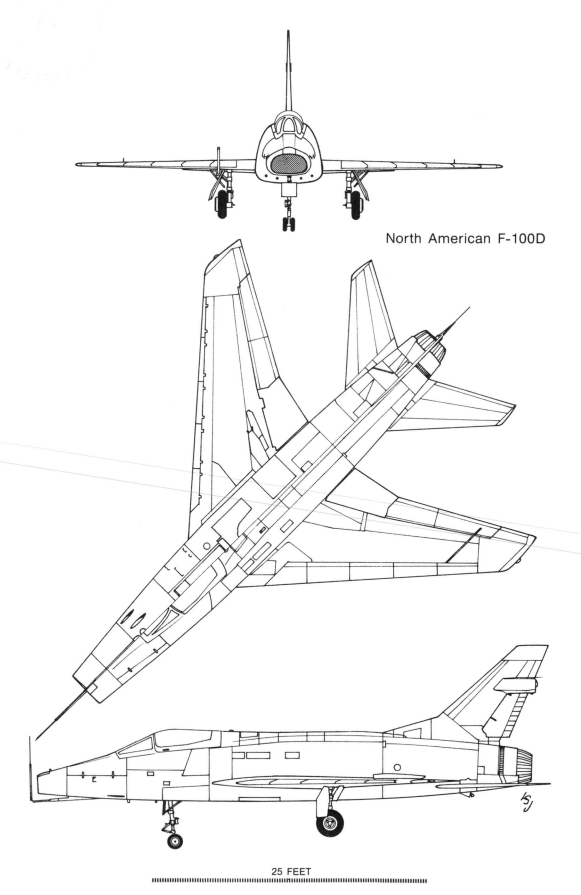

North American F-100D

25 FEET

One of the original F-100's with the short rudder.   North American (Rockwell)

An F-100D, the major production type of the Super Sabre series.

North American (Rockwell)

Three hundred thirty-three of these two-seat F-100F's were built.   North American (Rockwell)

tical tail compensated for this movement; but under certain conditions, the forces were too great for the tail surfaces to correct, leading to the complete loss of control. To correct this condition, the vertical area was increased by 27 percent and the wingspan was increased by 26 inches. Following these modifications, the planes were restored to flying status and began a long and successful career with the U. S. Air Force and several foreign air arms.

Production of the F-100A reached 203 planes, the last one being delivered in March 1954. These were powered by Pratt & Whitney J57-P-7 or -39 engines. The F-100B was so radically different from the series it was redesignated F-107. The next production model was the F-100C; 476 of this type were completed before the substantially improved F-100D began flying.

The F-100D has a wingspan of 38 feet 9 inches, fuselage length of 47 feet (the extended pitot tube adds another 6 feet 3 inches). Height is 16 feet 2 inches. Wing area

is 385 square feet. Empty weight is 21,000 pounds, normal loaded weight is 29,762 pounds, and maximum take-off weight is 34,832 pounds. The F-100D is fitted with in-flight refueling gear providing a range limited only by the pilot's endurance.

Armament of the Super Sabre is four M-39E 20 mm cannons with 200 rpg, to which a wide range of missiles and bombs can be added by means of six underwing hardpoints.

The F-100D is the major production version of the Super Sabre, production of this model reaching 1,274 units in 1958. Maximum speed of this model is 864 mph at 35,-000 feet (Mach 1.3). Power is obtained from a Pratt & Whitney J57-P-21A, rated at 11,-700 lbs. thrust with afterburning increasing available power to 16,950 lbs. Service ceiling is 50,000 feet.

A two-seat trainer version, the F-100F, was first flown on March 7, 1957. Of this type, 333 copies were built before production ceased.

The colorful F-100C's of the Thunderbird Flight Demonstration Team.   *North American (Rockwell)*

McDONNELL
F-101 VOODOO

An RF-101 photo-reconnaissance version of the Voodoo.   *McDonnell Douglas*

Construction of the first McDonnell F-101 began in May 1953, following a second study of the XF-88 penetration fighter project. The new Voodoo was based loosely on the XF-88 configuration, and a contract was issued for 29 pre-production F-101A's. They were to be built around a pair of afterburning Pratt & Whitney J57-P-13 engines of 14,500 lbs. of thrust each at full power. These first planes were all used in the development program. In May 1957, the first of 50 production F-101's was delivered to Tactical Air Command squadrons. With an unrefueled range of 1,700 miles at Mach .9, the USAF finally had a long-range escort fighter. Armament was three 20 mm M-39 cannons and provisions for a nuclear weapon.

The fifty-first Voodoo became the F-101C, followed by 47 more of the type. These differed from the first models by internal strengthening to permit their use as low-level fighter-bombers. All the F-101A and "C" models were assigned to the USAF's 81st Tactical Fighter Wing.

The principal production variant of the Voodoo is the two-place F-101B, of which 478 copies were made. The first of these was flown on March 27, 1957. The F-101B was developed specifically for the Air Defense Command and includes an MG-13 fire con-

trol system and all-missile armament. Three Hughes GAR-1, -2, -3 or -4 Falcon missiles are carried in an internal rotary weapons bay. In addition, two Douglas MB-1 Genie nuclear-tipped unguided missiles can be mounted beneath the fuselage.

Powerplant for the F-101B is comprised of two 11,990 lbs. thrust Pratt & Whitney J57-P-55's with lengthened afterburners which increase thrust to 14,990 lbs. With this energy, the two-place Voodoo can achieve a speed of 1,220 mph (Mach 1.85) at 40,000 feet. Service ceiling is 51,000 feet.

Dimensions of the F-101B are: wingspan - 39 feet 8 inches; length - 67 feet 4 inches; height - 18 feet. Wing area is 368 square feet. Unrefueled range is 1,550 miles while cruising at Mach .87 at 40,000 feet. Empty weight is 28,000 pounds, maximum gross at take-off is 46,673 pounds.

A photo-reconnaissance version of the Voodoo was developed as the RF-101A, later supplanted by the strengthened RF-101C model. These Voodoos were single-seaters carrying a battery of high-resolution cameras in an elongated nose. Thirty-five RF-101A's were built before the stronger RF-101C appeared. The total of 166 of the latter made it the major production model of single place Voodoos.

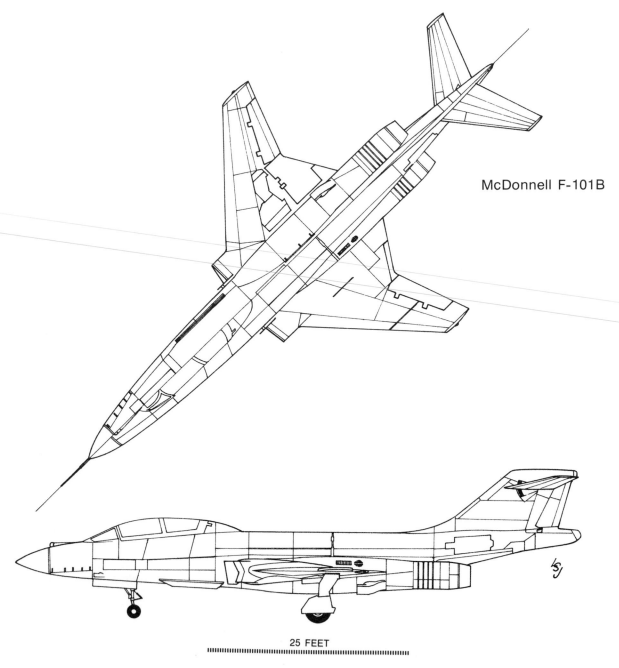

McDonnell F-101B

25 FEET

A pair of F-101B's of the Air Defense Command.   *U.S. Air Force*

This F-101A shows its relationship to the earlier XF-88.   *McDonnell Douglas*

CONVAIR
F-102 DELTA DAGGER

Here is the final shape of the F-102A Delta Dagger.   *Convair*

Invasion of the realm of supersonic flight was beset with unexpected problems and has created a strange new world of aerodynamic forms. Like the F-100, the Convair F-102 fell victim to the mysteries of the new flight regime.

In 1950, the Air Force held a design competition for a complete interceptor fire-control system. The objective was to provide a total weapons package by one designer instead of piecing together one from components of various manufacturers. The competition was won by Hughes Aircraft, resulting in the Falcon missile series. When the characteristics of the new weapons system could be determined, the Air Force requested proposals for an interceptor to utilize it. Among the designs submitted was one by Convair which was distinguished by a delta wing. This airplane was selected by the Air Force as the winning design.

The new interceptor was a refinement of the experimental XF-92A delta test vehicle, scaled up 1.22:1 and mounting a Pratt & Whitney J57-P-11 of 10,900 lbs., boosted to 14,500 lbs. with afterburning.. The designation YF-102 was assigned to the design, which underwent extensive wind tunnel

testing before the final shape was frozen. In the early 'fifties, supersonic wind tunnel testing was severely limited by the small size of the equipment, necessitating the use of miniature models. As a result, the conclusions of the tests contained several undetected flaws.

To facilitate rapid delivery of the new fighters, it was decided to establish a production line to build the planes at a slow rate while concentrating on an extensive test schedule. In this manner, any required modifications indicated by the flight tests could be incorporated into the production line.

The first of ten YF-102's (S.N. 52-7994) was ready for its maiden flight on October 24, 1953; but a flame-out eight days later caused a forced landing which damaged the prototype beyond repair. Three months passed before flight tests were resumed with the second aircraft. It soon became evident that the wind tunnel tests had been erroneous; the YF-102 was incapable of level supersonic flight because the transonic drag rise was greater than the available power. Since one of the USAF requirements was a speed in excess of Mach 1, Convair

Convair F-102A

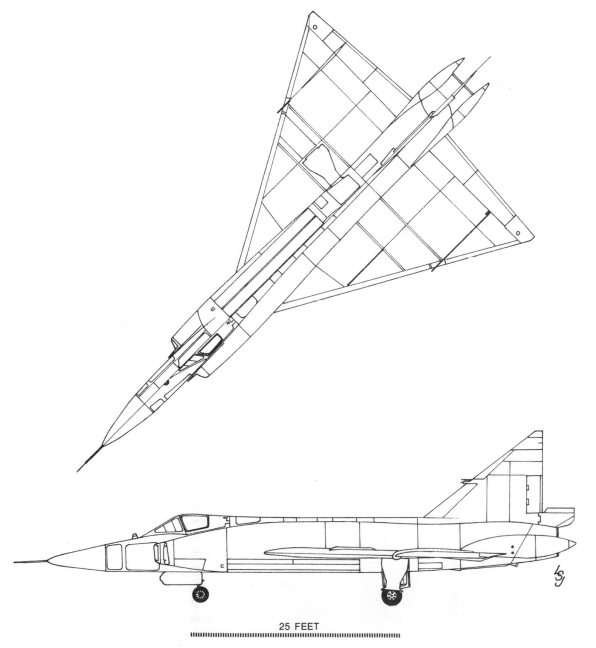

25 FEET

engineers were faced with a major redesign of the airframe—one that created a virtually new aircraft.

A new concept in supersonic configuration had been developed by Richard Whitcomb of NACA in which the shape of the fuselage was contoured in direct relation to the wing area. By reducing the fuselage cross section over the wing, drag could be drastically reduced. This principle became known as the area-rule and is now a feature of nearly all high-performance aircraft. In the case of the F-102, the fuselage was indented in the area over the wing, bulges were added behind the delta surfaces, and the nose was extended to give a higher fineness ratio. The wing itself was thinned down and the leading edge rolled over to create a conical-camber to improve low-speed handling. While the external changes were being made, a more powerful engine was also installed.

The transformation took 117 days, and the drastically altered YF-102A was lifted from the Edwards AFB runway on December 20, 1954. The next day, it easily slipped past Mach 1 on its second flight. A partial retrofit of the remaining YF-102's created some hybrid versions of the interceptor.

Production of the area-ruled F-102A was begun and the first plane was delivered to the Air Force in June 1955. A taller fin was added to the production line with the sixty-sixth plane. The last of 873 Delta Daggers

was completed in April 1958.

The F-102A's delta wing has a span of 38 feet 1 inch. Length over the nose probe is 68 feet 4 inches and height is 21 feet 2 inches. Wing area is 661.5 square feet. Normal gross weight is 27,700 pounds, maximum weight is 31,500 pounds.

The Delta Dagger has a maximum speed of 825 mph (Mach 1.25) at 40,000 feet. Power comes from a Pratt & Whitney J57-P-23 which has an afterburning thrust of 17,200 lbs. Service ceiling is 54,000 feet.

The all-missile armament of the F-102A consists of up to six Hughes Falcons of either infrared homing or beam riding types. The nuclear-tipped AIM-26A can also be carried. Originally, the F-102A mounted twenty-four 2.75 inch rockets in its missile doors. These were later deleted. A data link system in the F-102 permits the fighter to be flown by remote control from the ground. Guidance information is fed directly into the autopilot system.

A two-seat TF-102A combat proficiency trainer was test-flown on November 8, 1955. This is identical to the single-place model from the wing leading-edge back. The increased frontal area of the side-by-side cockpit, however, reduces the plane's maximum speed to 646 mph at 38,000 feet, but Mach 1 can be attained in a shallow dive. Although 111 TF-102A's were ordered, only 63 were completed.

The designation F-102B was temporarily assigned to the radically different F-106.

The two-place TF-102A is used as a tactical trainer. It can reach Mach 1 in a dive.   *Convair*

An artist's rendering of the proposed XF-103.   *Republic*

The heart of Republic's XF-103 advanced interceptor design was a unique dual-cycle turbo-ramjet engine which was intended to hurtle the big plane to a speed of Mach 4, approximately 2,600 mph. The engine, designated Wright XJ67-W-3/XRJ55-W-1, comprised a conventional turbojet and an afterburner which served the dual purpose of a ramjet engine.

The turbine segment of the turbo-ram engine was to be fed directly through a variable-inlet sugar-scoop intake in the lower fuselage. During take-off and acceleration, the turbojet exhaust would be augmented by the afterburner. As the speed built up, a pair of valves on either side of the turbo-jet would redirect the incoming air straight to the afterburner, changing it into a pure ramjet. This transition was to take place between Mach 2 and 3 at 50,000 feet. In actual tests, the cycle was completed in seven seconds. Above 50,000 feet, the ramjet was to provide 18,800 lbs. of thrust. The J67 portion of the powerplant was rated at a maximum of 15,000 lbs. thrust. The entire power unit weighed nearly 7,200 pounds and occupied more than half the fuselage length.

In its intended role, the XF-103 would be able to intercept an intruding bomber approaching over the North Pole at an altitude of 75,000 feet at Mach 2.2. After completing the interception, the XF-103 would return to its base on the power of the turbojet alone.

The Air Force became interested in the XF-103 during the competition which produced the Convair F-102. Two prototypes were ordered at that time. An intensive development program was undertaken and the XF-103 began to emerge as a monstrous creation of heat-resistant titanium and stainless steel weighing over 20 tons. Because of the great drag that would be caused by any protrusion, the conventional canopy over the cockpit was eliminated and the pilot was to be provided with a retractable periscope. The cockpit

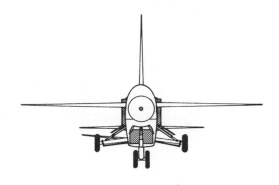

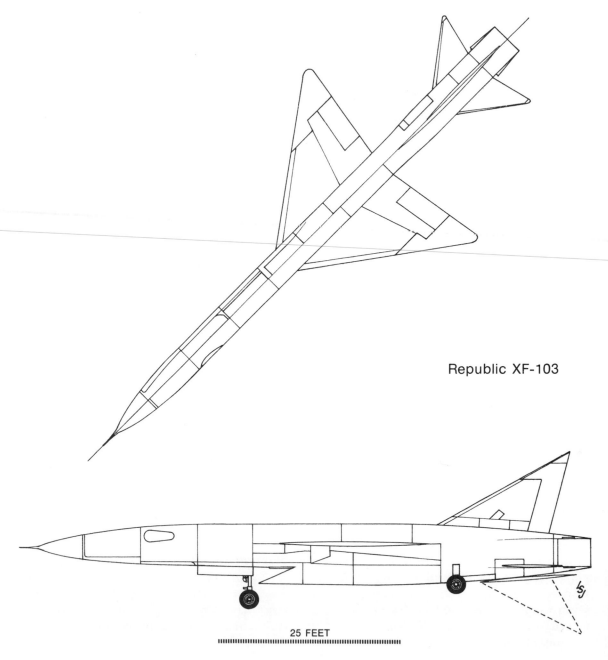

Republic XF-103

25 FEET

itself consisted of a capsule which could be lowered from the nose. In an emergency, the capsule could become an ejection seat.

Released information concerning the XF-103 shows a wingspan of 35 feet 10 inches, fuselage length of 81 feet 11 inches and a height of 18 feet 4 inches. Wing area was 401 square feet. Fuel capacity was a phenomenal 3,730 gallons. A ventral fin which retracted for take-off and landings was provided for stability at the high Mach numbers predicted. Combat radius was 431 miles with a service ceiling in excess of 75,-000 feet. The XF-103 design included provisions for housing six air-to-air missiles and thirty-six 2.75 inch Mighty Mouse FFAR rockets.

After a nine-year development period, the first example was under construction when, on August 21, 1957, the Air Force cancelled the project. Although the reason given was economic, it had become apparent that the Wright J65 would not provide adequate thrust for the proposed performance. At the time of the cancellation, Republic was working on the possibility of replacing the J65 with a 20,000 lb. thrust British-built Bristol Olympus. The low-mounted intake, with its complicated variable-inlet and bypass valves, was also cause for concern. Its location directly behind the nose wheel made it highly susceptible to foreign object ingestion.

The development of the XF-103 progressed as far as this metal mock-up before the project was abandoned in August, 1957.
Republic

The prototype F-104 did not have the intake shock wedges and was nearly 6 feet shorter than the production Starfighters. Lockheed

Following the discovery of the German research data on swept-wings after World War II, a sharply raked wing became the rule for high speed fighters. In contrast to this trend, Lockheed engineers designed a straight, but razor thin, lifting surface for their first supersonic fighter.

Design studies began in November 1952; and in March 1953, two examples were ordered as XF-104's. When it made its appearance, the first prototype bore a strong resemblance to a Lockheed-designed research missile, the X-7. In fact, the XF-104 owed a great deal of its design to the X-7 vehicle. The first flight took place on February 2, 1954, and the test program was conducted with a second XF-104 and 15 YF-104A's. The XF-104's were powered by afterburning Wright J65-W-6 engines. When delivery began on the YF-104A's, by then known as Starfighters, the powerplant was a General Electric J79-GE-3 with an afterburning power of 14,800 pounds. This engine provided fifty percent more thrust than the J65. Another item added to the YF-104's, and retained in production models,

was a shock-control cone on the air inlet to position the supersonic shock wave inside the duct. The overall length was increased from 49 feet to 54 feet 9 inches to house the new engine.

Shortly after production of 155 F-104A's had started, the planes were fitted with a ventral fin and arresting hook. Before deliveries of the Starfighter could begin, unexpected problems arose which required an intensive test program. Among these was the tendency of the aircraft to stabilize in a stalled condition—now called super stall. In this condition, the plane remains pitched up in a stalled attitude from which recovery is impossible. This flaw was corrected in April 1957. The tip-mounted fuel tanks were subject to modifications to eliminate a tendency to slam into the fuselage upon ejection. Finally, the sleek fighter was released for service, and the 83rd Fighter Wing received its first Starfighters on January 26, 1958. Within three months, the new planes were grounded due to engine failures. This was overcome by replacement with an improved J79-GE-3B, but the F-

278

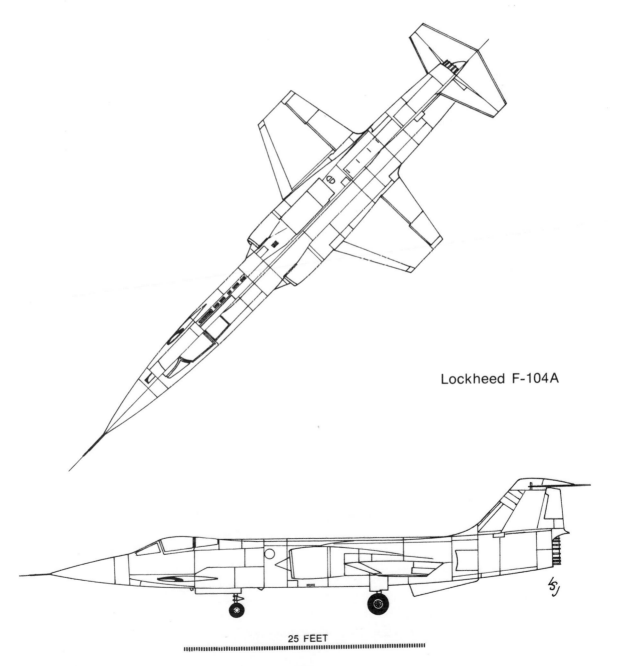

Lockheed F-104A

25 FEET

The Air Force acquired 77 of these F-104C's. A feature of the F-104A and C was a downward ejection seat.   *Lockheed*

Some F-104C's were used in Vietnam. They were camouflaged as shown here and fitted with refueling probes.   *Lockheed*

104A continued to be subject to a high accident rate. Suffering, also, from relatively short-range and without all-weather capabilities, the Air Force was compelled to withdraw the planes from first-line service. Many were sold to foreign countries, the remainder finding their way into the ranks of the Air National Guard. Others became QF-104A target drones, and three were equipped with 6,000 lb. thrust Rocketdyne AR-2 booster rockets for use by the Aerospace Research Pilot's School.

The F-104C was Lockheed's answer to the shortcomings of the "A" model. Seventy-seven of the improved Starfighters were delivered, the first of them arriving at a TAC squadron on October 16, 1958. This model was operated only by the 479th Tactical Fighter Wing before retirement.

The escape system used on the F-104A and "C" was of the downward-ejection type. The value of this method of ejection at low level is questionable, at best.

The F-104B is a tandem-seat trainer version of the Starfighter. The second seat was located in the area occupied by electronics, armament and one of the fuselage tanks. Twenty-six F-104B's were assembled.

Despite its initial difficulties, the Starfighter has proven to be an exceptional performer. It was the first operational combat plane to be able to sustain Mach 2 speeds. This speed was first reached on April 27,

1955. The F-104 was also the first plane to hold both speed and altitude records simultaneously, reaching a height of 91,243 feet on May 8, 1958, and a speed of 1,404.19 mph eight days later. The following year, an F-104 climbed to 103,396 feet.

The F-104's exceptionally-thin wing is so sharp, a felt cap is placed over it to protect the ground crew during servicing. The wingspan is 21 feet 11 inches. Length is 54 feet 9 inches, height is 13 feet 6 inches. Wing area is 179 square feet. Gross weight is 23,590 pounds, including 900 gallons of fuel in fuselage tanks, 390 gallons in two underwing tanks, and 340 gallons in two tip tanks. The F-104C can be refueled in flight. Maximum speed is 1,450 mph at 40,000 feet. Service ceiling is 58,000 feet.

A General Electric M61 Vulcan 20 mm rotary cannon, firing 6,000 rounds per minute, is mounted in the left side of the fuselage. Additional armament in the form of four Sidewinder heat-seeking missiles can be attached to the wings.

Although the Starfighter was not an outstanding success with the U. S. Air Force, the vastly improved export F-104G/J has more than proven the soundness of its design. This model has been built under license in Japan, Germany, Netherlands, Canada, Belgium and Italy. Over 1,000 examples of the export Starfighter have been constructed.

Sidewinders can be used interchangeably with fuel tanks on the F-104. The dark color of the missiles indicates these F-104C's are on a practice mission.
Lockheed

The "M" shaped wing was a characteristic of the Thunderchief.   *Republic*

By 1953, the Air Force had gained enough experience in jet operations to precisely define the requirements for a tactical fighter-bomber. Thus, the Republic F-105 became the first plane of its type designed specifically for the role. Virtually half fighter—half bomber, the F-105 design included a bomb-bay capable of containing a nuclear weapon.

In March 1953, Republic received an order for thirty-seven XF-105A's. The mock-up was ready for inspection seven months later. With the conclusion of the Korean War in mid-1953, the need for the new fighter was reduced, and consequently, the order was cut to fifteen aircraft, then to only three. Finally, the figure was restored to fifteen units.

While the first two XF-105A's were under construction, the difficulties encountered by the Convair F-102 were being studied by Republic. It was apparent that the same transonic drag rise problem discovered during the F-102 program could very well affect the performance of the F-105. New fuselage contours were drawn up,

but the first two airframes were nearly completed so the third plane received the revised shape and was designated F-105B. In addition to the area-ruling of the fuselage, a distinctive new two-dimensional air intake was mounted to the wing giving a unique "M" shape to the wing planform.

The first two F-105's were powered by a 10,000 lb. Pratt & Whitney J57-P-25; and on October 22, 1955, the Thunderchief began its flight testing, exceeding Mach 1 in the process. However, the transonic drag problem was confirmed as the prototype could only achieve Mach 1.2 in its unmodified form. The recontoured F-105B joined the test program in May 1956, and made its first flight on the 26th of that month. Employing a Pratt & Whitney J75-P-3 of 23,500 lbs. with afterburner, the F-105B reached a speed of 1,420 mph (Mach 2.15).

Seventy-five F-105B's were built, this type entering the Air Force inventory on May 27, 1958. The F-105D carries a General Electric FC-5 fully integrated automatic flight and fire control system giving it all-weather

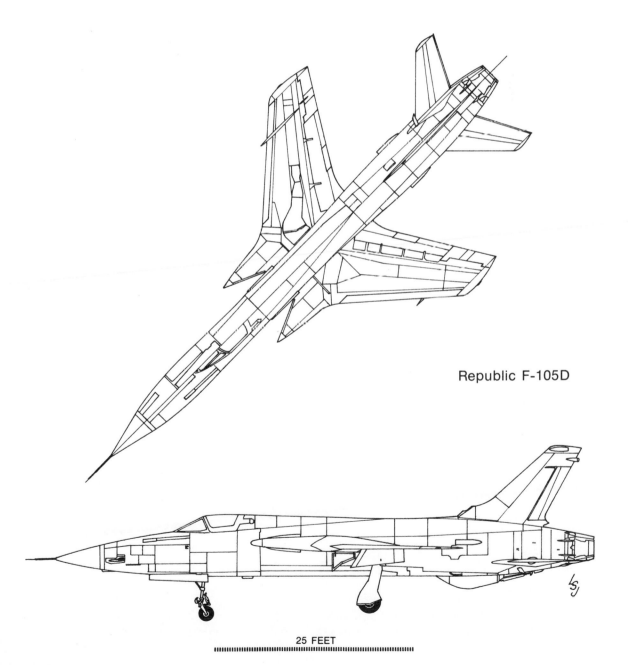

Republic F-105D

25 FEET

capabilities. A total of 610 of these make it it the major production version. Externally, it is 1 foot 3 inches longer than the "B."

The F-105F is a two-place Thunderchief, similar to an earlier F-105E which was cancelled while on the assembly line. The F-105F did reach the production line, however, and 143 of the two-seaters were completed. It was designed to help train pilots in the operation of the complex weapon system; but it became an operational combat weapon in Vietnam where the second seat was occupied by the operator of electronic counter-measures gear. In this role, an F-105F would accompany a flight of conventional Thunderchiefs which were armed with bombs. The two-seater mounted radar jamming gear to confuse the enemy's radar-directed anti-aircraft guns and SAM missiles.

In Vietnam, the F-105's were used as bombers—the usual load exceeded by fifty percent the amount carried by a World War II B-17. An extra fuel tank was fitted into the spacious bomb bay while up to 12,000 lbs. of bombs were suspended from five hardpoints. Though primarily used as a bomber, the Thunderchief still scored its share of downed Migs, 29 of which felt the bite of the big plane.

The F-105D's wing measures 34 feet 11 inches, tip to tip. Length is 64 feet 3 inches and height is 19 feet 8 inches. Wing area is 385 square feet. With its afterburning J75-P-9W, the F-105D has a maximum speed of 1,390 mph at 50,000 feet. Empty weight is 27,500 pounds, normal weight is 38,034 pounds, gross weight is 52,546 pounds.

The built-in armament of the F-105D consists of one 20 mm M61 Vulcan cannon with 1,029 rounds. A great variety of missiles can be suspended from the Thunderchief's hardpoints, the actual distribution would be determined by the particular mission at hand.

A Thunderchief between missions in Vietnam.　　　　　　　　　　　　*Republic*

CONVAIR
F-106 DELTA DART

A high angle of attack is typical of the take-off and landing attitude of a delta wing. *Convair*

Following the major redesign of the F-102 to produce a supersonic airframe, Convair engineers continued the refinements on the fighter to make the design even more efficient. The project was known as the F-102B. The result of their efforts differed so drastically from the F-102A that, in effect, only the wing remained the same. And that, too, was altered after production of the new model had commenced. By that time, the designation had been changed to F-106A, the name Delta Dart completed the transformation.

The F-106 design conforms to the area-rule formula with an entirely new fuselage which reduces the length of the engine intake ducts. To increase engine efficiency, the inlet ramps are adjustable to control the supersonic air before it enters the engine. A larger swept-back vertical stabilizer replaces the triangular surface of the F-102. Added to this was a change to the afterburning Pratt & Whitney J75-P-17—a fifty percent power increase over the F-102's J57.

Seventeen F-106A's were ordered in April 1956, and on December 26, 1956, the first of these was flown. By this time, another 18 planes had been ordered. In order to accelerate the test schedule, most of these planes were retained for development; the first of the actual production planes were delivered in mid-1959. The first F-106 squadron, the 539th FIS, became operational in June of that year. On July 20, 1961, the 277th and final F-106A was delivered to the Air Defense Command.

The F-106A carries one of the most sophisticated electronic and fire control systems devised. Designed by Hughes, the MA-1 system functions with the SAGE (Semi-Automatic Ground Environment) defense program in which the operation of the aircraft is controlled by ground stations. The MA-1 digital computer receives information on the required course, speed and altitude and translates it into electronic commands for the Automatic Flight Control System (AFCS). Thus guided, the Delta Dart approaches its target until its objective is picked up on radar. At this point, the F-106's radar locks on to the target and the missiles are fired automatically. During this time, the pilot acts as a monitor, tracking the course on a projected map in the cockpit. In the event of a loss of ground contact, or in an emergency, the pilot can override the MA-1 system.

The first F-106's were fitted with a pair

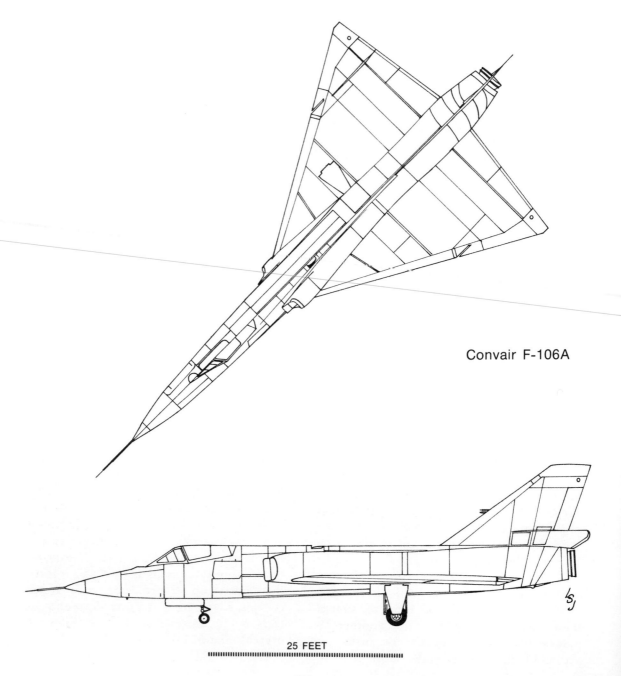

Convair F-106A

25 FEET

of fences on each wing as on the F-102A. These were later replaced by a slot cut into the leading edge of the delta surface. Another improvement made in the F-106 is the one-piece cockpit canopy (shown in the three-view drawing). This eliminated the heavy overhead framing used early in its life.

The two-place F-106B was ordered in June 1957, and became airborne on April 9, 1958. Aside from the second seat, which replaces one of the fuel cells, the "B" is identical in configuration and performance to its single-seat counterpart.

The Delta Dart has a wingspan of 38 feet 3 inches, overall length of 70 feet 9 inches, and is 20 feet 3 inches high. Wing area is 661.5 square feet. Empty weight is approximately 26,000 pounds, maximum take-off weight is 38,250 pounds. The F-106 can be fitted with drop tanks that permit supersonic operation, and has aerial refueling capabilities. Maximum speed is 1,525 mph (Mach 2.3) at 36,000 feet. Unrefueled range is 1,150 miles.

A combination of guided weapons is carried within the large bay located in front of the engine. These include the Douglas AIR-2A or -2B Genie, Hughes AIM-4F or -4G Super Falcons. The "Six Shooter" version mounts an M61 Vulcan rotary cannon.

Four Delta Darts from the 318th FIS on a mission over the Rockies.   *U.S. Air Force*

The F-107A used spoilers instead of ailerons for roll. Here they are extended during a bank.

North American (Rockwell)

The need for a tactical fighter-bomber with ground-attack ability led North American engineers to reappraise their new F-100 in this light. Certain modifications would be needed, of course, but the basic airframe would serve as the foundation for the attack craft. The designation F-100B was applied, and the engineering process began in June 1953. The first step was to provide room for radar. To accomplish this, the gaping nose intake was moved aft below the cockpit and the new nose tapered forward into a sharp-pointed radome. This concept was eventually revised to place the intake on top of the fuselage.

As the ground-attack fighter design took shape, it was clear that they had an entirely new airplane on the boards, and the Air Force redesignated it YF-107A. A contract creating three F-107's was signed in August 1954. Six more examples were also ordered but were ultimately cancelled.

When it first appeared in mid-1956, the F-107 was bound to attact attention. It displayed a tasteful blend of bold, yet graceful lines. The gaping exhaust orifice gave an indication of the potential power that would propel the F-107 to a speed of 1,300 mph (Mach 2.0). The first flight on September 10, 1956, concluded with a damaged nose gear when the braking parachute failed and the plane struck a depression on the dry lake bed at Edwards AFB. Damage was minor, though, and the big fighter was back in the air three days later.

Since the F-107 was designed to perform the same role as the Republic F-105, a competition was held between the two aircraft. The Republic ship emerged the victor, and the three F-107's were relegated to permanent test status. In this role, they proved several new features that were to find their way to other production aircraft. The one-piece all-moving rudder, as used on the A-5 Vigilante attack bomber, was said to be highly responsive on the F-107.

Another unique feature of the F-107 was the total absence of ailerons on the wings. The function of these controls was taken over by a series of spoilers on the wing sur-

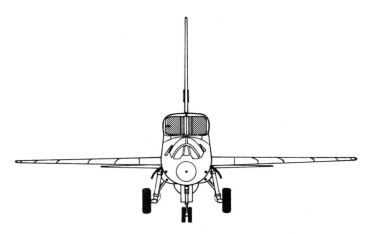

North American F-107A

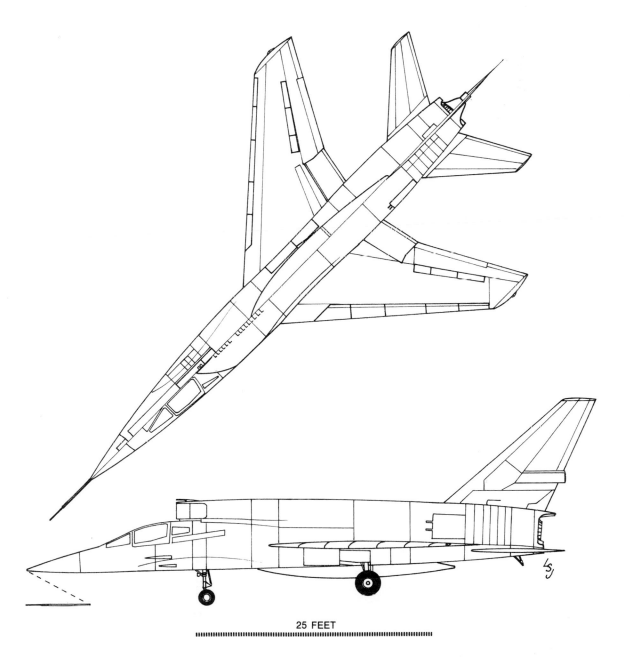

25 FEET

faces. This control system was also used on the F-11 Tiger.

The distinctive overhead inlet duct fed air to a Pratt & Whitney J75-P-11 afterburning engine giving 24,000 lbs. of thrust. Fuel for this engine was held in enclosed wing and fuselage tanks as well as underwing tanks and one centerline container mounted in the indented fuselage bottom. Total fuel capacity was 2,400 gallons.

It was planned to install an XMA-12 integrated fire control system to compute the necessary information to fire the four M-39E 20 mm cannons. Up to 10,000 pounds of offensive stores could be carried in place of the external fuel tanks. The full weapons gear was installed in the second F-107A, #55-5119.

The third prototype was transferred from the Air Force to NACA, where it was later written-off in a crash landing. The second F-107 is now on display at the Air Force Museum in Ohio. The first prototype was salvaged from the scrap pile with the intention of restoring it to flight status, or at least preserving this example of a significant step in aviation.

The F-107A wing, utilizing the basic F-100 lifting surface, has a span of 36 feet 7 inches. Wing area is 376.02 square feet. Length, exclusive of the nose probe, is 60 feet 10 inches, height is 19 feet 6 inches. Combat weight was 30,000 pounds and maximum take-off weight was over 40,000 pounds.

With the acquisition of North American by Rockwell International, the F-107 became the last fighter built to carry the North American name.

The third F-107A, shown here, was lost in a crash landing. The second plane is on display at the Air Force Museum in Ohio.   *North American (Rockwell)*

U.S. AIR FORCE

310107

USAF

JET INTAKE

U.S. AIR FORCE

YF-108

This drawing illustrates one of the configurations evaluated for the F-108 Rapier program. The three-view drawing shows the final configuration.

A competition in 1957, which cleared the way for design of the advanced XB-70 Valkyrie supersonic bomber, led to the creation of three other significant aircraft designs based on the same canard-delta configuration. In addition to the XB-70, North American built the aerodynamically-similar X-10 research craft and the XSM-64 Navaho intercontinental ramjet-powered missile. To this trio was added the unbuilt triple-sonic F-108 Rapier design.

The proposed F-108, which actually reached the mock-up stage, was a twin-engine, two place aircraft which was to weigh up to some 48,000 pounds empty and have a combat weight of more than 73,000 pounds. Maximum design gross weight was 102,000 pounds, a great deal of this poundage coming from the 7,100 gallons of internal fuel to be carried.

The configuration of the Rapier indicates that it was basically a half-scale Valkyrie, using only two of the General Electric J93-GE-3 engines mounted in the six-jet bomber. With each engine providing up to 30,000 lbs. of thrust with afterburning, the F-108 was to hurtle through the air at a speed of more than 2,000 mph (Mach 3). It would have been an appropriate escort for its giant sister, the XB-70, had the two reached the operational stage as originally intended. But this was not to be, as only a pair of XB-70's were constructed and further development of the F-108 was cancelled on September 23, 1959.

The Rapier's 52 foot 10½ inch span delta wing had an area of 1,400 square feet. A pair of vertical stabilizers was attached to the wings to provide the necessary stabilizing area when the fighter's speed exceeded Mach 2. Overall length was 84 feet 10½ inches and height was 22 feet 1 inch. Range of the F-108 was to be 1,150 miles at Mach 3. The Rapier design also provided for loiter missions in which the fighter would take-off and fly to a point 280 miles from its base, remain in the area for one hour, then proceed to intercept a target 750 miles away.

The two crewmen were to ride in individual ejection capsules of the type developed for the XB-70. If a prototype had been built, the scheduled first flight was to be in March 1961.

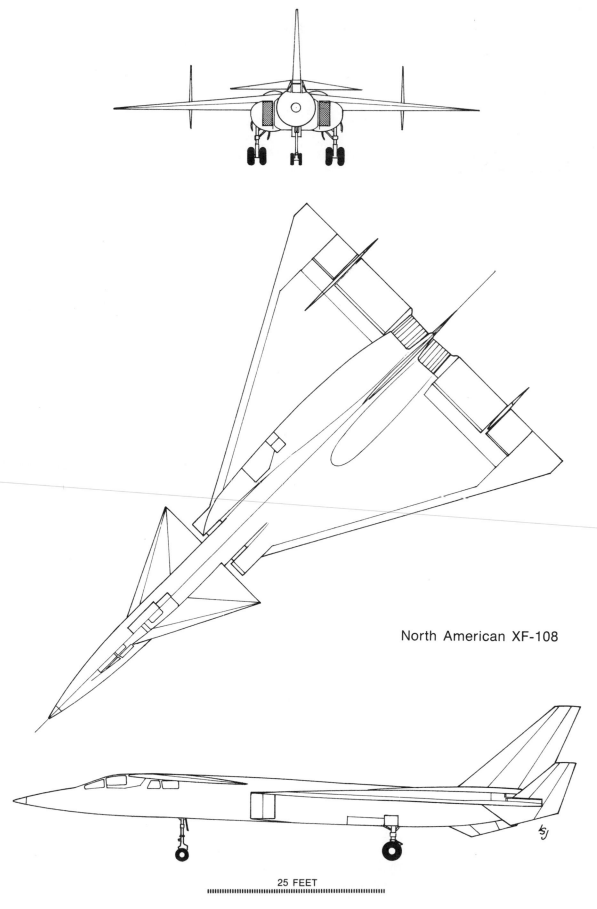

North American XF-108

25 FEET

This is how the XF-109 Mach 2.3 vertical take-off interceptor might have looked in flight.   *Bell*

With supersonic flight a matter of course, attention was directed toward increasing the versatility of the supersonic fighter. The ever-increasing size and weight of the fast planes dictated the use of lengthy runways and reinforced landing areas.

The Bell Company, at the request of both the Air Force and Navy, undertook the design of a Mach 2 fighter capable of taking-off and landing vertically and hovering motionless in the air. Known within the company as Bell Model D-188A, the Air Force assigned its F-109 designation to the project. A mock-up of the XF-109 was completed by the spring of 1961, but the actual aircraft was never constructed.

As planned, the XF-109 was to be propelled by eight General Electric J85-GE-5 engines of 2,600 lbs. thrust. Afterburners would raise the power to 3,850 lbs. on six of these. Two of the afterburning engines were to be located conventionally in the fuselage, fed by lateral intake ducts. Another two, without the afterburners, were to be installed upright in the fuselage behind the cockpit, exhausting downward to provide vertical lift only. The remaining four afterburning engines were to be paired in rotating wingtip nacelles providing either vertical or forward thrust as required. The rotational arc allowed the engines to be moved from horizontal to ten degrees beyond vertical, thus allowing the XF-109 to fly backwards.

For take-off, the tip-mounted engines would be raised to the vertical position and the two lift engines started. The combined thrust of the six turbojets would lift the fighter's 23,917 pound loaded weight into the air. Forward motion would be induced by lowering the nose as power was applied to the tail engines and the nacelles began to rotate to the level position. Simultaneously, the two lift engines would be shut down and their orifices covered to reduce drag. During the transitional phase, flight control and stabilization would be maintained by a reaction control system operated by bleed air from the compressors. This air would be ducted to four variable-exit nozzles. Conventional controls would be used in normal flight areas.

Once in level flight, the XF-109 would be able to accelerate to 1,520 mph (Mach 2.3), a speed which could be maintained for a distance of 390 miles. Sea level climb rate was estimated to be greater than 60,000 fpm. The XF-109 was to carry enough fuel to provide a subsonic range of 1,382 miles at 35,000 feet. Ferry range was 2,300 miles.

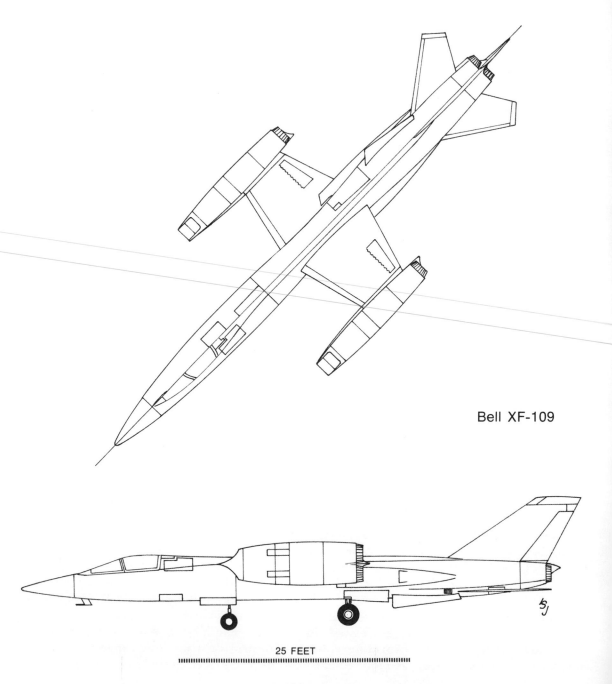

Bell XF-109

25 FEET

Had it been built, the XF-109 would have a wingspan of 23 feet 9 inches, a length of 62 feet and a height, with engines level, of 12 feet 9 inches. Area of the wing was to be 194 square feet. Empty weight would have been 13,791 pounds, gross 23,917 pounds.

A similar aircraft, the German VJ-101, was built and flown, using much of the technology developed by Bell in their XF-109 program.

The Bell XF-109 mock-up with its engines tilted as they would be for take-off or landing. *Bell*

McDONNELL
F-110 SPECTRE

The designation F-110 Spectre was assigned to the Air Force's first Phantoms. With the revision of the aircraft classification system on September 18, 1962, the F-110 and ten Navy types were renumbered to simplify their identification by both services. The F-110 became the F-4, under which heading it is described in this volume.

The fifth F-111A in maximum-speed configuration.   **General Dynamics**

Culminating an intensive competition, begun in February 1961, the General Dynamics F-111 was selected as the basic tactical fighter for both the Air Force and Navy on November 24, 1962. The purpose of the contest was to create a single aircraft which, with relatively few changes, could serve as the standard bearer for both services. In the case of the F-111, nearly 84 percent of the two planes were common. To the casual observer, the differences were in the lengths of the fuselage and wingspan. During the preliminary stages of the design study, the proposed fighter was designated "Tactical Fighter-Experimental," or TFX. The production of the Air Force version of the TFX was relegated to General Dynamics, this version being the F-111A. As co-designer in the competition, Grumman was given the production responsibility for the Navy's F-111B. The F-111A, first to be completed, was flown on December 21, 1964, and became the world's first combat plane to use variable-sweep wings.

Two experimental swing-wing planes had preceded the F-111 into the air, but these had been one-of-a-kind test vehicles. The Bell X-5, based on a captured German Messerschmitt design, was flown on June 20, 1951. The second plane to use the variable-position wing was Grumman's XF10F-1 Jaguar. In the case of the latter, the wings could be stopped at only two positions—fully swept or fully extended. The wings of the F-111 may be stopped at any point.

When the F-111 wings are fully forward, the leading edge sweep angle is 16 degrees. Within 24 seconds, they can be folded back to a sweep angle of 72.5 degrees.

The side-by-side cockpit is a self-contained ejectable capsule in which the crewmen remain should an emergency arise. The capsule is self-stabilizing and contains a parachute system which lowers the unit safely to earth. If ejection occurs over water, the sealed module will float until the crew can be removed.

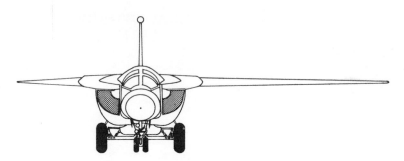

General Dynamics F-111E

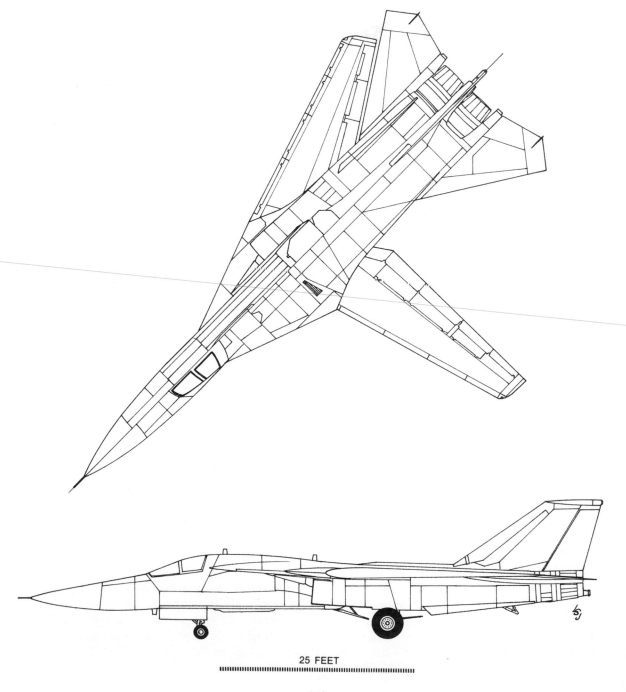

25 FEET

The F-111B was rejected by the Navy as unsuitable for its requirements. **Grumman**

This view of an unpainted F-111A shows the beefy main landing gear system. **U.S. Air Force**

Two of the Tactical Air Command's F-111D's. **General Dynamics**

The F-111A is powered by two afterburning Pratt & Whitney TF-30-P-3 turbofan engines of 18,500 lbs. of thrust. Later models use more powerful engines with ratings up to 25,100 lbs., as on the F-111F.

Assignment of the F-111 to Air Force squadrons began in October 1967, with the F-111A, of which 141 were constructed. The second Air Force type received for operations was the F-111E, of which 94 were delivered. This model had revised engine intakes. The F-111C designation was assigned to 24 of the planes built with longer wings for Australia. Advanced avionics are a feature of the 96 "D" models, which also include the improvements found in the F-111E. The latest fighter version of the series is the F-111F with the uprated TF30-P-100 engines.

The Navy version of the TFX, the F-111B, was rejected after extensive testing of seven prototypes because of several compromises in the design to permit its use by both services. The requirements for the two services are far enough apart as to make the development of a universal fighter unrealistic. The compromises could only result in a mediocre machine unsuitable for either role.

A tactical bomber development program created the FB-111A for the Strategic Air Command. Seventy-six of these planes used the long fuselage of the F-111A and the long span wings of the Navy model. These became operational with SAC on October 8, 1969. As a bomber, the FB-111A can carry two 750 lb. bombs in the enclosed weapon bay, with forty-eight more on eight underwing hardpoints, making a total load of 37,500 pounds. When underwing loads are carried, the wing sweep is restricted to 26 degrees. The power for the bomber is obtained from two 20,350 lb. thrust TF-30's.

The movable wing presented some unusual circumstances which required novel solutions. Roll control, for example, is the function of wing spoilers and the stabilators. With the wings extended, the spoilers are fully operational; as sweep-back begins, these controls are progressively locked until, in the fully swept condition, the roll function is taken over by the horizontal tail. In order to allow the wings to be moved while ordnance is suspended below them, swivelling pylon mounts were designed.

The F-111E wing measures 63 feet when outstretched; the span is reduced to 32 feet 11 inches with the tips all the way back. Length is 73 feet 6 inches and height is 17 feet. Wing area varies from 525 square feet to 657.3 square feet. Empty weight is 46,243 pounds, gross weight 91,500 pounds. Maximum speed is 1,650 mph (Mach 2.5) at 35,000 feet.

One of the most advanced systems of radar is installed in the F-111. Called Terrain Avoidance, it enables the big fighter to skim over the ground at low altitude while the system itself guides the plane over the contours of the terrain.

During the Vietnam War, the F-111 cut its teeth in combat. While some difficulties were encountered, they were overcome; and the plane has proven to be an outstanding piece of weaponry and the most advanced production fighter to date.

An FB-111A strategic bomber operated by SAC.

General Dynamics

A few of these FJ-3's were redesignated as F-1C's and D's.   *Rockwell*

The FJ-4 Fury, redesignated F-1 under the Defense Department ruling of 1962, was the final model of the navalized Sabre. The first of 152 FJ-4's was flown on October 28, 1954, and represented a total redesign of the earlier FJ-3 airframe. The wing was enlarged by 150 square feet and the span increased two feet. A 7,700 lb. thrust Wright J65-W-16A provided the F-1E with a maximum speed of 715 mph at sea level, a speed of 640 mph being attained at 35,000 feet.

The F-1E was the first of the Furies to utilize the "wet wing," in which fuel was carried between the wing skins instead of in fuel cells. This allowed for an increase in fuel capacity, reduction in weight and improved performance.

The AF-1E (FJ-4B) was intended for low-level assault operations. It incorporated a strengthened structure to withstand the stresses caused by high-speed performance at near surface altitudes. Two hundred twenty-two of this model were built by North American in Columbus, Ohio.

The stiffened wing allowed the AF-1E to carry five Martin Bullpup missiles and one missile-guidance pod for ground-attack missions. This was in addition to four nose-mounted MK-12 20 mm cannons. The AF-1E's externally mounted ordnance could include nuclear weapons.

The F-1E was 36 feet 4 inches long, had a wingspan of 39 feet 1 inch with an area of 338 square feet. Height was 13 feet 11 inches. Empty weight was 13,210 pounds, gross weight was 23,700 pounds. Service ceiling was 46,800 feet. Two FJ-4's were fitted with 6,000 lb. thrust Rocketdyne AR-1 rocket motors to test the power unit that was scheduled to be installed in the Vought Crusader III. These were known as FJ-4F's.

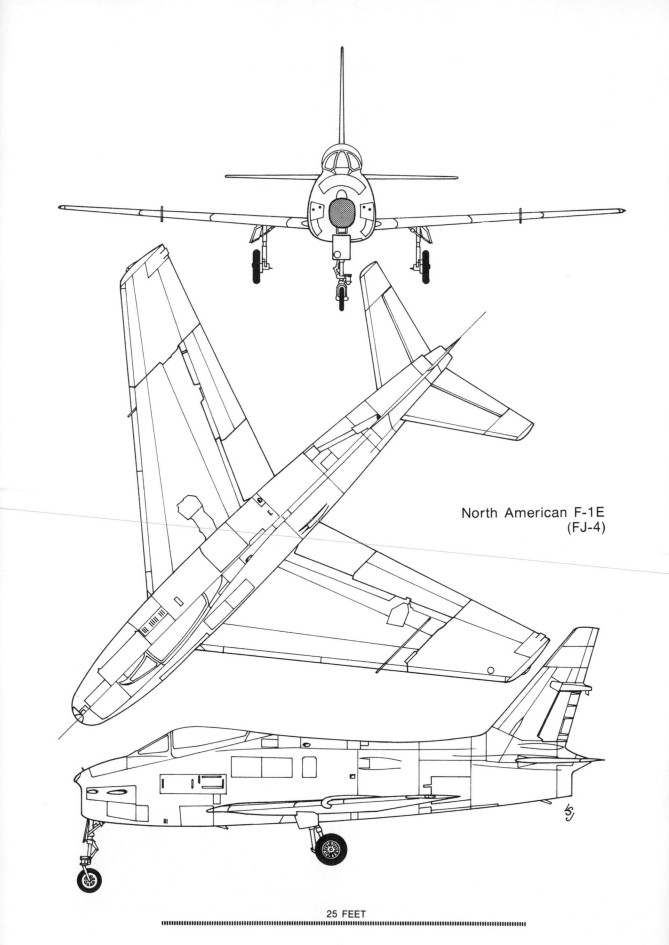

North American F-1E
(FJ-4)

25 FEET

This FJ-4 was fitted with a rocket engine booster for evaluation.   *Rockwell*

This heavily-laden F-1E is armed with Martin Bullpup missiles.   *Rockwell*

McDONNELL
F-2 BANSHEE (F2H)

An F2H 2P photo Banshee in the background is escorted by an F2H-3.   Hughes

The Navy's first jet fighter was the twin-engined FH-1 Phantom, destined, among other things, to become McDonnell's first production airplane.   On March 1945, two days before placing the production order for the Phantoms, the Navy authorized construction of two prototypes of a redesigned model of the FH-1. These became known as XF2H-1's, and were named Banshee. The Banshee was larger and heavier than the Phantom, but otherwise bore a strong resemblance to the FH-1. The XF2H-1 first went aloft on January 11, 1947, and a successful test program led to an order for 56 examples in May of the same year. The Banshee powerplant consisted of two Westinghouse J34-WE-22's of 3,000 lbs. thrust each.

A need to increase the range of its fighters resulted in a Navy order for 364 F2H-2's with a slightly lengthened fuselage housing additional fuel and fixed wingtip tanks. The installation of nose-mounted radar created 14 F2H-2N night fighters; and a camera-bay in the nose, instead of radar and armament, distinguished 58 F2H-2P reconnaissance craft. All versions of the -2 were powered by 3,200 lb. thrust J34-WE-34 engines.

Still seeking extended ranges, the stretched F2H-3 and -4 were ordered by the Navy, the added fuselage length housing the extra fuel. Both of these types were capable of all-weather operation. The solution to the problem of limited range came with the incorporation of in-flight refuelling gear in the -4 and retrofitted back to the -2's. One hundred seventy-five F2H-3's and 55 F2H-4's were completed. The F2H-3 and -4 were reclassed as F-2C and F-2D respectively.

The F2H-4 wingspan was 44 feet 11 inches, length was 47 feet 6 inches, and height was 14 feet 5 inches. Wing area was 294 square feet. Gross weight was 19,000 pounds. Maximum speed of the F2H-4 was 610 mph at sea level with a service ceiling of 56,000 feet. Four 20 mm cannons were located in the nose, and some Banshees were armed with two Sidewinder missiles.

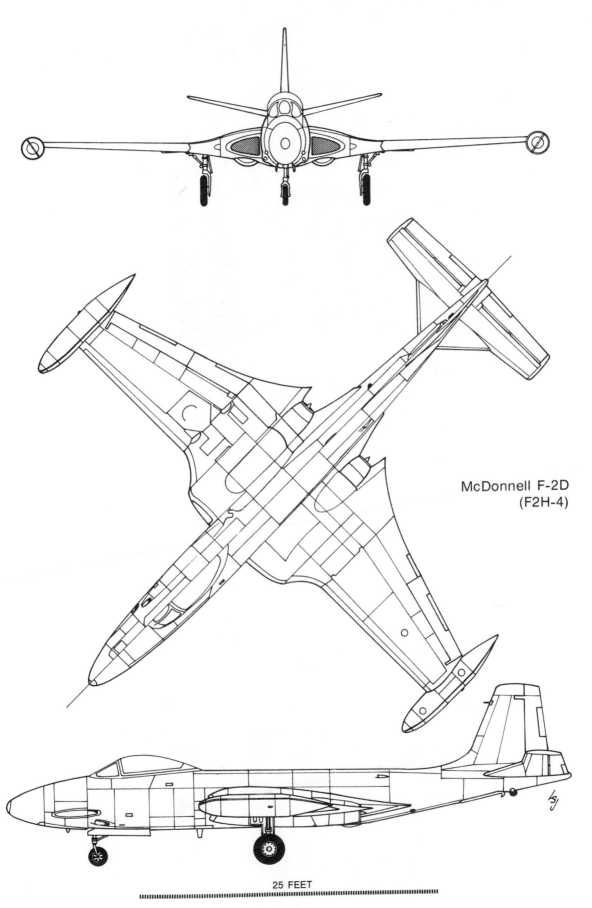

McDonnell F-2D
(F2H-4)

25 FEET

The F-2 Banshee was an outgrowth of McDonnell's first jet fighter, the FH-1 Phantom. McDonnell Douglas

This F2H-3 and the F2H-4 had their fuselages extended to carry additional fuel. McDonnell Douglas

McDONNELL
F-3 DEMON (F3H)

The missile carrying F3H-2M with four Sparrow AAM's. *McDonnell Douglas*

McDonnell's production momentum continued to increase with the selection of their swept-wing F3H Demon by the Navy as a missile platform. The company's Air Force designs were not moving beyond the prototype stage, but the Demon represented the third McDonnell plane to reach squadron status with the naval arm. Unfortunately, the story of the Demon is laced with tragedy and near cancellation due to circumstances beyond the designer's control.

The first XF3H-1 was ordered in July 1949, almost a year after the Air Force's XF-88 had begun flying. A strong resemblance to the early Voodoo could be found in the shape of the Demon's tail surfaces; but otherwise, the Navy plane was completely new. Most apparent was the selection of only one engine for the F3H-1, making it the sole operational McDonnell type to be thusly powered. It was this single engine that caused the near-demise of the Demon program.

By the time the XF3H-1 was ready for testing, the Navy had already ordered the production of 150 F3H-1N night fighters. This was increased to 528 examples when

the Demon flew on August 7, 1951. At this time, the fighter was deriving its power from a Westinghouse XJ40-WE-6 of 7,200 lbs., but it was intended to use a more powerful model of the engine for the heavier production Demons. Nine months later, the Westinghouse engine was suffering severe development problems. McDonnell suggested using an Allison J71-A-2 of 14,-250 lbs. with afterburning until the more powerful J40 could be perfected. The Navy decided the first 60 Demons would make use of the early J40, while the Allison was to be installed from number 61 on.

The Navy started accepting delivery of the F3H-1N in January 1954, and the underpowered J40 engine began taking its toll on the planes and their pilots. By July 1955, eleven crashes had destroyed six planes and killed four pilots. Of 56 F3H-1N Demons, twenty-nine were re-engined to become F3H-2N's, but twenty-one of the planes were permanently grounded and relegated to mechanics schools.

A redesign of the Demon to take the Allison J71 gave the Navy the fighter it had been seeking in the first place. The chord of the wing had been enlarged on the F3H-

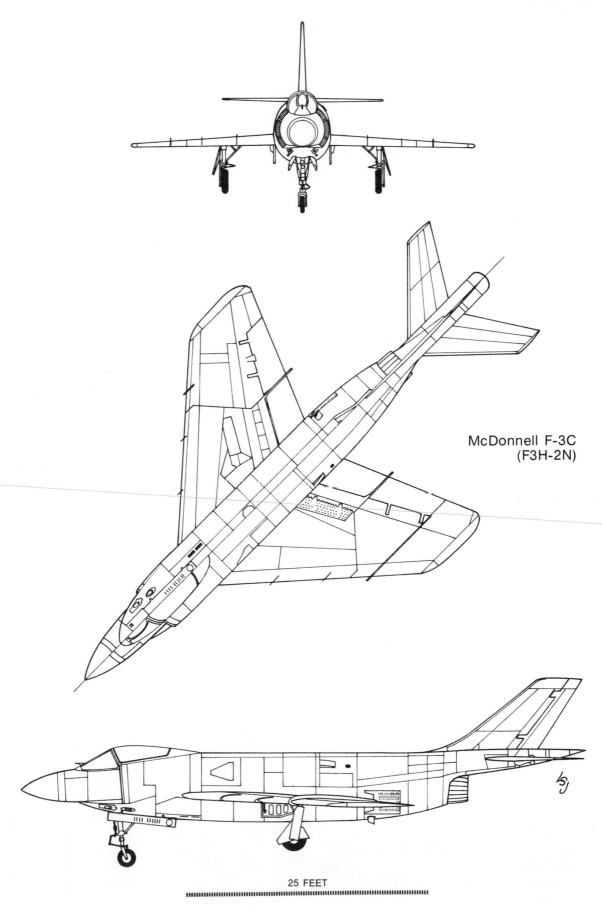

McDonnell F-3C
(F3H-2N)

25 FEET

308

2N's, increasing the area and making it a stable platform for launching its four Sparrow missiles. Four 20 mm cannons were carried in the nose.

Production ended in November 1959, with the 519th Demon. Despite its near-disastrous beginning, the F3H proved successful and remained operational until 1965.

The F3H-2N had a wingspan of 35 feet 4 inches, length of 58 feet 11 inches, was 14 feet 7 inches high, and had a wing area of 519 square feet. Empty weight was 22,133 pounds, gross weight was 33,900 pounds. Internal fuel amounted to 1,500 gallons. This model of the Demon could reach 647 mph at 30,000 feet. Service ceiling was 42,-650 feet. Range was 1,370 miles without air-to-air refueling.

The F3H-2 became the F-3B and the F3H-2N was the F-3C.

McDonnell's F3H-1N suffered from an underpowered engine.   *McDonnell Douglas*

When the Demon was designed to accept a more powerful engine, it became a successful front line fighter. This photo shows an F3H-2N.
McDonnell Douglas

McDONNELL
F-4 PHANTOM II (F4H)

The F-4J is the major Navy production model.

McDonnell Douglas

Fourth in McDonnell's unbroken line of successful Navy fighters is the F-4 Phantom II. Originally designed to fulfill an attack role, the designation AH-1 was assigned to the program. The projected fighter was to be a single-seat, twin engine craft armed with four 20 mm cannons. But a revision in the Navy's mission requirements resulted in a complete redesign of the plane to groom it for the role as missile-armed interceptor. The designation F4H-1 distinguished the altered design; and an order for two planes was placed in August of 1955. This was followed by another order a year later leading to the construction of 23 F4H-1's (F-4A) for evaluation.

When first seen, the Phantom II appears to have been designed by the proverbial "committee." Its wingtips sweep up and its tail droops to give a most unorthodox look; but both of these have a specific function. The twenty-three degree droop to the horizontal stabilizers places these surfaces away from the wing downwash which would tend to blanket them at high speeds. During the development of the Phantom II,

it was determined that a three degree dihedral angle would greatly improve lateral stability. However, to add the necessary dihedral would require an extensive rework of the wing and main landing gear structure. The designers ascertained that by adding twelve degrees of dihedral to the outer folding panels, the same effect would be obtained. Thus, the Phantom gained its most distinguishing characteristics.

The F-4 was first taken into its aerial environment on May 27, 1958, on the force of two General Electric J79-GE-3A engines of 14,800 lbs. of afterburning thrust. The Phantom II promptly set out to capture a basketful of world altitude and speed records. It climbed to 98,557 feet on one flight and set two closed-course records of 1,390.21 mph for 100 km. and 1,216 mph for 200 km.

After passing its carrier qualification trials in February 1960, the Phantom was ready to join the Navy. Transitional training began with pilots of VF-121 in February, 1961; the Marines of VMF-314

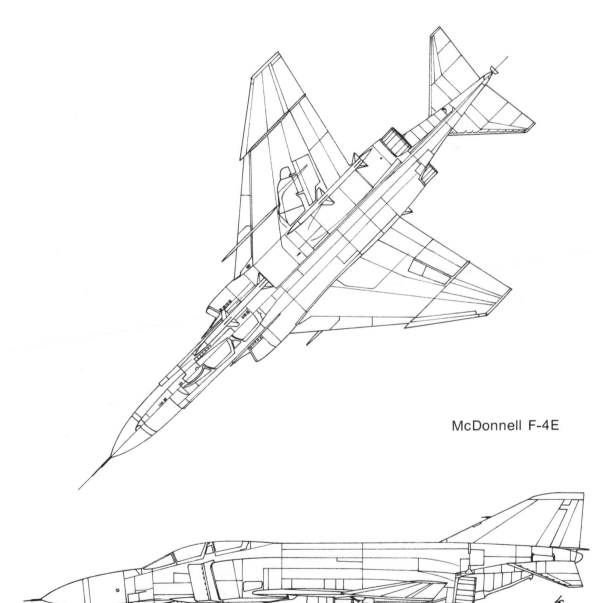

McDonnell F-4E

25 FEET

became the first of that service to receive the new fighter. F-4A production concluded when the 24th unit of the second order was completed, making a total of 47 of the type.

The F-4B became the Navy's first major production type, delivery beginning in 1961. During the same year, the Air Force was asked to compare the Phantom with its F-106A. The results of the trials showed the Navy fighter was superior in load carrying, had greater range, maintenance time was much lower, and the radar was more efficient than the Air Force plane. In March 1962, the Phantom was ordered by the Air Force to serve as an air superiority craft. These planes were originally known as F-110A Spectres, but became F-4C's with the classification change. The F-4B and F-4C are quite similar—the most obvious external difference is the use of wider tires on the Air Force plane, necessitating a bulged fairing over the wheel wells. This feature was adapted to all subsequent Phantoms as their weight increased.

The F-4E is the definitive Air Force model of the Phantom. It carries a nose-mounted Vulcan 20 mm rotary cannon as a result of deficiencies found in fighters armed only with missiles. During the Vietnam War, the lack of cannon armament was found to be a major disadvantage to the Air Force. Often, gunfire alone would have been sufficient for target destruction, and far less expensive than the sophisticated missiles. Missiles do have their place, of course, and the Vulcan cannon supplements the four Sparrow and/or Sidewinders usually carried by the Phantom.

The F-4J has supplanted the Navy/Marine F-4B as the production model. The designation F-4N is applied to upgraded "B's."

The F-4E Phantom II has a wingspan of 38 feet 5 inches, is 63 feet long and 16 feet 3 inches high. Wing area is 530 square feet. Empty, the F-4E weighs 30,073 pounds; gross is 57,400 pounds. With two 17,900 lb. General Electric J79-GE-17 turbojets, the F-4E can reach 1,450 mph (Mach 2.2) at 36,000 feet. As on nearly all supersonic types, the engine inlet is fitted with adjustable ramps for the most efficient air flow. Combat ceiling is 71,000 feet.

In addition to the Vulcan cannon, the F-4E can carry four Sparrow III missiles in troughs on the fuselage underside. Two more Sparrows or four Sidewinders can be fitted to underwing pylons. Up to 16,000 pounds of conventional or nuclear bombs can be carried on one fuselage and four wing hardpoints.

When the Phantom first joined the Air Force, it was designated F-110 Spectre. *McDonnell Douglas*

NORTHROP
F-5 FREEDOM FIGHTER, TIGER II

The F-5A became the Air Force's first "lightweight" jet fighter.   *Northrop*

As the speed of the modern jet fighter increased, its complexity, weight and cost have increased even more. In 1925, the Curtiss Company charged the Army $9,862 for each of its P-1C Hawks. In the mid-'forties, a P-51 Mustang cost $50,985. The first supersonic fighter, the F-100A, went for $663,354 a copy. Modern advanced fighters are costing up to fourteen million dollars apiece. To reverse this trend, Northrop devised a tiny Freedom Fighter at a cost within the budget of America's smaller Allies. The F-5E model is being offered for $2,147,000 each.

The Freedom Fighter began as a company funded project in November 1955. The development by General Electric of a lightweight, high velocity output engine caught the attention of Northrop's engineering staff. The engine was intended primarily for missiles, but Northrop's designers could see in it the potential for an uncomplicated supersonic fighter. When the Air Force issued a list of requirements for a supersonic trainer, Northrop began to conform their new fighter ideas around the trainer concept as well, designating their designs N-156F and N-156T. The latter was finally to emerge as the T-38 Talon.

In the meantime, the Air Force showed more than a passing interest in the N-156F; the Defense Department underwrote nearly $50 million for assembly of three aircraft and refinement of the engines. The first plane, 59-4987, was completed and flown on July 30, 1959. Power was provided by two General Electric J85-GE-5's of 3,850 lbs. with afterburning. The second N-156F was soon to join the test program, but the third was cancelled as official interest waned.

On April 25, 1962, the future of the Freedom Fighter was secured when it was selected for use by the Mutual Assistance Pact (MAP) countries. At this time, the official designation F-5A was given the fighter. The third prototype was reinstated and became the first production F-5A.

While the F-5 has been tailored to fit the needs of smaller air arms, the Freedom Fighter has also found favor in the U.S. Air Force; this service uses the F-5A and its two-

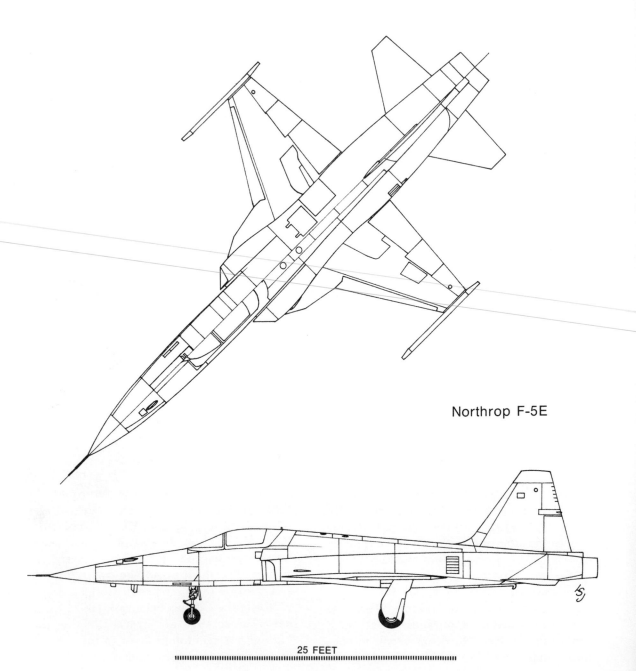

Northrop F-5E

25 FEET

314

The Tiger II two-seater is designated F-5F. *Northrop*

The N156F Freedom Fighter prototype was developed around a pair of missile engines. *Northrop*

A line-up of two-place F-5B's. *Northrop*

seat derivative, the F-5B. The latter can be used both as a tactical trainer or fighter.

The F-5A/B powerplant is a pair of J85-GE-13 engines rated at 3,050 lbs. normally, with 4,080 lbs. achieved with afterburning. This gives the plane a speed of 945 mph (Mach 1.43) at 36,860 feet.

The F-5 was designed for ease of maintenance and rapid serviceability. For its use in the MAP program, the ability to take-off from short unimproved fields is a requirement that the F-5 easily meets. Several of the countries flying F-5's are using the little interceptor in the all-weather role. No doubt, it is a lot of airplane for the relatively low cost per unit.

On August 11, 1972, the greatly improved F-5E was flown from Edwards AFB. This plane, labeled Tiger II, has 920 more

pounds of thrust per engine and a maximum speed of 1,056 mph at 36,090 feet. It has a wingspan of 26 feet 8½ inches, is 48 feet 2½ inches long, 13 feet 2½ inches high, and wing area is 186 square feet. Fully loaded weight is 21,834 pounds. Combat ceiling is 53,500 feet. Maximum range is 2,314 miles.

Two 20 mm M-39 cannons grace the nose of the F-5E and the earlier models. Supplemental armament includes nearly every contemporary weapon such as missiles and bombs. A total of 7,000 pounds of ordnance can be carried externally on seven hard-points.

As time would prove, the Northrop concept of lightweight and low cost was not a step backward, but a realistic approach to future fighter requirements.

"This way up." An F-5E Tiger II stands on its tail.

Northrop

DOUGLAS
F-6 SKYRAY (F4D-1)

The prototype Skyray with the Westinghouse engine.   *Douglas*

In selecting the name Skyray, Douglas could not have chosen a more descriptive title for their F4D-1. The Skyray was a compact design with smoothly flowing lines giving it an unmistakable planform. Its semi-delta wing was developed from the research done by Dr. Alexander Lippisch for Germany during World War II.

Design of a short-range, fast climbing, carrier-borne interceptor was requested by the Navy's Bureau of Aeronautics in 1947. The Bureau was intrigued with the potential offered by the delta configuration and asked Douglas engineers to investigate this shape. Extensive wind tunnel tests led to the creation of the bat-like form, which was not strictly a delta but a highly-swept wing of very low aspect ratio. All the horizontal flying controls were attached to the wing trailing edge classifying the Skyray as "tailless."

Two XF4D-1's were ordered in 1948, these to be built around the Westinghouse J40 then under development. The engines were not ready by the time the airframes were completed so Allison's 5,000 lb. J35-A-17 was substituted for the initial flights,

the first of these taking place on January 23, 1951. The alternate engine, with its lesser power output, complicated the flight test program and the Skyray was unable to reveal its potential performance until an XJ40-WE-6 was installed. However, with 2,000 lbs. more power, the XF4D-1 was still underpowered. On March 15, 1953, the Navy decided to install a Pratt & Whitney J57-P-2 on production Skyrays, eventually cancelling the Westinghouse engine.

The changeover to the Pratt & Whitney engine necessitated a redesign of nearly eighty percent of the airframe to accommodate the larger engine. To save time, the redesign was done while the first production planes were taking shape.

While the modifications were taking place on the production line, the second XF4D-1, reengined with an afterburning J40-WE-8, established a world's speed record of 753.4 mph on October 3, 1953, becoming the first carrier plane to hold that honor. Eventually, the Skyray set no less than seven official speed records.

The initial flight of the first production

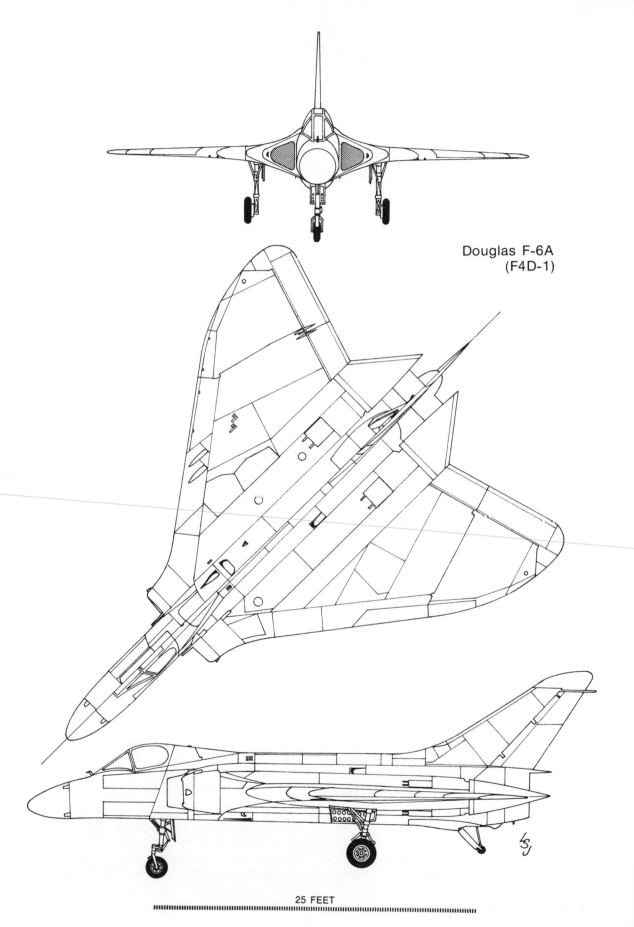

Douglas F-6A
(F4D-1)

25 FEET

F4D-1, with the Pratt & Whitney engine, took place on June 5, 1954; the plane easily slipped past Mach 1 in level flight. A change in the inlet duct to improve the engine air flow was required before the Skyray was ready for delivery; then the fighter was absorbed into Navy and Marine squadrons. The last Skyray was completed in December 1958, making a total of 420 F4D-1's.

The span of the Skyray's 557 square foot wing was 33 feet 6 inches. Overall length was 45 feet 8 inches, height was 13 feet.

Empty weight was 16,024 pounds, gross weight was 27,000 pounds with 1,240 gallons of fuel in both internal and drop tanks. Operational Skyrays had a maximum speed of 695 mph at 36,000 feet using the Pratt & Whitney J57-P-8B of 10,500 lbs. with the afterburner. Service ceiling was 55,000 feet.

Four 20 mm cannons were located in the Skyray's wing. Two Sidewinder missiles and two rocket pods carried nineteen 2.75 inch FFAR's supplementing the cannons on intercept missions.

The bat-like shape of the Skyray was unmistakable. The plane was very popular with its pilots.   Douglas

Two F4D-1's of VFAW-3, on a tactical mission for TAC. This squadron was on loan to the Air Force and operated with TAC squadrons for a time.
Douglas

CONVAIR
YF-7A SEA DART (YF2Y)

The F2Y-1 was troubled with a phenomenon known as ski-pounding. This ultimately led to its abandonment.
Convair

Water-based aircraft, and their ability to operate without prepared flying fields, have intrigued designers for years. One of the major drawbacks to the type was the excessive drag created by the floats needed for such operation. Floats which could be retracted, or even deflated, had been tried, but these were only partial solutions. The arrival of jet propulsion eliminated the need to place the fuselage far above the water to allow for propeller clearance.

Shortly after World War II, Convair engineers undertook the design of a jet fighter whose swept-wing blended smoothly into the fuselage. At rest, the plane would float on the lower wing surfaces. As power was applied to the two engines, the fuselage would rise out of the water and plane on a retractable step in the hull bottom. Convair titled this new fighter design "Skate" and built a radio-controlled model for preliminary testing.

At the same time Convair was developing the Skate concept, NACA was experimenting with a hydro-ski landing gear which seemed to offer some advantages over the blended-wing design. The principal advantage of the skis was that the airframe would not be subjected to the pounding of the water during take-off and landing. The skis themselves would absorb the shock. This would then permit the airframe to be lighter in structure; and since the skis could easily be retracted, the seaplane would then have the aerodynamic characteristics of a land-based plane.

On October 1, 1948, a competition was begun for a water-based fighter and Convair was selected to make a comparative study of the two concepts. It was determined that an airplane using the skis would be more compact and offer better performance than initially thought, and the Navy authorized a design along these lines.

Convair patterned their seaplane fighter after their delta-winged YF-102, which was then under development for the Air Force. On January 19, 1951, the Navy ordered two prototypes, each to use a pair of 3,400 lb. Westinghouse J34-WE-32 engines until a more powerful unit could be obtained. The planes were designated XF2Y-1, and Con-

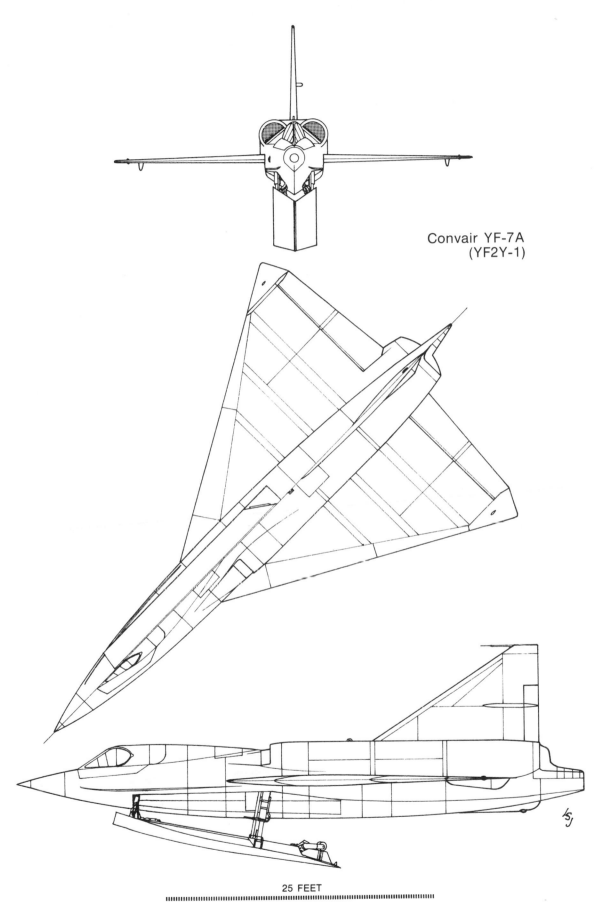

Convair YF-7A
(YF2Y-1)

25 FEET

321

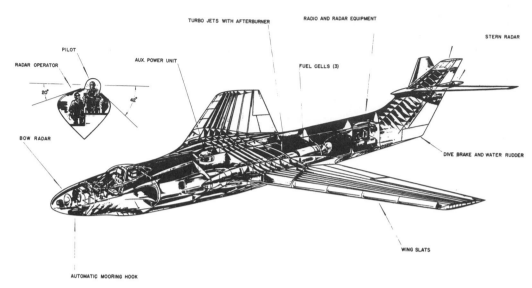

PLASTIC TIP ANTENNA

TURBO JETS WITH AFTERBURNER   RADIO AND RADAR EQUIPMENT

STERN RADAR

PILOT

RADAR OPERATOR   AUX. POWER UNIT   FUEL CELLS (3)

20°   42°

BOW RADAR

DIVE BRAKE AND WATER RUDDER

WING SLATS

AUTOMATIC MOORING HOOK

The Skate was Convair's original proposal for a seaplane fighter.   *Convair*

NAVY
137634

With its skis retracted, the XF2Y-1 presented a sleek picture.   *Convair*

Over one hundred types of skis were tested on the Sea Dart. Of interest are the numbers painted on the hull of this single-ski version.

B. J. Long

vair called them Sea Darts. On August 28, 1952, an order for 12 Sea Darts was placed.

During a series of taxi tests, the XF2Y-1 made an inadvertent flight of some 1,000 feet distance on January 14, 1953. The official first flight took place four months later, on April 9. The reason for the delayed flight was due to an unexpected ski-pounding occurring at planing speeds above 60 mph. The vibration was so severe, it was feared that the airframe would be damaged. A redesign of the skis and improved shock absorbers reduced this shortcoming, but during the span of the development program, over one hundred different ski configurations were tried in an attempt to eliminate the problem entirely.

Flight testing of the Sea Dart proved disappointing since the two Westinghouse engines did not provide sufficient power to achieve the desire performance. The engine proposed for the production Sea Darts was also in trouble. The Westinghouse XJ46-WE-2, which was supposed to provide 6,100 lbs. of power with an afterburner, could not reach its goal. The limited available power coupled with a high transonic drag rise reduced the anticipated maximum speed from Mach 1.5 to Mach .99. A complete redesign of the Sea Dart was proposed. As the F2Y-2, the seaplane fighter would use a single 15,000 lbs. Pratt & Whitney J75, or 12,000 lbs. Wright J67, with an improved single hydro-ski. But by this time, the mounting development difficulties were creating questions about the feasibility of the seaplane concept. On November 4, 1954, during a public demonstration of the Sea Dart, the plane was accidentally pushed beyond its limitations, causing it to disintegrate in front of the viewers. This tragedy, plus continuing setbacks with the hydro-skis, eventually led to the abandonment of the seaplane fighter concept in 1956. Only four of the aircraft were built.

Wingspan of the Sea Dart was 33 feet 8 inches, wing area was 563 square feet. Fuselage length was 52 feet 7 inches, height was 16 feet 2 inches. Empty weight was 12,625 pounds; gross weight was 16,527 pounds. It was estimated that the XF2Y-1 would have a maximum speed of 994 mph at 35,000 feet, but with the unexpected drag and engine problems, this was unlikely. On August 3, 1954, however, one Sea Dart did exceed Mach 1 in a shallow dive. Service ceiling was 50,200 feet, range was 513 miles.

It is interesting to note that the Sea Dart was given the F-7 designation nearly six years after its cancellation.

On this test, a dual-ski configuration was tried. Note RATO bottle under wing. This plane is designated YF2Y-1.
B. J. Long

CHANCE VOUGHT-LTV
F-8 CRUSADER (F8U)

The unique variable-incidence wing allows the Crusader's fuselage to remain relatively level during landing approaches.

LTV

The first carrier plane to exceed 1,000 mph; winner of the Collier Trophy for its design and development; recipient of the first Certificate of Merit to be awarded by the Bureau of Aeronautics; winner of the Thompson Trophy for just plain speed—the F-8 Crusader was born a champion.

The Crusader began taking shape on paper in September 1952, in answer to the Navy's requirement for a supersonic carrier fighter. Among the features the Navy liked was a unique method of tilting the wing to increase its incidence during take-off and landing. A hydraulic actuator moves the leading edge of the wing upward seven degrees while the camber is increased by drooping the leading and trailing edges. All of this action allows the fuselage to remain relatively level during the critical landing approach.

The XF8U-1 prototype was ready to show its capabilities on March 25, 1955, when it rose from the dry lake bed at Edwards AFB. When it again touched the baked desert earth, fifty-two minutes later, it had become a member of the Mach Buster's club.

Production of the Crusader, as it became known, was commenced, and the first of these planes was flown just six months after the prototype. Eight months later, the Navy received its first F-8—a remarkably short development period for such an advancement in fighter design.

The initial production run amounted to 318 F-8A day fighter types. This version used a Pratt & Whitney J57-P-4A of 16,200 lbs. thrust with afterburning. Internal armament consisted of four 20 mm cannons and thirty-two 2.75 inch missiles in a retracting launch tray. This model could reach Mach 1.67. On July 16, 1957, Major John Glenn, later to become an astronaut, made the first non-stop transcontinental flight at an average speed above Mach 1 in an RF-8A.

The F-8B was devised for limited all-weather operations. A small radar scanner was installed in the nose of this Crusader. A total of 130 F-8B's were completed before the appearance of the "Air Superiority" F-8C's. This model has an increase of 700 lbs. engine thrust, but is limited to Mach 1.7

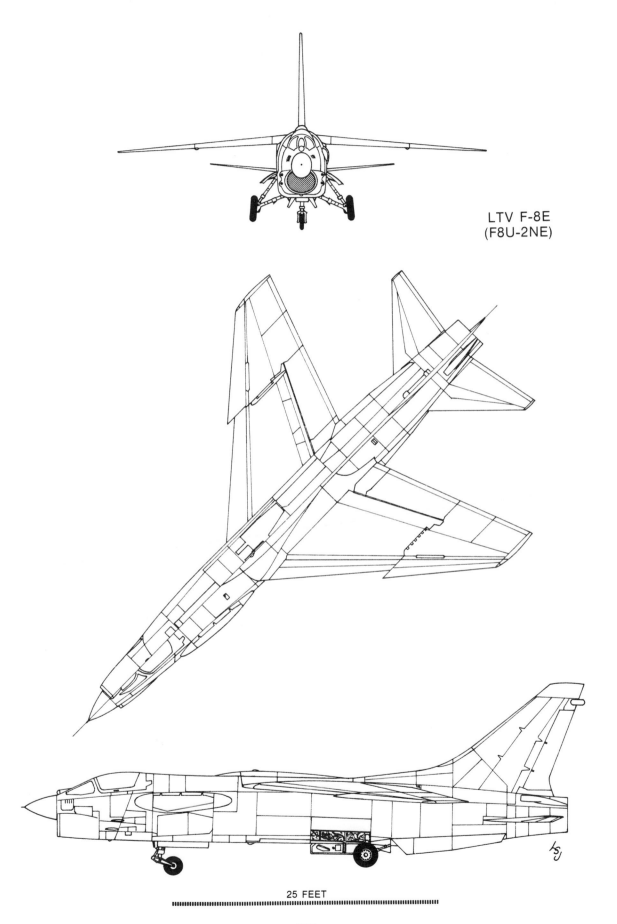

LTV F-8E
(F8U-2NE)

25 FEET

because of instability at higher speeds despite the addition of two ventral fins on the aft fuselage. One hundred eighty-seven "C's" were delivered. The retracting rocket tray was deleted on the next series, the F-8D, to provide for increased fuel tankage. The F-8D designation is carried by 152 Crusaders.

Underwing attachment points allow the 286 F-8E's to carry external ordnance in ground-attack operations. All-weather ability was increased with an enlarged search and fire control radar in the nose. New electronics for the revised operations are located in a hump on the fuselage spine.

In September, 1955, the Navy made inflight refueling capability mandatory on all their aircraft. To achieve this on the Crusader, the refueling probe was fitted to the left fuselage behind the cockpit. Since the plumbing was mounted outside the fuselage skin, a streamlined fairing was placed over it.

The F-8E Crusader is propelled by a Pratt & Whitney J57-P-20A with 10,700 lbs. normal and 18,000 lbs. with afterburning. Maximum speed is 1,120 mph (Mach 1.7) at 40,000 feet. Service ceiling is 58,000 feet. Wingspan is 35 feet 2 inches, length is 54 feet 6 inches, height is 15 feet 9 inches. Wing area is 350 square feet. The F-8E, fully loaded with fuel and external weapons, weighs 34,000 pounds. Supplementing its four 20 mm cannons, the F-8E can also carry up to 5,000 pounds of attack weapons.

The F-8's ailerons are mounted on the inboard segment of the wings. The outer panels fold upward for carrier storage, as on most Navy fighters. On occasion, the Crusader has been flown, unintentionally of course, with the wings folded. In one instance, when it was realized that the wings were folded, the pilot quickly rolled his plane right and left, actually snapping the wings in place. This is not the recommended procedure, however, as it tends to distort the lifting surfaces.

The F-8E is fitted with underwing racks permitting it to carry external weapons.   *LTV*

GRUMMAN
F-9 COUGAR (F9F)

The Grumman Cougar was an interim design used by the Navy until higher performance swept-wing jets were available.
Grumman

The Navy's first swept-winged carrier fighter was Grumman's F9F-6 Cougar. Basically a continuation of the straight-winged Panther series, the Cougar differed externally in the angle of the wing and stabilizer surfaces. The short fuselage and raked tail were those of the Panther.

The prototype Cougar resulted from a Navy contract dated March 2, 1951, and made its aerial debut on September 20, 1951. Because of its relationship to the preceding Panthers, the production Cougars were rolling from the assembly lines only five months later.

Sweeping the flying surfaces back thirty-five degrees and increasing the thrust by 1,000 lbs. gave the Cougar a maximum speed over 85 mph greater than that of the Panther. The original production order covered 706 F9F-6's using a Pratt & Whitney J48-P-8 of 7,250 lbs. A second contract gave the Navy 168 Allison-powered F9F-7's. These used J33-A-16A engines of 6,350 lbs. thrust. With water injection, the thrust rate increased to 7,000 lbs.

Although the performance of the Cougar was satisfactory, especially compared to the Panther, both Grumman and the Navy felt there was still some untapped performance in the basic concept. To enhance low-speed handling, an important characteristic of a carrier plane, the wing leading edge was cambered and the chord of the outer panels increased. More area was added at the trailing edge resulting in a proportionately thinner wing section and raising the critical Mach number. The larger wing also provided space for more fuel to increase the Cougar's range. To further refine the new Cougar, the fuselage was lengthened 8 inches, improving the fineness ratio and permitting the installation of still more fuel tanks. The extra wing and fuselage tanks added 140 gallons of fuel. The new F9F-8 flew on December 18, 1953, and paved the way for 711 more -8's. The effectiveness of the redesign was shown when the F9F-8 was able to reach a maximum speed of 714 mph, as compared to 690 mph achieved by the -7 types. Mach 1 could be reached in a slight dive. A production line upgrade added a bulge for search radar under the nose and in-flight refueling provisions.

To teach pilots how to handle the unique characteristics of swept-wing aircraft, Grumman built 399 two-place F9F-8T (TF-

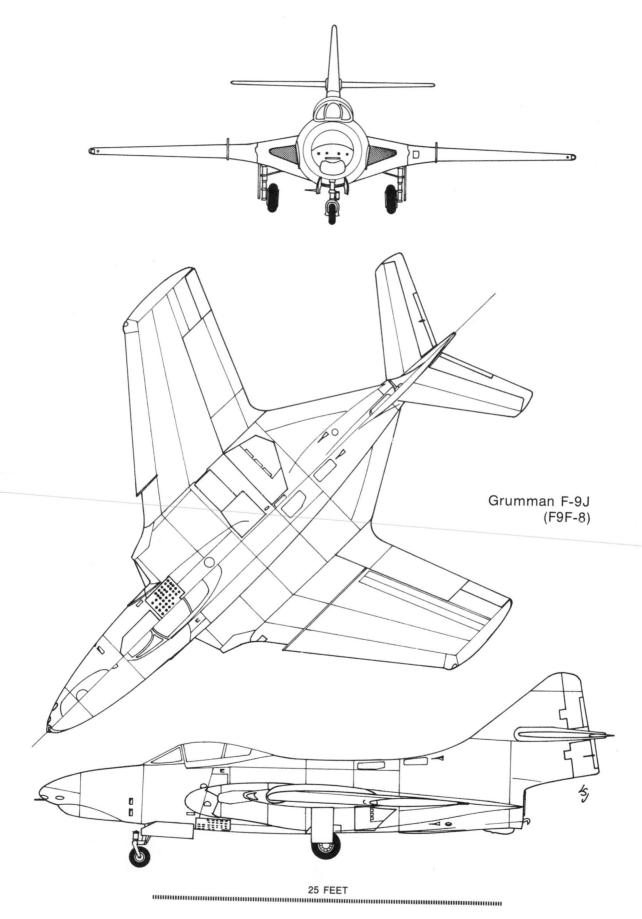

Grumman F-9J
(F9F-8)

25 FEET

9J) trainers which could reach 705 mph. The trainer was 2 feet 10 inches longer than the fighter Cougars.

In its final form the F9F-8 (F-9J) had a wingspan of 34 feet 6 inches, length of 40 feet 10 inches and a height of 15 feet. Fully loaded for launch, the Cougar weighed 20,000 pounds. Service ceiling was 50,000 feet, range was 1,300 miles.

The Cougar's nose held four 20 mm M3 cannons and underwing attachment points could carry up to 4,000 pounds of bombs or missiles.

While most of the Panthers had been retired by the time the designations were changed, several of them were classed as F-9's.

The probe extending from the nose of this Cougar permits air-to-air refueling.   *U.S. Navy*

Grumman's Panther, straight-winged progenitor of the Cougar series. This one is an F9F-2.   *Grumman*

DOUGLAS
F-10 SKYKNIGHT (F3D)

A production F3D-1 awaits delivery to the Navy. The marks on the rudder are used to determine the plane's approach angle during carrier landings.
Douglas

The value of a night interception aircraft can be judged by the fact that the Douglas F3D Skyknight was responsible for the destruction of more enemy aircraft in Korea than all other Navy types. The F3D also has the distinction of making the first nighttime jet-to-jet kill when, on November 2, 1952, a Marine Skyknight downed a Mig 15.

An order for three planes on April 3, 1946, set Douglas engineers to the task of building the Navy's first night fighter. The Skyknight was an uncomplicated State-of-the-Art machine with two 3,000 lb. Westinghouse J34-WE-22's attached to the fuselage sides beneath the wings. The pilot and radar operator sat beside each other in a pressurized cockpit. The side-by-side positioning of the crew created a wide fuselage with a bulbous nose, ideal for the large amount of radar needed for tracking its prey in the dark. Reliable ejection seats were still under development so a novel method of exiting was devised—the crew slid down a tunnel beneath the cockpit and dropped from the airplane through a hatch between the engines. This system could be safely used even at high speeds.

The XF3D-1 made its initial flight on March 23, 1948. Twenty-eight F3D-1's were ordered following the successful test program, the first of these flying on February 13, 1950. A pair of 4,600 lb. Westinghouse J46-WE-3 engines were to be installed in seventy F3D-2's. The larger size of the engines required a redesign of the engine nacelles, but failure of the engine to overcome its shortcomings resulted, instead, in the use of two 3,400 lb. J34-WE-36 units in the larger nacelles. Two hundred thirty-seven of this variant were produced.

The Skyknight was capable of carrier operations, but the type was operated in combat only by the Marines from land bases.

A swept-wing Skyknight was designed, as the F3D-3, to use the J46 engines. This model was to have a speed of 515 mph at 40,000 feet and a gross weight of 34,000 pounds. An order for 102 of this type was cancelled before the first example was completed.

Not only did the Skyknight prove its worth in combat, it became the basis of several conversions which maintained its value into the 1960's. Among the new duties performed by the F3D, were missile

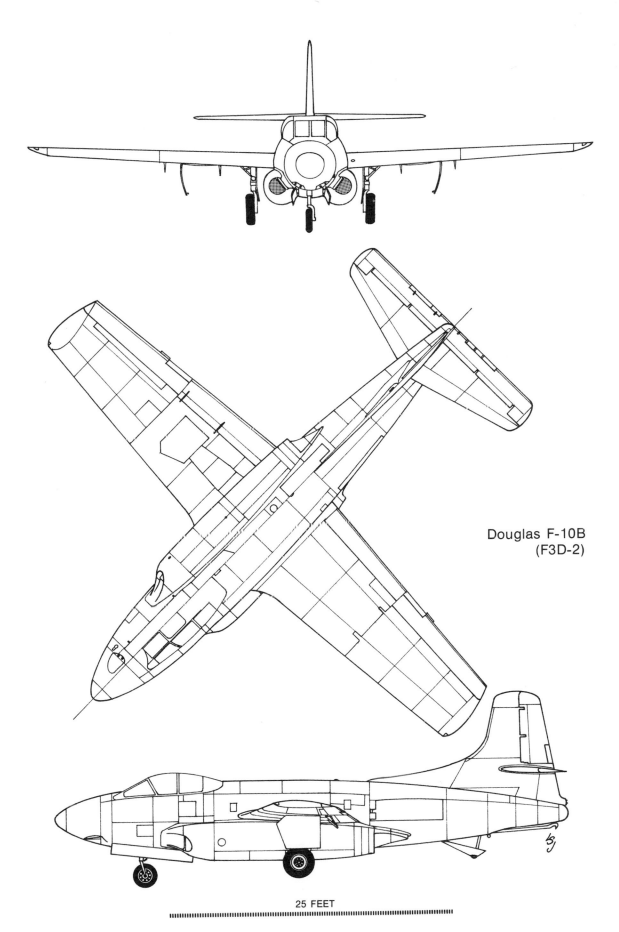

Douglas F-10B
(F3D-2)

25 FEET

launchers (F3D-2M) which could carry and fire four Sparrow AAM's. Sixteen of this type were made. Thirty F3D-2Q's carried electronics countermeasures. The second seat was ideal for crew practice, thus the F3D-T2 trainer was created.

Proportions of the Skyknight were: wingspan of 50 feet; length of 45 feet 6 in-ches; height of 16 feet 6 inches; wing area of 400 square feet. The F3D-2 weighed 18,160 pounds empty and grossed out at 26,850 pounds. Maximum speed was 560 mph at 20,000 feet. Service ceiling was 42,800 feet. Fuel capacity was 1,290 gallons giving the Skyknight a maximum range of 1,120 miles.

Marine-operated Skyknights, such as this, were credited with more enemy planes destroyed in Korea than all other Navy types. This one is an F3D-2M, one of sixteen built.   *Douglas*

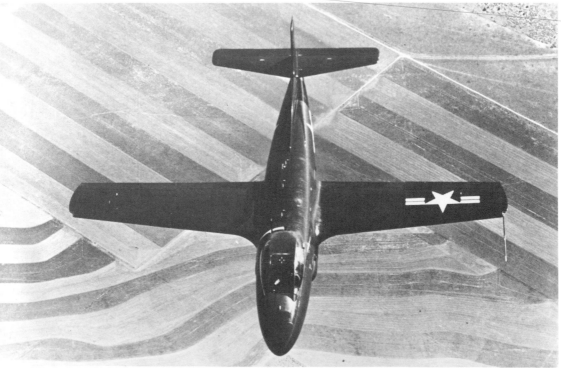

The XF3D-1 prototype of the Skyknight series.   *Douglas*

GRUMMAN
F-11 TIGER (F11F)

Grumman's Tiger was the first Navy plane to use the area-rule principle.   *Grumman*

The fighter that was to become Grumman's Tiger actually began as a continuation of the Panther/Cougar series. The company model number 98 was applied to the design, but the military designation was F9F-8—later changed to F9F-9 when the Cougar was obtained by the Navy.

Four basic changes to the original concept were required to make this offspring of the Cougar into a successful fighter on a par with its contemporaries. First, the fat fillets, housing the engine intakes, had to be eliminated to reduce drag. These were moved forward to the fuselage sides. Next, the wing was thinned in cross-section. This necessitated the relocation of the main landing gear, which was placed in the fuselage. Finally, the high-mounted stabilizer was lowered to the fuselage and the newly discovered area-rule principle applied to the fuselage, creating the characteristic coke bottle shape of a supersonic airplane.

All these features were then compacted into the smallest possible airframe wrapped around a Wright J65-W-7 of 7,500 lbs. No afterburner was available for the engine at

that time, but provisions were made for later installation of the device. With regard to its size, the Tiger was so small that only the wingtips needed folding for carrier stowage.

The first two flights of the F9F-9 were made on July 30, 1954. The lack of the afterburner was immediately apparent. In January 1955, the Tiger flew with an afterburning J65. The improved performance was quite obvious, but the design still needed refining to make the plane a suitable combat machine. The J65 afterburner had not been perfected, the cockpit visibility needed improving, and several obstacles common to a new aircraft were yet to be overcome.

A production contract had been approved for 44 F11F-1's, as the Tiger was finally designated, and these planes were used as development craft. A second contract produced another 157 planes making a total of 210 Tigers in all. The Tiger was accepted for operations in March 1957; its mission to be that of a day fighter.

Even during its service life, the Tiger was

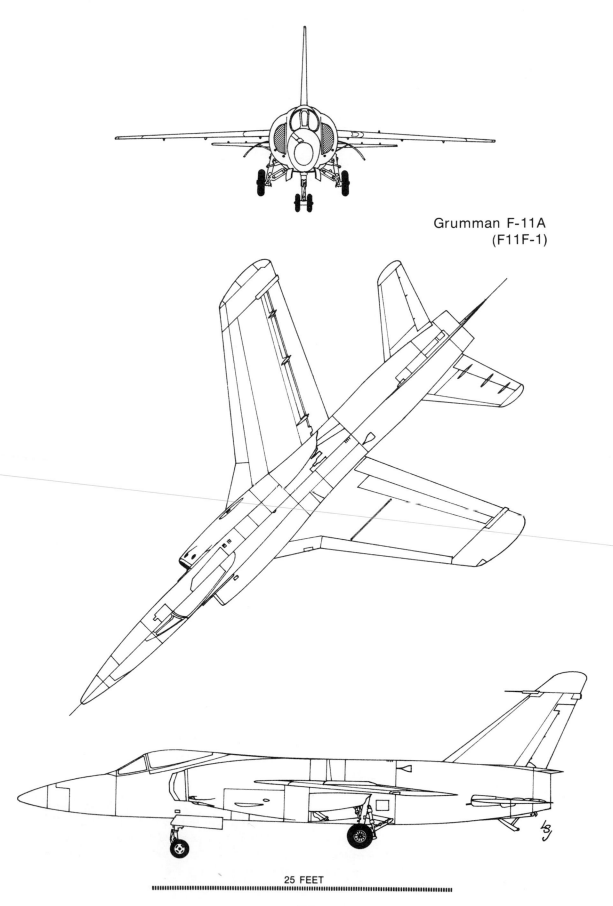

Grumman F-11A
(F11F-1)

25 FEET

The F11F-1 was designed to be a compact carrier fighter and was so small that only the wingtips needed to be folded for carrier stowage.   *Grumman*

Two Tigers were converted to the F11F-1F configuration and were capable of Mach 2 performance. Note the full span flaps in this view. The Tiger did not have ailerons but used wing-mounted spoilers for the same purpose.   *Grumman*

subjected to continuing changes. The main fault was more in the engine performance than the airframe design, though a great number of minor changes were made to the plane itself. Two Tigers were fitted with afterburning General Electric J79-GE-3A engines of 15,000 lbs. These two F11F-1F's could reach 1,220 mph and climb to an altitude of 76,939 feet under test conditions, but could not serve as combat types because the Tiger's small wing would not support their higher gross weight with combat gear at the slow speed required for a carrier approach.

It was during flight testing of the Tiger that one of aviation's most bizarre events occurred. During a weapons-firing test, one of the Tigers had discharged its cannons while in a shallow dive. A few seconds after firing its guns, the plane was shaken by the impact of its own cannon shells. The Tiger had actually overflown the shells and passed through their trajectory, shooting itself down. The pilot was able to maintain sufficient control of the plane to make a crashlanding without serious injury to himself, but the Tiger was destroyed by fire.

Acquisition of the Tiger by the famed Blue Angels flight demonstration team made the F11F a familiar sight to millions of thrilled spectators for several years. The light, maneuverable Tiger was ideally suited to the team's requirements; and in the long run, it is a fitting tribute to the plane's designers that it be immortalized in this manner.

The Tiger's 31 foot 7½ inch wing was equipped with spoilers instead of conventional ailerons. Roll was achieved by raising the spoiler from one or the other wing. Full-span flaps were fitted to the wing trailing edges. Speed brakes were located under the nose and between the landing gear doors.

Overall length of the F-11, as it was ultimately designated, was 46 feet 11 inches, and the plane stood 13 feet 3 inches high. Wing area was 250 square feet. Empty weight was 13,428 pounds; maximum take-off weight was 24,078 pounds. Operational

Tigers could reach a speed of 752 mph at sea level. Fuel capacity was 1,049 gallons for a range of 1,250 miles. Service ceiling was 41,900 feet. Four 20 mm cannons were built into the sides of the engine intakes and four Sidewinder AAM's could be carried on underwing pylons.

The famous Blue Angels performing in their Tigers.
Grumman

LOCKHEED
YF-12A

The SR-71 is a Mach 3 reconnaissance plane which was evolved from the YF-12A.   *Lockheed*

On December 22, 1964, a huge lance-like shape parted company with its shadow on a desert air strip in Nevada as the sky became the recipient of the most awesome fighting machine yet devised. Its proportions made it the largest fighter type to fly, and its weight exceeded by a great margin that of any other interceptor. For its first flight, the aircraft bore the designation A-11, assigned by Lockheed, but the official Air Force designation YF-12A has since been applied.

The design of the YF-12A was initiated when Lockheed won a competition for an advanced interceptor and received a contract in 1960. The requirements specified a cruise speed greater than Mach 3 and a sustained altitude higher than 80,000 feet. A plane capable of this performance had to be designed from the beginning. It was bound to be different, and it is.

Not long after the YF-12's began flying, airline pilots reported seeing strange-shaped aircraft flashing past them. Since the new interceptor had been conceived and built under the utmost secrecy, it is easy to

imagine what these pilots thought they saw. Its extraordinary performance and un-orthodox shape certainly would tend to place it in the category with other uniden-tified flying vehicles. But the YF-12A is very tangible indeed.

The YF-12A is virtually a titanium shell around a huge fuel tank. It is approximately 101 feet long, supported by a 1,800 square foot wing spanning 55 feet 7 inches. The top of the canted rudders are 18 feet 6 inches from the ground. The empty weight of this immense fighter is near 60,000 pounds; its gross weight is more than 140,000 pounds.

The sharp edge along the forward fuselage actually forms a forward lifting surface, as on a canard, thereby letting the fuselage itself generate aerodynamic lift. Inside this widened area are the bays which can house four Hughes AIM-47A Falcon AAM's. These missiles were originally intended to arm the cancelled XF-108 Rapier. The leading edge of the forward lifting plane contains infrared sensors, and the needle-like nose houses the necessary radar

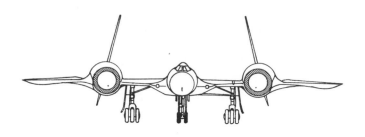

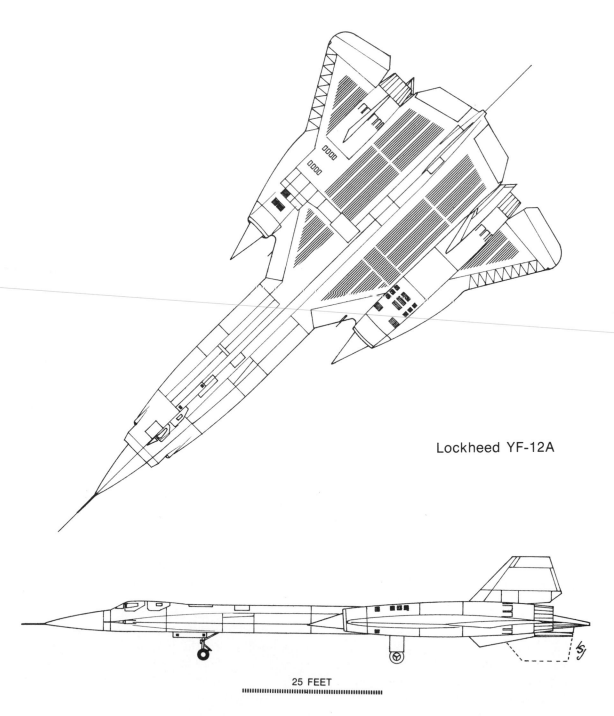

Lockheed YF-12A

25 FEET

and fire control systems. The highly responsive radar used in the YF-12A has a detection range of nearly 800 miles, or in terms of the YF-12's speed, about 20 minutes travel time.

Two YF-12A's established no less than twelve official world records on May 1st, 1965. Among these were the absolute speed of 2,070.102 mph and sustained altitude of 80,257.86 feet. At Mach 3 speeds, the heat generated by the YF-12A can reach 1,100 degrees F. To reduce this high temperature, the planes are coated with 60 pounds of a special black paint which helps dissipate the heat. But despite this, parts of the airplane still remain extremely hot for a while after the plane has landed. This great heat also has an effect on the airframe itself. As heated metal expands, it can distort the precise aerodynamic shapes of a Mach 3 aircraft. An ingenious method of overcoming this was the use of corrugations in the wing surfaces. These ripples allow the flexing of the metal skin without impairing the flying characteristics.

High performance flight, of the type undertaken by the YF-12A, requires a powerplant of phenomenal output. The huge 32,500 lb. Pratt & Whitney J58 engines were made specifically for the big fighter; they are equally as advanced in concept as well as performance. To attain the necessary Mach 3 cruise speed, the afterburner has to be in continuous operation. To achieve this, Pratt & Whitney designed the unit to function as a ramjet, reminiscent of the engine devised for the XF-103 interceptor. A complex sensing mechanism positions the inlet cone on each nacelle for the most efficient air flow to the engines. The fuel used is JP-7, a hydrocarbon-type developed for the YF-12A. Eighty thousand pounds of fuel are carried in five tanks.

At Mach 3, the YF-12A must make a turn of 180 miles radius to reverse its direction. In the high speed regime, most of the flight operations are performed by automatic systems. Because the plane was designed expressly for extremely high speeds, it is unusual to find that the YF-12A has very conventional low-speed characteristics. Approach speed is approximately 200 mph; touch-down is 172 mph.

The SR-71 is the production version of the A-11. Its primary duty is reconnaissance, and it differs mainly in electronic gear. The SR-71, nicknamed "Blackbird," has been refined for greater aerodynamic efficiency. The foreplane extends in an unbroken line to the nose, and the empennage protrudes six feet behind the delta wing. This increased area permits the elimination of the large retractable and two fixed ventral fins used on the YF-12A for high-speed stability.

Total quantities of the YF-12A have not been officially disclosed, but at least three planes were built as interceptors. SR-71 production has exceeded 21 units; but here again, the actual number is classified. In recognition of the advanced engineering involved in the development of the YF-12A/SR-71, the radical "Blackbird" became the recipient of the Collier Trophy in 1964.

The first A-11 as it appeared in a bare metal finish.   *Lockheed*

Lockheed's YF-12A, world's fastest fighter.   *U.S. Air Force*

The YF-12A is the largest fighter ever built for the Air Force.   *Lockheed*

The YF-12 port missile bays are open in this view. The teardrop pods suspended from the engines housed cameras used in tracking the missiles. Also seen are the folded ventral fin and the unique three-wheel main land -ing gear.
                    U.S. Air Force

GRUMMAN
F-14 TOMCAT

Grumman's Tomcat was the Navy's first operational swing-wing aircraft.   *Grumman*

The failure of the F-111B to meet the requirements set forth by the Navy resulted in a new competition for a suitable carrier-based fighter. Although variable-sweep wings were not required under the new specifications, Grumman proposed such a feature on their entry. By virtue of their involvement with the XF10F-1 Jaguar and the F-111B, Grumman had accumulated more experience with movable wings than any of the competing companies. On January 15, 1969, Grumman's Model 303 was selected to become the Navy's new F-14A air superiority fighter; the designation F-13 was bypassed. Six planes were to be built for the development program, followed by six more pre-production F-14A's. By the end of 1970, the prototype F-14A was completed, and given the name Tomcat.

Following the necessary ground tests, the F-14A was readied for its first flight on December 21, 1970—a full month ahead of the program. Unfortunately, the time gained by the earlier test schedule was lost when, on the second flight, the hydraulic system failed and the first Tomcat was destroyed. The ejection system functioned as advertised, however, and the crew safely abandoned the stricken plane.

Flight testing was continued on May 24, 1971, with the second Tomcat, and the program was accelerated as seven more planes were completed by the beginning of 1972. The F-14A was introduced into the fleet at NAS Miramar, California, on October 12, 1972. The first squadrons receiving the planes were VF-1 and VF-2.

An interesting feature of the F-14 is the pair of retractable vanes mounted in the leading edge of the glove which blends the movable wings into the fuselage. These triangular glove vanes extend outward for added stability as needed and can be operated manually or programmed by a computer. The Tomcat is also unusual in being the first production plane to use strong, but lightweight, composite boron-epoxy in its construction. The horizontal stabilizer structure features this material.

The F-14A reflects a return to fixed cannon armament with the inclusion of an M61A-1 20 mm rotary cannon, with 675

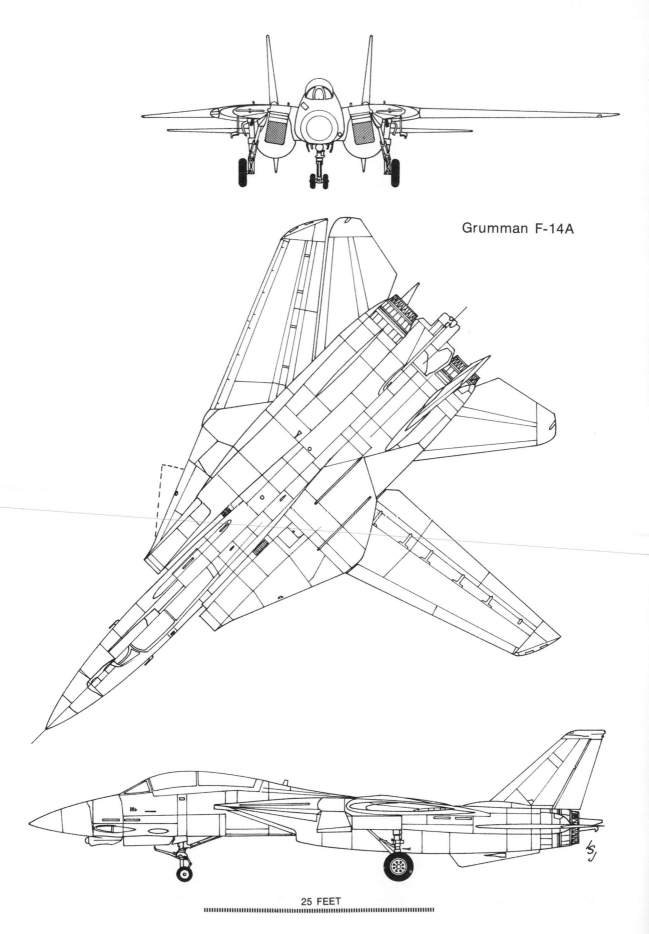

Grumman F-14A

25 FEET

rounds, in the port side of the fuselage. Six Phoenix AIM-54A missiles can be carried and launched simultaneously—each one directed to a different target. All the hardpoints are situated on the rigid portion of the glove and fuselage, obviating the need for swiveling pylons on the wings.

Nacelles mounted beneath the glove house a pair of Pratt & Whitney TF30-P-412 turbofans with an afterburning rating of 20,900 lbs. Internal fuel capacity is 16,-445 pounds. The unloaded weight of a Tomcat is 40,070 pounds; take-off gross weight is 55,000 pounds.

In order to provide the necessary keel area for supersonic flight, yet keep the overall height at a minimum for stowage below the deck of a carrier, two vertical stabilizers are carried on the F-14. They also provide an aerodynamic benefit by counteracting the unstable air flow over the intakes at high angles of attack.

With its wings in the forward position, the F-14A has a span of 64 feet 1½ inches. In normal swept condition, the span reduces to 38 feet 2 inches. For carrier stowage, the wings can be positioned over the stabilizers reducing the span to only 33 feet 3½ inches. Wing area is 565 square feet. In flight, the sweep angles range from 20 to 68 degrees. Overall length is 61 feet 11½ inches; height is 16 feet even. The Tomcat's maximum design speed is Mach 2.34, or over 1,500 mph.

Two F-14B's were built, using Pratt & Whitney F401-PW-400 turbofans providing 28,096 lbs. of thrust. The first of these flew on September 12, 1973, but the Navy had already cancelled a production order for the type due to delays in delivery of the engines.

An unusual view of the second F-14 in the Grumman paint shop.   *Grumman*

A Tomcat of the Wolf Pack, VF-1.   *Grumman*

McDONNELL DOUGLAS
F-15 EAGLE

The modified wingtips are apparent in this view of the TF-15.　　　　　　*McDonnell Douglas*

As we have seen, the modern jet fighter has become a technological wonder, filled with complex electronic gear that virtually relieves the pilot of all his duties except filling out the log book. This is an exaggeration, of course; but the current role of the fighting plane has become so far removed from its original precepts that it bears almost no resemblance to the typical combat situations of World War II, for example. In Vietnam, our highly refined Phantoms were often at a disadvantage when engaging the more nimble Mig 21, and the need for cannon armament was clearly demonstrated. In aerial conflicts, supersonic speed is not nearly as advantageous as fast response and maneuverability. The F-15 Eagle has become the first of a generation of modern "dogfighters."

Simplification was the keynote in the design of the F-15. Maintenance time has been reduced to nearly half that of the Phantom by using less complicated systems yet retaining essential automatic controls, such as engine inlet positioning. To enhance its dogfighting ability, the wing loading has been kept to a minimum and the engine thrust exceeds the Eagle's gross weight by some 10,000 lbs. This permits an extremely tight turning radius without losing precious airspeed.

To keep the overall weight at the lowest possible level, the F-15 structure uses composite boron-epoxy, a very lightweight but extremely strong material allowing much thinner control surfaces. Titanium comprises about 25 percent of the entire airframe structure.

The F-15 is the first design to appear following the merger of the McDonnell and the Douglas aircraft companies. Their proposal was selected from among three competitors for an experimental fighter (FX) project. A contract for 18 production F-15A's and two TF-15A two-place trainers was approved in the spring of 1973 following the fighter's first flight on July 27, 1972, from Edwards AFB.

To ensure that no major unexpected characteristics appeared as the F-15 program proceeded, a series of 3/8 scale model gliders were launched from a B-52 flying at 45,000 feet. They were controlled by radio from the ground but recovered in flight by a helicopter after deploying parachutes.

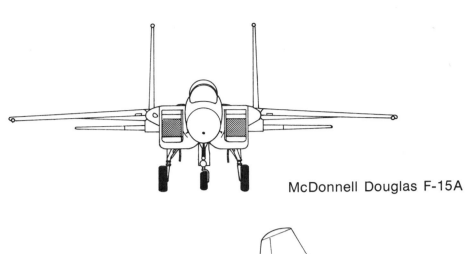

McDonnell Douglas F-15A

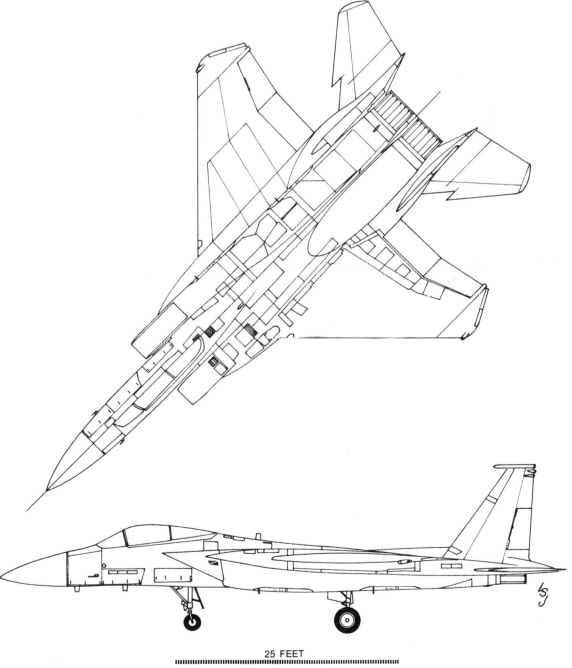

25 FEET

Two 23,400 lb. Pratt & Whitney F100-PW-100 afterburning turbo-fans are mounted between the twin vertical stabilizers. Air for the engines passes through a variable inlet that is adjusted by moving the entire leading edge of the duct in conjunction with internal ramps. The intakes are situated away from the fuselage by several inches to avoid the complication of a boundary-layer separator.

The "talons" of the Eagle consist of an M61A-1 rotary cannon fitted into the right wing/fuselage fairing. This weapon is provided with 1,000 rounds of 20 mm ammunition. Permanent attachment points for four AIM-7F Sparrows are located on the outside bottom edge of the fuselage. Four AIM-9L Sidewinders can be placed on underwing pylons. A centerline pylon is also available.

A zero speed, zero altitude ejection seat, of the type now standard on American jets, is mounted in the cockpit. This unit permits safe ejection through all flight regimes.

The first F-15's carried square-tipped wings spanning 42 feet 10 inches with an area of 610.6 square feet. This has been supplanted by a recontoured tip which reduces the area by about 20 square feet, the span remaining the same. Overall length is 63 feet 10 inches and height is 18 feet 7 inches.

Maximum design speed is 1,530 mph (Mach 2.3) at 60,000 feet.

The wedge-shaped air intake, which partially obscures the insignia in this view, moves up and down according to engine demand.   *McDonnell Douglas*

Delivery of the first production Eagle, a TF-15, at Luke AFB, Arizona, on November 14, 1974. The F-15 Eagle was designed specifically as a dogfighter.   *McDonnell Douglas*

Many parts of the F-16 are interchangeable from right to left in order to keep costs down. General Dynamics

Five airframe manufacturers accepted the Air Force's request for a simple, inexpensive but effective fighter on February 18, 1972. The planes were to be light in weight (20,-000 pounds), have a high thrust-weight ratio to provide rapid acceleration, and the cost should average $3,000,000 per unit for 300 planes. The offerings made by General Dynamics and Northrop were accepted and contracts for two examples of each plane were authorized. A large production contract was on the horizon for the plane winning a comparative fly-off. General Dynamics Model 401 received the official designation YF-16.

Work began immediately on the lightweight fighter. To keep costs at a minimum, GD engineers elected to use only a single engine—the Pratt & Whitney F100 which was proving itself in the F-15. Also the standardization of powerplants between the two planes was bound to appeal to the Air Force. In keeping with this standardization, some fifty-eight percent of the YF-16 components are interchangeable with other

aircraft. Many of the parts are reversible, such as stabilators, flaperons, and most of the landing gear.

A blended wing-fuselage design, similar to the one examined during the Skate seaplane studies (described under the F-7 heading in this book), was adopted for the YF-16. This blending created a pair of forebody strakes similar to those on the YF-12A, although the purpose of the F-16's strakes is to generate a controlled vortex which allows a reduction in wing area. In addition, it improves stability at low speeds. The wings themselves are variable in camber to conform the surface to the most efficient shape under a given circumstance.

A great deal of innovation went into the design of the cockpit. During the tight, high-speed turns of which the F-16 is capable, the pilot is subjected to unusually high g loads. To increase his resistance to these forces, his ejection seat is tilted rearward thirty degrees and his heels are raised. To further aid the pilot under these conditions, he has been provided with a control stick mounted on the right side of the cockpit instead of on the centerline. This side stick controller requires a minimum of movement for full control. The cockpit bubble is large enough to provide 360 degrees of visibility around the upper hemisphere.

Another weight saving feature of the F-16 is the fly-by-wire control system in which mechanical pushrods and linkages are replaced by electrical wires feeding control commands directly to the servos for instantaneous response.

The low mounted position of the engine intake was selected to place it in the area of the least disturbed air and reduce the length of the duct. It is also located ahead of the gun muzzle and is less susceptible to gas ingestion when the gun is fired. In conjunction with the inlet placement, the nose gear was mounted behind the intake to avoid foreign object damage to the engine.

The YF-16 made a rather surprising first flight on January 20, 1974, during what was intended to be a routine taxi test. An unexpected roll tilted the plane rapidly to the right and left, scraping a wing and stabilizer. Rather than try to regain control on the ground, the pilot quickly lifted the prototype into the air and circled the field before making a normal landing. The second YF-16 made a conventional maiden flight on May 9, 1974.

Aside from a few minor incidents, the F-16 testing proceeded as scheduled, and on January 13, 1975, the Air Force announced that the General Dynamics fighter had won the competition. Initial production contracts have approved construction of 11 F-16A's and four two-seat F-16B's. The fuselage of the F-16B is 2½ feet longer than the single-place F-16A. The second seat replaces some internal fuel, but with aerial refueling, the reduction in capacity is negligible.

The General Dynamics F-16A lightweight fighter has a 300 square foot wing with a span of 30 feet without missile launchers. Its length is 49 feet 10½ inches, of which 21½ inches is nose probe. Height is 16 feet 3 inches. Design gross weight is 16,500 pounds; maximum take-off weight is 27,000 pounds. Maximum speed of the F-16 is approximately 1,466 mph (Mach 2.2) with an absolute ceiling over 60,000 feet. The F-16's Pratt & Whitney F100-PW-100 turbofan has an output of nearly 23,500 lbs. Range is 500 miles at 30,000 feet.

The now standard M61 rotary cannon, with 500 rounds of 20 mm shells, is faired into the left foreplane behind the cockpit. Supplemental armament consists of up to four air-to-air missiles on the wingtips and underwing mountings.

The large bubble canopy affords excellent visibility for the F-16 pilot.   *General Dynamics*

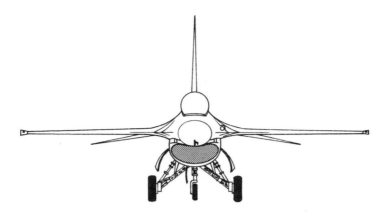

General Dynamics F-16A

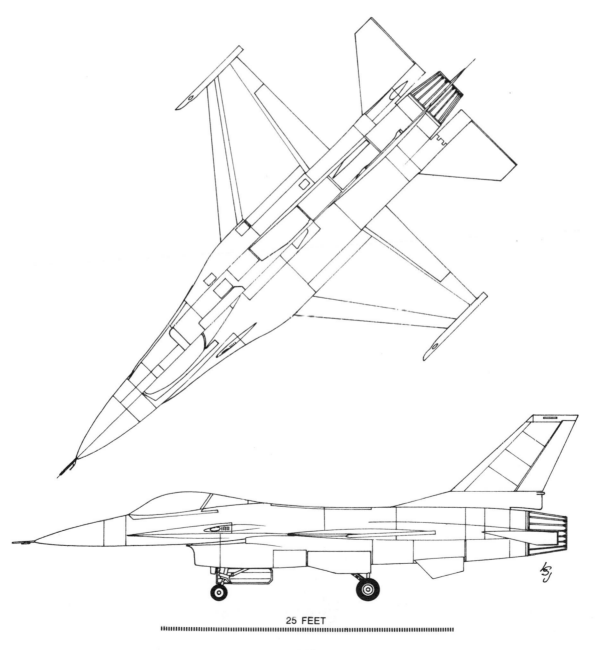

25 FEET

Northrop's YF-17 was based upon the design of an earlier company study, the P-530 Cobra.   Northrop

The second contender in the Air Force's lightweight fighter competition was Northrop with their Model P-600, a derivation of an earlier design they had named Cobra (Model P-530). This fighter has been build around a pair of General Electric YJ101-GE-100 turbojets designed to develop 15,000 lbs. of thrust each with their afterburners. The designation YF-17 was applied to the two prototypes authorized on April 13, 1972.

Distinctive characteristics of the YF-17 include a cobra-like fairing sweeping forward from the wing to set up a controlled vortex over the lifting surfaces. This fairing contains slots for bleeding off boundary layer air. Two large vertical stabilizers cant outward into the free airstream. The wings of this Northrop fighter bear a strong resemblance to those used on their F-5 series; and, like the F-5, also include similar combat flaps for maneuverability. The latter consist of leading and trailing edge flaps, controlled by the aircraft's angle of attack and Mach number, which vary wing lift to match the maneuver.

Aerial evaluation of the YF-17 began on June 9, 1974, when the prototype was lifted from the desert floor at Edwards AFB. Although some obstacles were encountered, flight testing progressed normally. The major shortcoming displayed during the evaluation flights between the two competing lightweight fighters was the inability of the experimental YJ101 engines to deliver full rated power. This placed the YF-17 at a decided disadvantage during the flyoff, but it was only one of the factors involved in the final selection.

The YF-17 has a wingspan of 35 feet with an area of 350 square feet. Length of the aircraft without the nose probe is 55 feet 6 inches, and the YF-17 stands 14 feet 6 inches high. Normal take-off weight is 21,000 pounds. Design maximum speed is 1,320 mph (Mach 2.0) at 40,000 feet.

A single General Electric M61A-1 rotary 20 mm cannon is built into the nose in front of the pilot. Two air-to-air missiles are normally attached to each wingtip.

Following the announcement that the Air Force had selected the YF-16 for production, Northrop, in conjunction with McDonnell Douglas, undertook a modifica-

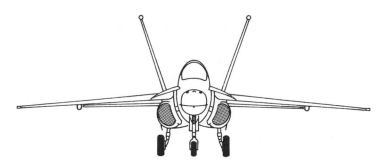

Northrop YF-17

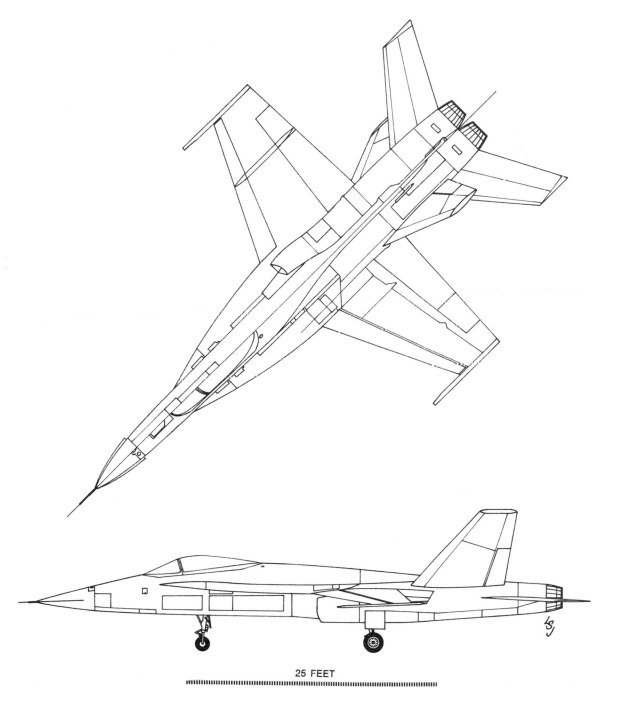

25 FEET

tion of the YF-17 to make a fighter suitable for use by the Navy. In June of 1975, the Navy announced its decision to acquire the revised version, designating it F-18.

At this writing, the McDonnell Douglas F-18 design has not been frozen, but the description which follows gives a good representation of its physical characteristics. Using the same configuration as the YF-17 on which it is based, the F-18 wingspan has been increased to 37 feet 3 inches with a 400 square foot area. Length is 55 feet 6 inches and height is 14 feet 6 inches, as on the YF-17. The main landing gear is strengthened for carrier operations and the tread widened. Also, a dual-wheel nose gear is fitted. Power is obtained from two 15,000 lb. afterburning General Electric J101-GE-100 turbojets to provide Mach 2 speeds. The single M61 rotary cannon in the nose has provisions for up to 500 rounds. In addition to the wingtip-mounted Sidewinder AAM's, fixtures for a Sparrow missile are attached to each fuselage side similar to those used on the F-15 Eagle.

On August 1, 1975, the U. S. Marines announced plans to outfit four squadrons with the new F-18 early in the 1980's.

Following the Air Force rejection, the Navy selected the Northrop fighter as the basis for their carrier based interceptor.   *Northrop*

The two YF-17 prototypes during a 1974 lightweight fighter competition.   *Northrop*

U.S. FIGHTERS

by Lloyd S. Jones

25 FEET

Northrop XP-79B

Lockheed F-80B

Convair XF-81

Republic F-84F
YF-96A

Republic XF-84H

McDonnell XF-85

McDonnell XF-88A

Northrop F-89C

Lockheed XF-90

Lockheed F-94A

Lockheed F-94C
F-97A

Hughes GAR-1D (F-98)

Boeing IM-99 (F-99)

Republic XF-103

Lockheed F-104A

North American F-107A

North American XF-108

McDonnell F-2D (F2H-4)

McDonnell F-3C (F3H-2N)

McDonnell F-4E F-110

LTV F-8E (F8U-2NE)

Grumman F-9J (F9F-8)

Douglas F-10B (F3D-2)

Grumman F-14A

McDonnell Douglas F-15A

General Dynamics

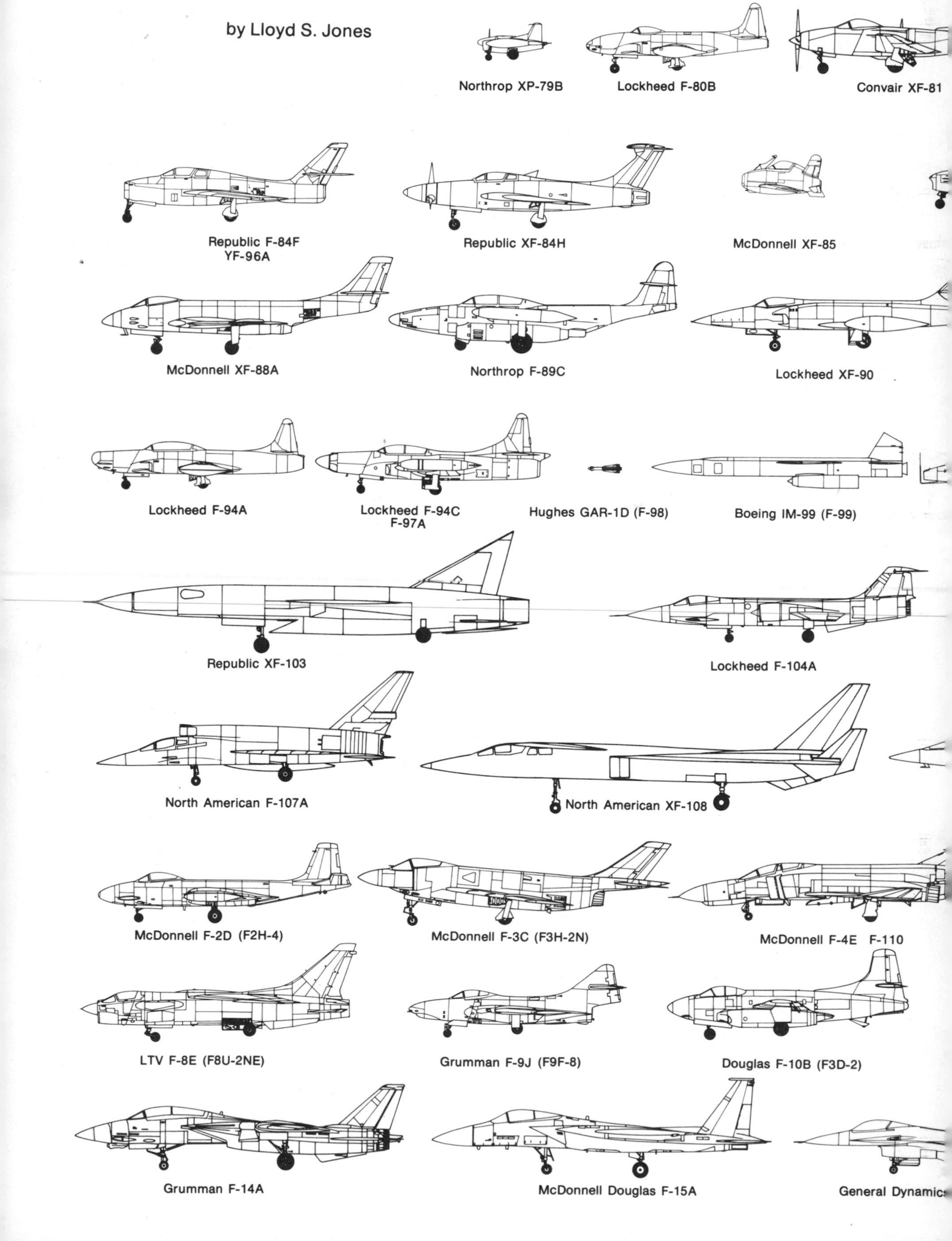